The Tragedy of American School Reform

Also by Ronald W. Evans

The Hope for American School Reform: The Cold War Pursuit of Inquiry Learning in Social Studies
This Happened in America: Harold Rugg and the Censure of Social Studies
The Social Studies Wars: What Should We Teach the Children?
The Handbook on Teaching Social Issues (coeditor)

The Tragedy of American School Reform

How Curriculum Politics and Entrenched Dilemmas Have Diverted Us from Democracy

Ronald W. Evans

palgrave
macmillan

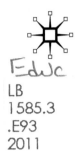

THE TRAGEDY OF AMERICAN SCHOOL REFORM
Copyright © Ronald W. Evans, 2011.

All rights reserved.

Portions of Chapter 1 are adapted from "National Security Trumps Social Progress: The Era of the New Social Studies in Retrospect." by Ronald W. Evans, 2010, in Barbara Slater-Stern, (ed.), *The New Social Studies: People, Politics and Perspectives*, 1–40. Copyright 2010 by Information Age Publishing. Adapted with permission.

First published in 2011 by
PALGRAVE MACMILLAN®
in the United States—a division of St. Martin's Press LLC,
175 Fifth Avenue, New York, NY 10010.

Where this book is distributed in the UK, Europe and the rest of the world, this is by Palgrave Macmillan, a division of Macmillan Publishers Limited, registered in England, company number 785998, of Houndmills, Basingstoke, Hampshire RG21 6XS.

Palgrave Macmillan is the global academic imprint of the above companies and has companies and representatives throughout the world.

Palgrave® and Macmillan® are registered trademarks in the United States, the United Kingdom, Europe and other countries.

ISBN: 978–0–230–10798–4

Library of Congress Cataloging-in-Publication Data

Evans, Ronald W.
    The tragedy of American school reform : how curriculum politics and entrenched dilemmas have diverted us from democracy / Ronald W. Evans.
        p. cm.
    ISBN-13: 978–0–230–10798–4 (hardback)
    ISBN-10: 0–230–10798–2
        1. Social studies—Study and teaching—United States.
    2. Educational change—United States. I. Title.

LB1585.3.E93 2011
300.71'073—dc22   2011005469

A catalogue record of the book is available from the British Library.

Design by Newgen Imaging Systems (P) Ltd., Chennai, India.

First edition: May 2011

10 9 8 7 6 5 4 3 2 1

Printed in the United States of America.

This book is dedicated to my late mentor, Richard E. Gross, who read a previous draft manuscript and remarked, "This is what we've been up against for all these years."

Contents

List of Illustrations   ix

Acknowledgments   xi

Introduction: Challenges of Curriculum Development   1
The Problem   4

Part I   Changes

1 The New Social Studies   9
Cold War Origins   9
Emergence   15
The Projects   20
Concerns and Critiques   23
Reform in Perspective   24

2 The Newer Social Studies   27
1968: The Year Everything Changed   28
The New-Wave Critique of Schooling   35
New Trends in Social Studies   46
Conclusion   57

3 Larger Trends in Schools   59
Open Education   60
Multicultural Education   64
Critical Pedagogy   68
Behind the Newer Social Studies   72
Influence in Schools   75
Conclusion   79

Part II   Reaction

4 Aftermath: "We Face a National Conspiracy"   83
Academic Freedom Cases   84
The Fenton Textbook Controversy   86

The Kanawha County War   91
Conclusion   97

5 The MACOS Controversy and Beyond   99
Initial Confrontations   100
Nationwide Controversy   114
Who Were the Critics?   119
Controversy in Congress   127
Conclusion   146

6 The Conservative Restoration   149
Books Burning in Indiana   149
The Conservative Restoration in School and Society   155
A Nation at Risk?   165
The Revival of Traditional History   171
Explaining the Conservative Restoration   178
Conclusion   182

Part III   Making Sense

7 Can We Transcend the Grammar of Social Studies?   185
Status Studies   186
Constancy and Change   192
The Grammar of Social Studies   196
Failure of the New and Newer Social Studies   203

Conclusion: Reflections on Education for Democracy   209
Dissonance   210
Can We Make a Difference?   211
Lasting Impressions   213

List of Abbreviations   217

List of Manuscript Collections Abbreviated in Notes   221

Notes   223

Index   251

Illustrations

(Following Page 98)

1 Jerome S. Bruner
2 Edwin P. Fenton
3 Alice Moore Reelection Poster
4 Mel and Norma Gabler
5 Robert Welch, founder of the John Birch Society
6 Peter B. Dow
7 Jigging for lake trout
8 John Steinbacher
9 Congressman John B. Conlan
10 Legislative aide George H. Archibald, with Vice President Gerald R. Ford, at a 1973 fundraiser for Congressman Conlan
11 Ed Feulner introducing President Ronald Reagan at a Heritage Foundation dinner, November 30, 1987
12 Joseph Coors and President Ronald Reagan shaking hands while attending a dinner for the board of governors of the Ronald Reagan Library Foundation at the Ritz-Carlton Hotel in Washington, DC, December 14, 1985
13 George C. Wallace announces he is a presidential candidate, February 8, 1968
14 William J. Bennett, Secretary of Education, 1985–1988
15 Diane Ravitch, with Barbara Bush

Cover photograph: Demonstrator holding sign in front of Kanawha County Board of Education, 1974. Courtesy of Bill Tiernan, photographer, Nanya Friend, editor and publisher of the *Charleston Daily Mail*, and Trey Kay.

Acknowledgments

As I send this book to press, I would like to acknowledge all of the people who made contributions to this project. First, the work could not have been completed without the helpful assistance of many archivists and the access to materials they provided. I would like to express my deep gratitude to Jennie Benford at Carnegie Mellon University Archives; Nora Murphy of the Massachusetts Institute of Technology Institute Archives; David Ment at Milbank Memorial Library and Archives at Teachers College, Columbia University; Janice Goldblum at the National Academy of Sciences Archives; Sharon Kelly of the John F. Kennedy Presidential Library; and the reference staff at Harvard University Archives. I thank the many archivists and support staff at each of these institutions and elsewhere who endured my endless requests, helped locate materials, and offered many wise suggestions. I would particularly like to acknowledge the helpful assistance of Alan Walker at the National Archives Civilian Record Unit, College Park, Maryland, who guided me to many helpful materials, and Peter Dow, who gave me full access to the EDC materials while they were in his care. Both were extremely helpful.

I would also like to acknowledge the assistance of several archivists and others who supplied photographs and permissions including Bill Tiernan and Nanya Friend of the *Charleston Daily Mail*; Trey Kay, producer of "The Great Textbook War"; Jennie Benford of Carnegie Mellon University Archives; Debra Basham of the West Virginia State Archives; Danny Turner of Danny Turner Photography, Dallas, Texas; Scott Rook of the Oregon Historical Society; Peter Dow of Buffalo, New York; William Hulsey of the Education Development Center, Inc. (EDC); Wendy Saul and Inda Sachaenen of the University of Missouri-St. Louis; Wendy Goen of the Arizona State Historical Archive; Kathy White of the Ludwig von Mises Institute, Auburn, Alabama; Bonnie Burlbaw of the George H. W. Bush Presidential Library; Steve Branch and Michael Pinckney of the Ronald Reagan Presidential Library; John Steinbacher; Ted Fenton; and George H. Archibald. I would also like to thank Trey

Kay, Carole Mason, Jim Haught, Ron Miller, Kay Michael, Stan Bumgardner, Steve Fesenmaier, Debra Basham, Karl Priest and the many others who helped in tracking photos and permissions.

I would also like to thank Jerome Bruner, Peter Dow, and Ted Fenton for generously agreeing to interviews and for their many helpful insights. As key leaders of in the new social studies, nothing could substitute for meeting them in person and hearing their stories and answers to my questions. I found each extremely generous with time, resources, memories, and perspectives. In each case, my visit was a memorable experience. I am very appreciative.

My colleagues at San Diego State University have been very supportive of my research for many years, and of this project as well. I received consistent and invaluable support in the form of research assigned time, small grants to fund archival visits, and a sabbatical leave, which provided ample time for writing. I would especially like to thank David Strom and Nancy Farnan for their support and encouragement. I would also like to acknowledge the support I received from countless other colleagues and staff, and the steadfast assistance of John Rizzo, Marc Pastor, Jim Edwards, and Ricardo Fitipaldi at Instructional Technology Services.

Several colleagues provided thoughtful comments on various portions of this work, or offered helpful comments and resources. In that regard, I would especially like to thank Geoff Scheurman, Barbara Slater-Stern, Gregg Jorgensen, Barry Franklin, Catherine Broom, Lynn Burlbaw, and Jared Stallones. The path-breaking work of several other scholars contributed in laying a strong foundation for this work, notably books by Peter Dow, John Rudolph, and Eugene Provenzo, Jr. I would like to thank Gene Maeroff, William Reese, and John Rudolph for their wise counsel as I negotiated the path to publication. I would also like to express my gratitude to my colleagues in the Issues-Centered Education Community of the National Council for the Social Studies for their friendship and support. I would especially like to thank Mike Dorfi, Kim Cohn, Jason Leichter, Kris Wardwell, and Gregg Jorgensen for their generous and careful help with proofreading. While many others contributed to the work, I take full responsibility for any errors or omissions.

I would also like to acknowledge the support of my family and friends who put up with this preoccupation over many years and offered encouragement as well as supportive questions and comments. I would especially like to thank my wife Mika, and my children, Kathryn, Mira, and Kai who have patiently endured many rambling discussions of this project. I would also like to express my appreciation to my men's support group and the Men's Fellowship of the First Unitarian Universalist

Church of San Diego for listening to me talk at length about this project and offering their generous and unflagging support.

The research project behind this book aimed to cover the entire era of social studies curriculum reform from its inception in the 1950s through its undoing in the late 1970s. Because the initial draft was quite lengthy, my editor at Palgrave Macmillan asked whether I had considered breaking the work into two volumes. The first volume, *The Hope for American School Reform: The Cold War Pursuit of Inquiry Learning*, examines the origins and development of the reform, the projects, and reactions from academics through the early 1970s. This, the second volume, focuses on changes in the direction of reform from the late 1960s through the 1970s, and the academic freedom battles and entrenched dilemmas that brought the era of the new social studies to a close. I will be forever grateful to my editor at Palgrave, Burke Gerstenschlager, editorial assistants Samantha Hasey and Kaylan Connally, and production assistants Richard Bellis and Rohini Krishnan, for the opportunity to publish my full treatment of the topic and for their efforts to help bring the project to completion.

RONALD W. EVANS
San Diego, California

Introduction: Challenges of Curriculum Development

As a social studies teacher in the 1970s and early 1980s, I found that students were often excited by my experiments with inquiry and issues-oriented approaches to teaching. I was given tremendous freedom to create interesting lessons and courses within broad parameters. That freedom allowed me to explore a variety of modes of teaching, to go for depth when warranted, to engage students frequently in wide ranging discussions of inquiry and value questions, Socratic seminars, debates, mock trials, and simulations. Teaching was a compelling, dynamic, and creative experience, deeply intellectual work combined with the opportunity to influence a rising generation.

This history of the new social studies, the newer social studies, and its aftermath, the conservative restoration, highlights two important dilemmas in the fields of social studies and curriculum, both of which are related to my early teaching experience and the experiences of teachers today. The first quandary, curriculum politics, is colorful and controversial, especially in social studies. It is, in essence, a blood sport in which armies of citizens struggle over whose version of the American way will prevail in our schools and culture. The second puzzle, which I am calling the "grammar" of social studies, embodies the entrenched dilemmas of schooling, the institutional obstacles that seem to stifle attempts at reform, and against which we have made little progress. Both of these dilemmas have profoundly influenced the landscape of social studies practice in recent decades. Unfortunately, in many schools today teachers are constrained by scripted lessons, pacing guides, and the pressures of standards and testing. In many instances, teachers are not given the requisite freedom for democratic education to flourish.

The reforms of the 1960s were not the earliest attempt to transform schooling. Efforts of the progressive era, and ensuing sidetracks, had tried and largely failed in their quest to transform the school from an institution marked by tradition and social control to a dynamic center of interest and growth for all children. As illustrated in the first volume of this work, *The Hope for American School Reform*, the story of efforts to reform the American school began to change and emerge into something similar to its present form during the 1950s and 1960s, driven by collaboration among big science, government, business, and prestigious universities.

My thesis in this book, *The Tragedy of American School Reform*, is that improvement in social studies is constrained by two main factors: curriculum politics and the entrenched dilemma of classroom constancy. The first factor is well represented by the origins of the new social studies, the rise of the humanistic newer social studies, and the academic freedom cases and controversies of the 1970s that were a key element in bringing an end to reform and establishing a conservative restoration in schools. That restoration gradually led to the imposition of accountability reforms. The second factor is embodied in the failure of classroom practice to live up to its potential for interesting, engaging teaching worthy of our nation and the questions, social issues, and problems we face as citizens.

The curriculum reform movement that spawned the new social studies emerged as a response to a perceived external threat and to the perception of anti-intellectualism and quackery in public schools. University scholars served as the model for reform. However, the patterns of inquiry and concepts drawn from university scholarship, which might be seen as logical components of the "church of reason," were not congruent with the traditions and culture of the schools.[1] The reform, linked to empire, and the military-industrial-academic-complex, which served its interests, was artificially induced and imposed from above, an innovative "fix" or solution for schools that were assumed to be dysfunctional. The new social studies was partially superceded in the late 1960s by the newer social studies, a progressive and reconstructionist oriented movement that focused on relevance, activism, and values clarification as schools sought to develop a more humanistic approach.

Beginning in the late 1960s, the era of reform resulted in a number of academic freedom cases involving teachers and several major controversies that received significant national attention. In cases involving individual teachers who applied the newer techniques in classrooms, the new social studies was literally put on trial. Confrontations emerged over key new social studies materials, including the Fenton textbook controversy in Georgia and the conflict over MACOS, which erupted in numerous cities and towns during the 1970s and led to debate in the halls of Congress.

Critics of the new social studies included an array of conservative activists: ultraconservative textbook watchdogs Mel and Norma Gabler, a network of activists linked to the John Birch Society, the Heritage Foundation, the Council for Basic Education, the American Party, journalist John Steinbacher, and others. It was to some extent an interlocking network that shared resources and information. At least a few of the players were well financed. These controversies resulted in termination of funding for MACOS and other projects and dealt a serious blow to freedom for teaching and learning in the 1970s that has had continuing consequences.

Similar pendulum swings are a regular attribute of the curricular landscape, toward traditional and discipline-based curricula during conservative times; toward experimentation, child-centered, inquiry, or issues-oriented curricula during liberal times. Despite ever changing curricular fashions and trends, a set of competing interest groups is a semipermanent feature of the social studies arena. The major competing camps, as I describe them in a recent book, *The Social Studies Wars*, endeavoring to influence the field include the following: traditional historians, who support history as the core of social studies; mandarins, intellectuals who advocate social studies as social science; social efficiency educators, who hope to create a smoothly controlled and more efficient society; social meliorists, Deweyan experimentalists who want to develop students' reflective thinking capabilities and contribute to social improvement; and social reconstructionists, who cast social studies in schools in a leading role in the transformation of American society. Many scholars and teachers choose to meld aspects of two or more traditions in a consensus or eclectic approach.[2]

Aside from how the interest groups are described, their comparative rank and influence over the rhetoric of schooling changes slowly over the years. One may be dominant, then recede as another comes to prominence. None disappear, but remain present with a lower profile, as if parallel streams; while one is flooded, another may be dry. Each stream has a history of promoters and defenders, leaders and pretenders. Citizens, scholars, and teachers can learn a great deal about their own affinities and deepen curricular identities by examining the strands in some depth.

Frequently, the social studies curriculum, or its accompanying textbooks and materials have served as a lightning rod, attracting comment and criticism, as if the curriculum is a screen on which critics of various stripes project visions of a preferred future. These rhetorical battles and accompanying propaganda often inspire dramatic episodes filled with harsh oratory and marked with confrontation. This was never more true than during the 1970s, when educational innovations were literally put on trial in a number of cities and towns across the nation. Given ever-changing curriculum politics, and the stubborn nature of schools as an institution, it is a somber challenge to make schooling a genuine force for human growth and potential, to create forms of education that contribute to the cause of freedom and social justice.

The Problem

The main, long-term problem posed by the social studies curriculum is centered on the difficulty of reform or improvement. Perhaps more than any other curricular area, the field of social studies is constrained by curriculum politics, seared by conflict. As we have seen, the rhetoric of the social studies arena is composed of multiple theories and interest groups, each vying for power over the future of the field. From the era of the new social studies, social science inquiry received its greatest boost. During the episode of the newer social studies a revitalized progressivism emerged. By the mid-1970s and beyond, interest groups supporting traditional history and social efficiency began to reassert their dominance. Through it all, the field was limited by the institutional and cultural obstacles to change that I am calling the "grammar" of social studies.

In an ideal world, schools would serve as a church of reason, developing in students not only basic knowledge and skills, but also a critical facility and broad understanding of the social world, its competing influences and interests, and entrée to a host of issues and questions. Walter Parker summarized this forward-looking notion and its implications in the introduction to a recent book:

> Social studies is at the center of a good school curriculum because it is where students learn to see and interpret the world—its peoples, places, cultures, systems, and problems; its dreams and calamities—now and long ago. In social studies lessons and units of study, students don't simply experience the world...but are helped systematically to understand it, to care for it, to think deeply and critically about it, and to take their place on the public stage, standing on equal footing with others. This, at any rate, is the goal.[3]

However, most schools in the world we inhabit are a long way from this ideal. Instead of serving as a church of reason, schools function primarily as an institution of control, social efficiency, and cultural transmission. We have, for the most part, lost sight of a compelling vision of democratic education, driven by high purposes, and instead seem bent on application of a business model for reform. How and why we have lost our way is a difficult question deserving long and thoughtful study, especially if we are ever to make social studies what it potentially could be.

This history of the new social studies and its aftermath is a case study of an era, examining issues related to purposes and practices in education. As such, it raises several broad questions pertinent to our understanding of social studies, schools as an institution, and the social context:

> Who controls the schools? To what ends?
> Whose interests are served? Who benefits?
> To what extent is schooling an arm of the state? Controlled by government, business, science, or some other influence?
> To what extent do schools serve the people and the democratic impulse?
> How does social studies function in schools? To what ends?
> What role do censorship battles play in shaping school curricula?
> Can we reform social studies to enhance the level of meaningful learning?

From its origins, the new social studies was an establishment turn, driven by concerns over manpower and national security. Its essence was rooted in cold war fears. Despite, and perhaps partly because of its origins, the founders of the reform and the projects they directed contributed powerful, inquiry oriented theories and materials that made a strong contribution to the rhetoric of reform. With the advent of the newer social studies in the late 1960s, the direction of reform took a progressive, even revolutionary turn, driven by conflict, hope, and the human potential movements of the time. In its aftermath, a counter-revolution materialized and both movements for reform were censured by a fervent coalition of neoconservatives, the new right, and ultraconservative evangelicals who wanted to turn back the clock on the people's revolutions of the 1960s. Meanwhile, as they played out in schools, both movements for reform were stifled by the "grammar" of social studies, persistent patterns of instruction and institutional constraints that seem to deflect most efforts at reform.

In the end, the new social studies failed to reach the lofty expectations of its creators. Despite a high level of research and development activity, there was little lasting change. And, unfortunately, the immediate aftermath of the era saw a great deal of support for the reinstitution of more traditional forms of education. As this study illustrates, schools are highly permeable institutions. Reforms are motivated largely by forces outside the classroom and school, deflected, mediated, or partially incorporated into the ways schools operate. From studying this episode in some depth, we can learn a great deal about an important attempt at social studies reform and the counter-revolution it inspired. Both remain relevant to our current situation. Hopefully this study can help lead to better understanding of a remarkable era, offer a healthy contrast to current accountability measures, provide historical perspective on the possibilities and dilemmas of school reform, and assist in the ongoing effort to improve schools.

I

Changes

1

The New Social Studies

The new social studies came to fruition during the 1960s, but was, in most ways, an artifact of the 1950s and the cold war struggle over communism. It was rooted in cold war manpower development anxieties and was an expansion of trends in science and mathematics education. Chiefly discipline-centered, the social studies projects of the period, supported by record federal and private financial backing, were a direct consequence of critiques of education and progressive social studies that had been brewing over many years. In a very real sense, this was an extension of the war on social studies and the climax of decades of disdain.

In a recent book, I develop the argument that controversies and criticism over the social studies curriculum developed in a sequential pattern, with the controversy becoming broader and more damaging to progressive social studies as the years went on. Criticism of progressive social studies emerged and intensified in three major episodes that preceded the era of the new social studies, including the Rugg textbook controversy that spanned 1939–1942, the controversy over American history, 1942–1944, and the controversy over progressive education, 1947–1958. As I have argued previously, these three controversies were instrumental in the eventual evolution of the era of the new social studies and were a strong reflection of the historical context.[1] In the postwar era, the controversy would spread to encompass all of progressive education.

Cold War Origins

In the late 1940s and early 1950s, a growing crescendo of criticisms of progressive education emerged—with many of the most negative observations focused on social studies—packaged and marketed under colorful titles such as *Educational Wastelands* (1953), *Quackery in the Public Schools* (1953), *Progressive Education is REDucation* (1956), and "Who Owns Your Child's Mind?" (1951).[2] Arthur Bestor, author of *Educational Wastelands* and perhaps the most respected critic, called social studies an anti-intellectual "social stew."[3] Bestor and others critiqued the "scrambling" of history, geography, and government into the social studies; they bemoaned the "anti-intellectualism" of educators who they derisively called "educationists"; and, they frequently linked progressive education to communism, all critiques that had been raised during the Rugg and Nevins controversies, only this time, the deluge of attacks was longer and more intense. Educators responded with articles and books countering the charges—though it was a relatively muted response, reflecting the times.

The social milieu of the cold war era is especially pertinent to a deeper understanding of the origins of the new social studies. With the dropping of atomic bombs on Japan, and the subsequent development of the nuclear arms race, the world had entered the nuclear age, and the threat of global holocaust was very real. Competition with the Soviet Union, growing national security concerns, the development of McCarthyism, and the deluge of intellectual and red-baiting attacks on progressive education were all conditioned by this context.

Manpower Concerns. The impetus for the broader curriculum reform movement that gave rise to the new social studies also grew, in part, out of cold war manpower studies conducted by the Central Intelligence Agency (CIA). Manpower concerns were raised beginning in the late 1940s and early 1950s and were partly behind creation of the National Science Foundation (NSF). The NSF, established by Congress in 1950 with the aim of promoting basic research and education in the sciences, initially had little to do with the lower schools, though it did begin to sponsor science fairs and summer institutes for teachers in science and mathematics. Manpower concerns were heightened by a series of confidential CIA reports on developments in the Soviet Union. The first of these reports provided evidence that the Soviets were training scientists, engineers, and technical manpower at a rapid rate and employing the "Stakhanov" movement or "socialist competition" to spur productivity gains. They were giving monetary awards for innovation and "Stalin Prizes" and "Hero of Socialist Labor" awards. In short, the report showed that the Soviet Union was an awakening industrial giant. A later report confirmed the earlier findings and indicated that the Soviets were devoting "large sums to education, especially in the fields of science and engineering," and that in many fields, "Soviet technology equals or even exceeds that of the west."[4] By 1963, a "secret" report found that Soviet productivity was "second only to the U.S." and that the Soviets had made especially rapid progress in "development of engineering and other professional and technical manpower," with a 237 percent increase in engineers from 1939 to 1959.[5]

Among US policy makers, the CIA manpower reports were cause for alarm at the highest levels and led to a manpower report from the Office of Defense Mobilization (ODM) commissioned by President Dwight D. Eisenhower.[6] The ODM study reported on the "availability of manpower simultaneously to operate a military training program, to supply military personnel for active service, and to meet the needs of the civilian economy." In essence, civilian scientific and technical manpower was viewed as an adjunct to military power and as an essential part of national security.[7] The report stated that manpower resources, especially "our supply of highly trained and skilled workers" was not "keeping abreast of the current and potential requirements of the rapidly expanding technology" on which the nation's "growth and security depend." The authors of the report cast manpower as a key ingredient for "success on the diplomatic front."[8] By the fall of 1954, national security and manpower concerns had become the subject of alarming media coverage. An interview with NSF Director Alan T. Waterman published in *Nation's Business*, organ of the US Chamber of Commerce, was titled "Russian Science Threatens the West," and a *New York Times* article reported "Russia Is Overtaking U.S. in Training of Technicians."[9] Manpower concerns continued to loom large throughout the cold war era and stood behind government and business-led efforts to develop more scientific and technical personnel and better trained citizens.

The curriculum reform movement that would eventually result in creation of the new social studies also had its seeds in two projects that began, almost unnoticed, at two universities in the 1950s. The University of Illinois Committee on School Mathematics (UICSM) was formed in 1951 out of concerns over the math deficiencies of entering freshmen at the University of Illinois. Based on similar concerns in science, Jerrold Zacharias at the Massachusetts Institute of Technology (MIT) wrote a memo in 1956 to James Killian, MIT president, titled "Movie Aids for Teaching Physics in High School," in which he proposed a project for the improvement of physics teaching by creating ninety twenty-minute films as the heart of the curriculum, each with a "real physicist."[10] Zacharias's memorandum led to the creation of what was called the Physical Science Study Committee (PSSC) that received NSF funding. In each case, the rationale for the development of the curriculum improvement projects was rooted in manpower concerns that surfaced earlier, and which continued to be aired, in one form or another, throughout the period.

These early curriculum development programs established initial patterns for the funding of national curriculum development projects that would largely continue for the next fifteen to twenty years. One pattern, represented by the University of Illinois Committee, was initial funding by private foundations (often Carnegie or Ford) followed by support from the NSF or the United States Office of Education (USOE). A second pattern, represented by the MIT Committee, was long-term funding by the NSF or USOE from start-up to publication. By 1956, six national projects were established and funded in science and math, five of which aimed at curriculum reform. By this time, it was apparent that several broad assumptions or guidelines were shared by virtually all of these endeavors, and included the following: the need to change the content, materials, and methods of instruction; a focus on the textbook or learning materials; directors of projects drawn from the academic disciplines; a focus on courses for the academically talented and gifted because it was seen as more critical to the national interest; overriding concern about the integrity of the academic disciplines and their "structures"; learning by discovery and inquiry; and a focus on the cognitive over affective, personal, or social action dimensions.[11] Another shared assumption: if the problem with schools was the shoddy stuff they taught, then the solution was to bypass the teacher by creating new and innovative materials under the direction of some of the leading minds in each discipline.

Wartime Research Model. Virtually all of the later curriculum development projects involved an application of the same innovative model of research and development embodied in the initial projects. Reformers, most of whom had little previous experience with educational reform efforts, imported methods of research and development from military research programs to the field of education. In effect, the projects owed much of their form to the military-industrial research complex as it evolved during and after World War II. The reforms of the era were "designed and implemented by a small cadre of scientists," led by Zacharias of MIT, who transferred techniques "almost seamlessly" from military weapons research and development programs of the postwar period to the field of education.

Though the push for a more rigorous and academic education originated in critiques of progressivism and cold war manpower concerns, the trend was enhanced and given its "fundamental operational characteristics," along with its conception of the essential "problem of education, and the means of its solution," by the newer research and development techniques drawn from wartime weapons research. The particular "intellectual skills and technical methods" involved had proven their worth during World War II.[12]

In the eyes of scientists and policy makers during the cold war era, there seemed no limit to the power of these techniques to solve virtually any problem. Partly due to its origins in wartime research and development, the reform strategy took little account of the culture, history, mores, or social and economic context of the school. If its reform implementation strategies were flawed, an oversimplification that failed to understand the complexities of schools and teaching, few inside the growing reform juggernaut were aware of its limitations. Indeed, through the myopic vantage point of those most involved and guided by a vision of omnipotence, the educational possibilities seemed limitless, even "revolutionary."[13]

The ideological turn behind passage of the National Defense Education Act (NDEA) developed over many years of red-baiting and criticism of progressive education from academic critics. The stage was set and the launching of Sputnik, the Soviet satellite, on October 4, 1957, affirmed the criticism and unleashed funds for educational reform. Sputnik served as a clarion call for education in science and math, and other studies that would strengthen US brainpower for the cold war. That call was answered by the NDEA, passed in early 1958, providing unprecedented categorical aid in the hundreds of millions of dollars for the improvement of mathematics, science, and foreign language instruction. The NDEA was supported by two main arguments: that national security required the "fullest development of the mental resources and technical skills" of American youth, and that the national interest required federal "assistance to education for programs which are important to our national defense."[14]

Following Sputnik, national magazines and a new round of books stoked the fires of a renewed "crisis" in education. Critics such as Vice Admiral Hyman G. Rickover, father of the nuclear submarine, blamed the schools for our nation falling behind the Russians in science, math, and engineering, endangering national security. In his criticisms of American education, published in a book entitled *Education and Freedom* (1959), he called attention to Soviet successes and described the superiority of the Soviet and European educational systems.[15] Another vociferous critic, E. Merrill Root, authored a critique of textbooks that exemplified the anticommunist tenor of the times and contributed to the crisis mentality. In *Brainwashing in the High Schools* (1958), Root sought to demonstrate that the United States was losing the cold war because of unpatriotic textbooks filled with misleading propaganda for socialism and communism.[16] Another book that appeared shortly after Sputnik seemed to sum up many of the criticisms of education spawned by cold war fears and competition. *Second Rate Brains* (1958) contained a compendium of thought on Soviet schools and scientists and offered critiques of the mediocrity in American schools.[17] The cumulative effect of these persistent and strident attacks on education supported new directions and a renewed emphasis on discipline-based academic study.

A Broadened Agenda. Following Sputnik, and passage of the NDEA, the growth of research and development for curriculum improvement that began in the technical fields, in math and science, was gradually broadened to include the humanities and social sciences. Two important meetings took place in April 1958, six months after the launch of Sputnik, and shortly after passage of the NDEA, which would have an important influence on the direction of curriculum reform. The first of these was a conference on Psychological Research in Education aimed at investigating better approaches to teaching science and math "than are now being utilized."[18] The second was a meeting held at the National Academy of Sciences (NAS) at which virtually all of the major decision makers in funding the growing curriculum reform movement were present. At that meeting it was decided to broaden the PSSC curriculum reform model to other science areas. That decision would open the door to curriculum reform in social studies. At the same meeting, it was agreed that the PSSC would form a small corporation known as Educational Services Incorporated (ESI).[19]

The furor and flurry of interest in education that followed Sputnik provided an invaluable assist to those who wanted schools to raise academic standards and give more attention to gifted students. At the NSF, the "crisis" in education and the intense interest following Sputnik increased the Foundation's role in secondary school reform. Projects proliferated, made possible by increased funding from the NSF and the USOE following passage of the NDEA in 1958, and inspired by Sputnik. At the heart of the curriculum reform movement was Zacharias. As Jerome Bruner later recalled, "I think it was Zach more than anybody else who converted Sputnik shock into the curriculum reform movement that it became rather than taking some other form."[20] Gradually, the directors of funded projects became the new "leadership" in American education. With the backing of the national government, these new reforms represented a sort of "official" direction for the creation and transmission of knowledge in the nation's schools, one that was built around the academic disciplines and the cold war aim of manpower development, even if few of those involved seldom seemed to explicitly acknowledge it at the time.

Emergence

The aim of the new social studies movement was to transform students into "junior" historians and "little league" social scientists. The developments of the 1960s rested, in part, on a small, influential book, *The Process of Education* (1960), written by Jerome Bruner, reporting on the proceedings of the Woods Hole Conference.

Woods Hole. The Woods Hole Conference, held in September 1959, at Woods Hole, Massachusetts, at a large mansion that was summer headquarters of the NAS, brought together leaders in the new reforms in science and math and led to a concise and well-crafted formulation of the principles of curriculum development shared in the new movement. Among the thirty-five participants were luminaries such as conference director Jerome Bruner, Richard Alpert, Lee Cronbach, Robert Gagne, Zacharias, and John Morton Blum. Key participants included curriculum-makers, biologists, mathematicians, and physicists, along with a few psychologists, several educators, a couple of historians, and a classicist. The National Academy of Sciences, the institution behind putting the conference together, wanted to have a closer look at the curriculum reform movement and infuse some new thinking from psychology. Other sponsors of the conference included the USOE Cooperative Research Program, the Rand Corporation, the Air Research and Development Command, and the NSF. From a larger perspective, the conference was fueled by the reaction to Sputnik and the complaints of critics such as Vice Admiral Rickover and was funded by a range of federal agencies. In a sense, what was emerging was a manufactured consensus, paid for by stakeholders with an interest in education conducted on behalf of national security.

In *The Process of Education*, Bruner summarized his own "sense of the meeting" based on the reports of five working groups formed at the conference. The conference took the "structure of the disciplines" as its central theme and overriding assumption and examined in some depth, "the role of structure in learning and how it may be made central in teaching." The conferees assumed the goal of "giving students an understanding of the fundamental structure of whatever subjects we choose to teach" and the "teaching and learning of structure" rather than simply the "mastery of facts and techniques."[21]

The second theme of the conference had to do with readiness for learning and "the hypothesis that any subject can be taught effectively in some intellectually honest form to any child at any stage of development."[22] A third theme involved the nature of intuition and the training of hunches. "The shrewd guess, the fertile hypothesis," Bruner asserted, "is a much-neglected and essential feature of productive thinking." These three themes, Bruner wrote, were all premised on a central conviction "that intellectual activity anywhere is the same, whether at the frontier of knowledge or in a third-grade classroom...The difference is in degree, not in kind."[23] A fourth theme centered on how to stimulate student motivation through interest in the material. The essence of the reform centered on finding means that would help the learner to get through the "surface clutter" of details "to the pure, unflawed idea behind it: the deep structure."[24] That meant, in the case of history, for example, "You don't just think *about* history, you think history." In other words, history was not just a description of the past, but a way of getting to that description, a process. As Bruner would frame it later, "Knowing how something is put together...allows you to go beyond it."[25]

Not all of these ideas were new. The concept of inquiry or discovery oriented teaching had been around at least since the days of the scientific historians in the nineteenth century and was increasingly championed by many progressive educators. Motivation through student interest was also an old song. Parts of the new curriculum movement were a recapitulation of common ideas in the rhetoric of education. The focus on the "structures" of the disciplines was a reformulation, though what it actually meant in terms of classroom practice remained somewhat unclear.

Though there was little explicit acknowledgment of the cold war backdrop to which the conferees at Woods Hole owed their existence, Bruner, a cold war liberal in politics, did refer somewhat obliquely to the social milieu. He wrote, "If all students are helped to the full utilization of their intellectual powers, we will have a better chance of surviving as a democracy in an age of enormous technological and social complexity."[26] A part of that "complexity" was no doubt entangled in the cold war struggle with totalitarian communism in the minds of Bruner and his colleagues.

In his role as director, during the conference Bruner wrote memos to each of five working groups on the apparatus of teaching; the sequence of the curriculum; the motivation of learning; the role of intuition; and, cognitive processes. One of the most telling comments was contained in Bruner's memo to the work group on the apparatus of teaching. "Perhaps rather unfortunately," the memo began, "we introduced this subject for discussion today by suggesting the analogy to a weapon system—proposing that the teacher, the book, the laboratory, the teaching machine, the film, and the organization of the craft might serve together to form a balanced teaching system."[27] It was a revealing comment. It alluded to the cold war backdrop through which the entire program of curriculum reform might be seen as both a weapons system and an outgrowth of national security concerns, and it made an implicit connection to the earlier involvement of Bruner and Zacharias in the development of weapons systems. Bruner's initial direct involvement with the wartime research model apparently came with his work on Project Troy, a highly classified summer study invited by the State Department and ostensibly created to find a way to overcome Soviet jamming of Radio Free Europe, but with the broader aim of getting "the truth behind the Iron Curtain" by bringing together some of the "best brains in the country" to work on the problem and to counter the Soviet propaganda program.[28] Zacharias was also deeply involved in similar wartime government projects and had been for some time, with key leadership roles in the MIT Radiation Lab and the Manhattan Project, as a consultant on Project Troy, and notably, as director of Project Hartwell, focused initially on antisubmarine warfare and completed at MIT in 1950 with funding from the Office of Navy Research.[29] These involvements provided a model and many of the personnel for what would become large-scale consultancies involving scientists, social scientists, the US military, intelligence, and propaganda agencies. The model was later applied to social studies education as an arm of the propaganda effort, that is, improve manpower development on a broad scale, improve social science instruction, and win the cold war, assuming, of course, that students gain strong inquiry skills and reach the proper conclusions. In the case of Bruner, participation in Project Troy was "a rather heady experience" and led to a regular monthly dinner meeting at the St. Botolph's Club in Boston the first Friday evening of each month for the next fifteen years, which he later described as "the best club I ever belonged to."[30]

This is not to confuse the contextual influences and circumstances that gave rise to the reform with the motivations of reformers. While reformers, especially in the early years of the reform movement, were establishment figures with strong links to the military and wartime research, they believed strongly in the power of scientific thinking and sought to imbue students with critical thinking skills, as junior scientists, mathematicians, historians, and social scientists. Zacharias stated this motivational belief clearly:

> The reason I was willing to do it [PSSC] was not because I wanted more physics or more physicists or more science; it was because I believed then, and I believe now, that in order to get people to be decent in this world, they have to have some kind of intellectual training that involves knowing [about] Observation, Evidence, the Basis for Belief.[31]

Following Woods Hole, other theorists added to the mix, creating building blocks for the new reform and fleshing out the rationale.

The era of the new social studies was introduced most clearly when an article by Charles R. Keller, director of the John Hay Fellows Program, and a former college history teacher, appeared in the *Saturday Review*. Keller's article was titled "Needed: Revolution in Social Studies" and appeared in 1961. His thesis was that social studies was "in the educational doldrums," partly traceable to the fact that "social studies" was a "federation of subjects...often merged in inexact and confusing ways."[32] Social studies teachers too frequently "depend on textbooks," leading to "unimaginative, unenthusiastic, pedantic teaching." The remedy, according to Keller, was "a possible revolution in social studies," beginning with "eliminating the term 'social studies,' which is vague, murky, and too all-inclusive and substitute for it the term 'history and the social sciences,' which is exact and hence meaningful."[33] Keller then echoed many of Bruner's recommendations, a clarion call for a social studies reform movement along the lines already begun in other subject areas.

Before the appearance of Keller's article, social studies reformers were already engaged in pioneering work in a few isolated places. Lawrence Senesh, a scholar in economics at Purdue University, was busily creating an economics program for elementary age students, drawing on the disciplines in creating a progressive-oriented program and textbook series, *Our Working World*. Edwin Fenton, a historian at Carnegie Institute of Technology in Pittsburgh, who had been given responsibility for preservice teacher education in history, was bothered by the pat assertions found in high school history textbooks and by the boredom and loathing of his own students for many history and social science courses. In an attempt to bring history to life and rekindle student curiosity, he introduced primary source documents as a means of stimulating students, asking them to experience the work of historians, and to make sense of raw data. Fenton's experiences with using primary source documents led to publication of a book titled *32 Problems in World History* and an eventual leadership role in the new social studies movement.[34]

Endicott House. During the period before and after the Woods Hole conference, a series of meetings took place with the general theme of broadening the curriculum reform projects to include other areas such as English and social studies. Perhaps the single most interesting and relevant of these meeting occurred at Endicott House in Dedham, Massachusetts, in June 1962. The Endicott House meeting was the first comprehensive meeting to grow out of the reform movement to examine the need for curriculum reform in social studies in some depth. During the Kennedy administration, Zacharias served as chair of the President's Science Advisory Committee (PSAC) and sponsored a number of meetings on a variety of topics aimed at further developing and broadening the educational reform movement. The Endicott House meeting was a more immediate and direct outgrowth of a January 1962 meeting at which Zacharias recommended development of an ESI social studies program.

The Endicott House Conference was held in June 1962 at a secluded estate ten miles from Harvard Square with forty-seven scholars and teachers representing a broad spectrum of disciplines in the social sciences and humanities, and a wide range of views. Controversy emerged almost immediately after Robert Feldmesser, a sociologist, blamed the poor condition of social studies teaching in the schools on historians and the dominance of history in the curriculum. "We shall make no progress in transforming the social studies into social science," he said, "until we slaughter the sacred cow of history."[35] Feldmesser proposed inclusion of more social science materials at all levels, and that children be introduced to the inquiry methods and conceptual structure of the social sciences so that they could develop a more critical attitude toward the social world. Most of the historians at the meeting were offended by Feldmesser's comments, and for a time the conference descended into a turf battle over whose content was most valuable. Edwin Fenton, the historian from Carnegie Institute of Technology, was one of the few historians at the meeting who agreed with Feldmesser that traditional history had dominated the curriculum for too long.

Gradually, however, as the two-week session went on, and other voices were heard, a consensus began to develop around the notion that the problem in the schools had more to do with how history was typically taught, rather than with the subject matter itself. What emerged from the Endicott House meeting was a proposal for more in-depth study, later given the name "postholing," that would engage students in source material and the process of inquiry and that would expose them to the uncertainty, speculation, and imagination that are part of scientific and historical investigation. As at Woods Hole, the latter part of the conference was devoted to presentations by working groups that had been meeting regularly throughout the two weeks to develop concrete suggestions for curriculum reform. In the end, the meeting produced a few suggestions about where the emerging reform of social studies might head, but did not create a blueprint for reform.[36] Following the conference, Zacharias's new ESI social studies group began meeting regularly to develop a refined and concrete proposal to submit to the Ford Foundation, eventually evolving into the Man: A Course of Study (MACOS) curriculum.

The Projects

In the October 1962 issue of *Social Education*, the same month as the Cuban missile crisis, a small, two paragraph, "Announcement for Project Social Studies," appeared on the bottom half of one page. The announcement read, in part, "The United States Office of Education has announced the initiation of Project Social Studies, which is designed to improve research, instruction, teacher education, and the dissemination of information in this field." The announcement also stated that funds were available for research projects, curriculum study centers, conferences and seminars.[37] The fact that the announcement coincided with the height of cold war tension is not lost in hindsight, though at the time the depoliticization of education made it appear a rather innocuous research and development notice, with exciting possibilities for scholars and teachers.

The earliest social science projects had begun to receive funding before the announcement of Project Social Studies and received support from the NSF as well as private foundations such as Ford or Carnegie. Senesh and Fenton had already begun work on their projects in the

1950s and had received at least some private funding for their efforts. A similar endeavor, the Amherst History Project, had its beginnings in the 1959–1960 school year under the leadership of Van Halsey.[38]

Three additional projects were launched in 1961, all emanating from professional associations. All three eventually received funding from the NSF. These included the High School Geography Project, Sociological Resources for the Secondary Schools, and the Anthropology Curriculum Study Project.

Following up on the announcement of Project Social Studies, in July 1963, USOE reported that seven curriculum centers, eleven research projects, and two developmental activities had been approved for funding.[39] These included Fenton's project in American history, and Donald Oliver's project at Harvard focused on analysis of public issues. Four additional new projects were funded in 1964. By 1965, there were some two-dozen projects that made up the new social studies movement, funded by the NSF, the USOE, or private foundations. Most notable among the new additions was the Harvard Education Development Center's (EDC's, formerly ESI) MACOS, for which Jerome Bruner served as the intellectual architect. The vast majority of the projects fit the general theme of the "structure of the disciplines," but there was some diversity in orientation. Perhaps the least compatible with the discipline-based focus was the Harvard Project, with its focus on public issues as the heart of citizenship education.

Clearly, a revolution of sorts was brewing, but what was its nature? In April 1965, *Social Education* devoted virtually the entire issue to a "Report on Project Social Studies," with an overview provided by Edwin Fenton and John Good. Their report began with a bold and confident statement: "The curriculum revolution which began in mathematics, the natural sciences, and modern foreign languages about a decade ago has at last reached the social studies. More than 40 curriculum development projects of national significance promise to revolutionize teaching about man and society."[40]

Calling the sum of the projects "the new social studies," in what appears to be the first use of this term, Fenton and Good provide a succinct summary of some of the general themes of the activities supported by Project Social Studies and other funding sources, including the emphasis on structure, inductive teaching, the disciplines, sequential learning, new types of materials, new subjects, and emphases on evaluation. Though the article gave a concise overview of the new reform, the authors demonstrated little awareness of the contextual origins of the movement.

After 1965 another wave of projects was christened. By 1967 more than fifty national projects were in progress, though curricular materials were slow to appear and were not issued in significant amounts until 1967. The projects created after 1967 all claimed loyalty to the principles of the new social studies, but in actuality, seemed to move off in all imaginable directions. Though there were many variations and permutations on the general themes of the new social studies, the defining parameter of discipline-based inquiry appears to have held fairly constant as a working guideline for the vast majority of projects.

From a distance, it appears that the new social studies movement reached its zenith in 1967. In this year, the total number of funded projects appears to have peaked, and new social studies topics and concerns dominated both *Social Education* and the National Council for the Social Studies (NCSS) annual conference. Moreover, for many of the initial projects, funding periods were at or near their end. The years after 1967 would be spent dealing with publication, dissemination, and diffusion of materials.

A second wave of projects received initial funding from 1968 to 1972. Several of the newly funded projects added selected use of contemporary social problems as topics for study and as criteria for selection of social science content. Adding to the general ferment, nonproject social studies curriculum workers, teachers, and teacher educators labored in the field, often providing conferences and workshops and receiving funds from the USOE, state departments of education, and local school districts.

If 1967 was the zenith of enthusiasm for the new movement, the years following, through the early to mid-1970s, represented a continuing presence with activity at a lower level of intensity. As we shall see, events in the society, many of which impinged directly on schools, may have diluted teacher enthusiasm for the new social studies and its general focus on inquiry based in the disciplines, a step removed from the conflicts and dilemmas of the social world.

In retrospect, the materials produced in the era of the new social studies were among the most innovative and influential commodities ever produced for use in social studies classrooms. Despite the historical context out of which they were born, and perhaps partly because of it, projects funded by millions of grant dollars from the NSF, the USOE, and other sources contributed to creation of a rich and multifaceted explosion of curriculum development the likes of which may never be seen again. The projects and materials set a tone for an era of innovation and inquiry that spread to other curriculum materials, textbooks, and curriculum guides. Yet, as in each of the previous attempts to reform social studies, this one too had its problems.

Concerns and Critiques

The profession was far from united behind the new reform movement. In fact, there were many contemporary critiques of what came to be called the new social studies, and they originated from several different quarters. Perhaps the earliest published critique of the new social studies came from Donald Robinson in an article that appeared in 1963, shortly after the launch of Project Social Studies, which cautioned that "everyone has a different notion of what the social studies should attempt" and concluded that social studies curricular practice would continue to be fashioned by "a combination of national tradition, suggestive state programs, locally prescribed curricula, the considerable influence of textbooks, universities, and professional organizations."[41]

Another similar caution came from James Becker who observed, in 1965, that there was a new consensus emerging on the need for reform in social studies. Yet, ironically, he noted that "never before in our history has there been less general agreement about precisely what needs changing" and described a "nearly total confusion" on goals. Becker cautioned that prospects were slim for any kind of radical change.[42]

Also among the earliest critiques were those voiced in a group of letters published in *Social Education*. Fred M. Newmann wrote that "we must be cautious to avoid seduction by the fashionable emphasis on 'inductive thinking' or 'discovery method'" when the major objectives of most of the projects centered on "communication of the structure of one discipline," and too frequently aimed at guiding students to predetermined generalizations. Byron G. Massialas charged that the projects "concentrate on the empirical and cognitive dimensions of learning" neglecting the "normative and affective components" and assumed that "what is good for the social scientist acting as a researcher is good for the child." Richard E. Gross suggested that the projects suffered from a failure to clearly delineate purposes, a tendency to concentrate on average and above average students, and development of "teacher-proof" materials that could reduce the teacher's role to that of technician.[43]

Another critique by Mark M. Krug charged that the new reforms had conceptual flaws, that there was no logical structure of ideas in the social sciences, and asked why all children should explore "the kinds of questions that interest historians, political scientists (and) economists?" Krug charged that Bruner slighted this need and urged a restoration of traditional history.[44] James P. Shaver lamented the new social studies projects' "general failure...to examine the basic rationale for social studies instruction" and labeled them "scholacentric."[45]

Somewhat surprisingly, another contemporary critique of the new curriculum movement was written by one of its founders, Jerome Bruner. Bruner wrote in 1971 that the rational structuralism of the *Process of Education* "was based on a formula of faith: that learning was what students wanted to do, that they wanted to achieve an expertise in some particular subject matter. Their motivation was taken for granted."[46]

Reform in Perspective

As we have seen, the origins of the new social studies may be found in the confluence of at least four concurrent trends: critiques of progressive education; cold war manpower fears; the increasing power of the military-industrial-academic-government complex and the wartime research model it employed; and, scientists and social scientists' belief in inquiry—as an act of faith—to transform schooling and remake schools and schoolchildren in their own image, conceptualizing schools as sort of a minor league extension of the research university.

As a movement to improve schooling, the new social studies had a number of strengths. Numerous leading scholars were involved. The period illustrates that time, money, and brainpower devoted to curriculum development can have influence. The unprecedented amounts of money devoted to the reform suggests that for that time, social education was taken quite seriously by the society. The reform created a new language and had influence on many teachers. Especially prominent was the belief that an inquiry orientation is one key to meaningful learning. This belief has a good deal of continuing influence on scholarship in social studies, and to a lesser extent, on mainstream practice in social studies classrooms.

Unfortunately, leaders of the broader reform and the new social studies movement made a number of mistakes that may have limited their influence to some extent. Key leaders chose to bypass educators with knowledge of schools, including professors of education and curriculum leaders. Moreover, a number of the leaders of the reform exhibited a high level of arrogance—and made the assumption that their ideas and materials would catch on because of their high quality and inquiry orientation. In many cases, teachers involved in the projects were treated as window dressing—and the resulting materials, in some cases, had a "teacher proof" quality. Most projects aimed at an elite, the upper quarter of students, and neglected others, thus the reform had an elitist, antidemocratic tone. The reform lacked an explicit and fully developed rationale for citizen education. Reformers failed to fully respect the grammar of schooling and obstacles to reform—and consequently, it had relatively low influence in schools—and did not meet the expectations of reformers. Though critics pointed out many of the reform's flaws—it was to little avail.

By 1968 the growing turmoil in the society centered on civil rights, the war in Vietnam, and a host of protest movements as pressing issues began to influence social studies rhetoric, theory, and practice. As we shall see in the next chapter, a grassroots movement emerged in education reprising the progressive and social reconstructionist trends of earlier decades, but in new forms and with new language and materials, as the rebellion in the streets began to enter the classroom.

2

The Newer Social Studies

The projects and materials of the new social studies ran into problems almost instantaneously, in part because their vocabulary and conceptual level were high, but largely because they frequently failed to address the pressing matters of the 1960s: civil rights, the war in Vietnam, and campus turmoil. During the late 1960s and early 1970s, social studies changed in numerous ways. Both the rhetoric and the practice of social studies instruction were deeply altered in many classrooms by the events and issues of the times, albeit temporarily. During the 1960s, the war in Vietnam had grown from a relatively minor police action engaging a contingent of US advisors to a major American overseas involvement that included a military draft, half a million US troops in Vietnam, and massive protests at home. The struggle for civil rights changed from a period of marches, protests, and sit-ins to the era of Black Power and morphed from a focus on Black civil rights to a multicultural effort for equality and justice involving several historically oppressed groups, including Latino Americans, Asian Pacific Americans, and Native Americans. The struggle for civil rights also crossed gender lines and spread into the women's liberation and gay rights movements. From the early 1960s, university students pressed for greater freedom and the right to make decisions over their own education and inspired the nation to live up to its democratic ideals. What began among a few student radicals gradually became a counterculture movement that would lead to a significant cultural shift. During a relatively short span of time, the United States went from an age of conformity in the 1950s to an age of rebellion and questioning that, it seemed, was pulling the country apart.[1]

The dramatic events and issues of the period became part of the culture of schooling. At its heart, many members of the baby boomer generation that came of age in the 1960s and early 1970s embodied a spirit of rebellion, an antiauthoritarian ethos, and a strong sense that America was not living up to its ideals, that the authorities were not telling the whole truth, and that something had to be done. From the perspective of many youth of the time, the traditional social studies curriculum and beyond that, the school as an institution, were seen as a major arm of the establishment and part of the problem, a repressive and authoritarian institution that needed profound reform, if not dissolution. In total, the social movements and changes of the time, while often romantic and sometimes revolutionary in tone, were a revolt against complacency and the moral compromise that had for so long marked American society. They were, largely, an embodiment of a movement for the greater realization of human potential and freedom. However, because the "movement" was splintered around so many different issues and interest groups, there was a tendency toward fragmentation. Social studies reform of the period was a strong reflection of that splintering and was, in hindsight, largely fragmentary, partial, and only temporarily effective.

1968: The Year Everything Changed

The events of 1968 seemed the zenith of the building turmoil of a decade. The assassination of the Rev. Dr. Martin Luther King, Jr., rioting in many cities, student strikes, antiwar marches and confrontations, and growing militancy by minorities contributed to a climate of crisis in the nation and calls for substantial social change.[2] The social studies rejoinder to this turbulence took form in the code word "relevance" and spiked interest in social problems and social activism. Probably the most noteworthy effect of this new trend was its influence on course offerings, giving impetus to a short-term flurry of development in which many high schools swiftly created minicourses on a cornucopia of topics: Black history, Native American history, and women's history, among others. Though the minicourse explosion was relatively short lived, it had a considerable impact on the problems curriculum later on, as we shall see.

National Council for the Social Studies (NCSS) and *Social Education*: Evidence of Change. The commotion in the streets was accompanied by dramatic changes in the journal *Social Education* in both style and substance. While a reflection of the times, the alterations in the pages of *Social Education* were also instigated by a change of editors, from Lewis Paul Todd to Daniel Roselle, and from staid tradition to a journal and field suddenly obsessed by the concerns of youth for relevance, engagement, and social transformation. There was a crescendo toward change from the early 1960s and before. In the newer movement, the notion of student as minor-league social scientist was superseded by student as social activist. The newer social studies stressed an issues-centered, largely pre-sentist direction. Following the initial blast, a new wave of topical interest evolved, including a focus on urbanization, environmentalism, population, futurism, women's studies, and area studies, with a special focus on Africa and Asia, areas long neglected. Concomitant with the topical focus on issues was a growing stress on newer methods and pedagogical techniques, including simulation, small group discussion, values education, concepts and inquiry, and active learning. These pedagogical changes were, in part, extensions of the new social studies and, in some cases, well-known progressive reforms under new labels. Most of the innovations of the time employed the new social studies terminology of inquiry, concepts, valuing, and decision making and were assisted by the increased availability of a new and varied array of classroom materials in a range of mediums.

The NCSS annual conference was also enlivened with the newer trends. NCSS presidential addresses were a reflection of the time, with titles such as "Activism in Social Studies Education," "The Choice Before Us," and "A Social Studies Manifesto." Many presidential addresses mirrored the focus on issues and the confrontations of the "student revolution." At the 1968 NCSS conference, attendees held an "almost spontaneous speakout" following the Friday night banquet with nearly 100 participating. According to one observer, "Those who spoke did so out of concern for and disappointment with the vitality of the NCSS convention." A participant in the "speak-out" captured the general tone: "This meeting is supposed to have the theme of Urban Education. Does this conference have anything to do with this theme? I haven't seen...any real urgency about the world passing us by in the cities and beginning to go awry."[3]

The 1969 NCSS House of Delegates passed a resolution demanding that the US government "exert every effort to withdraw from military engagement in the Republic of Vietnam." Later, the NCSS board of directors passed a revised and slightly toned-down version also calling for withdrawal.[4] By 1972, the NCSS board of directors was considering a question at the very heart of the new movement: "What should be the role of the NCSS as an activist in connection with social, political, and economic issues in our society?"[5]

Although there had been quite a bit of critical commentary on schooling during the early and middle parts of the decade, urging school reform and a stronger role for schools in curing the ills of society, by the late 1960s many critics of schooling declared that schools were as much a cause of the nation's social ills as were other "establishment" institutions. Critics of American schooling, stirred by rebellious and revolutionary events and the zeitgeist of the times, came in various stripes, but tended to fall into one of two main categories: multiculturalists who included Black Power advocates, along with representatives of a host of other oppressed groups; and humanists, who tended to embody what might be referred to as the new progressivism, which also took a variety of forms.

Then there were the issues. Perhaps never before in American history had a confluence of issues exploded upon the scene the way they did in the 1960s. Most prominent were the multicultural issues of race, class, and gender, with the antiwar movement equally if not more powerful in generating a growing opposition to mainstream culture.

Although social studies journals and literature had given occasional though often superficial attention to racial issues, in the late 1960s, there was a burst of activity. An article by James A. Banks in 1968 recommended that "inquiries into black power, poverty, racism, the black revolt, and historical reactions to oppression should characterize social studies for black pupils." The April 1969 issue of *Social Education* was devoted in its entirety to "Black Americans and Social Studies" and "minority groups in American society." Other special issues and articles followed, devoted to American Indians and women in history. There were articles on "Women and the Language of Inequality" and "Clarifying Sexist Values." Later, there was a special section on "Eliminating Sexism from the Schools."

Black Power. The effort to gain equal educational opportunity for Black children was one of the guiding forces of the period. Although curricular issues were generally subsumed under the quest for integration, a number of Black leaders began examining the policies and practices of schools, and the Black Power critique of schools resulted. The most powerful expression of the Black Power position came in a book entitled *Black Power* by Stokely Carmichael (who later changed his name to Kwame Ture) and Charles V. Hamilton. In the view of Carmichael and Hamilton, "Black people in this country form a colony, and it is not in the interest of the colonial power to liberate them." The educational system was an arm of that colonial power, and it continued to "reinforce the entrenched values of the society... [and] support a racist system." This analysis led Carmichael and Hamilton, and other advocates, to demand an end to White control of Black schools. As they put it, "White decision-makers have been running those schools with injustice, indifference, and inadequacy for too long; the result has been an educationally crippled black child turned out onto the labor market equipped to do little more than stand in welfare lines to receive his miserable dole." Instead, they argued, "Black parents should seek... actual control of the schools in their community; hiring and firing of teachers, selection of teaching materials, determination of standards, etc." A second and related objective focused on the transformation of the curriculum. Rejecting the "traditional," "irrelevant" and white-dominated curriculum used in schools, the Black Power advocates demanded that schools revise their programs, especially in those schools serving Black children, to reflect the history and culture of African American people. Earlier, Malcolm X had argued that the school program was part of a deliberate effort to hide the true history of African Americans. Even critics of Black Power such as Martin Luther King, Jr., denounced traditional history books that "completely ignored the contribution of the Negro in American history" and advocated an end to what he described as "cultural homicide."[6]

Black Power advocates argued persuasively that if schools were given over to community control, and if the curriculum were revised to more accurately reflect the history and contributions of African Americans, and if new methods and materials were created that would provide greater relevance for Black children, then African American children would quite naturally strive for higher levels of achievement and success. By the late 1960s, the journal *Social Education* quickly filled with articles on what was labeled, "the black experience." The 1968 article by James A. Banks, mentioned earlier, affirmed the essence of the Black Power thesis with the argument that social studies for African American pupils should emphasize inquiry into "black power, poverty, racism" and the historic struggle against oppression. Banks projected a new identity for African American students and called on social studies teachers to "promote this identity quest" by examining racism past and present, by stressing the contributions of Black people, and by developing positive self-images and higher expectations among Black youth. Banks drew on the language and ideas of the new social studies and suggested use of historical documents, inquiry, and concepts in implementing the new approach.[7]

In the April 1969 issue of *Social Education*, devoted to "black Americans" and "minority groups," Nathan Hare advocated courses in Black history and culture that would focus on "the struggle and aspirations of the black race" and proposed a Black History Week to begin with the date of Malcolm X's assassination, February 21, and include February 23, the birthday of W. E. B. DuBois. Emily Gibson argued that mainstream historians had "distorted the image of black people" and omitted people, episodes, and contributions that did not fit the stereotype, "and thereby denied black people the right to pride in their heritage." She described several examples of neglected aspects of African American history, including slave revolts, Black African empires, Black contributions to American life, and examples of "the white man's inhumanity to other human beings." Moreover, she reported that Black youth were "demanding that school curriculums and textbooks be revised to 'tell it like it is.'"

Two contributors attacked the Black biography approach as insufficient. Edwin Fenton suggested that knowledge of the achievements of black individuals would do little to change attitudes, and that focus on a biographical approach might limit the learning of inquiry skills, which required a greater range of materials. Instead, he urged a broader treatment of Black history rather than a focus on individual contributions. Louis Harlan, historian and biographer of Booker T. Washington, largely agreed with Fenton, and wrote that he considered the Black version of "cherry tree history" to be misleading and unrealistic. Instead, he proposed five interpretive themes to guide the study of Black history in schools, beginning with the historical repression and subordination of Blacks, and including Black cultural history and Black urbanization among other topics.

That issue of *Social Education* also included articles on teaching about other groups that had been historically oppressed and denied equality, including Native Americans, Latinos, and Asian Pacific Americans. Subsequent issues of *Social Education* were devoted to further depth on the topic of ethnic studies or multiethnic education, as it was frequently called. For example, the May 1972 issue of *Social Education* was devoted to "teaching about American Indians," and it included articles aimed at "teaching non-Indian students about American Indians." Edited by Hazel W. Hertzberg, a longtime scholar of American Indian history, the special section was a plea for balanced treatment and greater knowledge of the Native American past. In an introduction to the special issue, Hertzberg warned against "the tendency to overcompensate for past errors of omission and commission" and argued that it could lead to a range of problems, including the assumption that victims of discrimination "are thereby free of prejudices of their own," the tendency to treat ethnic groups as "much more monolithic than they actually are," the tendency to treat them as "virtually time-free, unchanging entities," and the failure to recognize "the tremendous amount of mixing that has taken place."[8]

The lead article of the section, which was also authored by Hertzberg, addressed issues in teaching about American Indians. She challenged teachers to help students gain knowledge and to overcome "three major images of the Indian," which are widespread and frequently presented in a stereotyped fashion: "The noble savage, the ignoble savage, and the victim." She warned that school experiences that further these images could be "counter-educational" and suggested that students needed "far more balanced and rounded pictures of Indian historical development," one that goes beyond political history, one that sees the past through "new and more complex perspectives," meaning that "the frontier will be seen from both sides. The winning of the West will also be the losing of the West. The Civil War will also be a civil war among the tribes." She warned against "overcompensating" for the biased treatment of the past and of "peopling the past with stereotypes of whites which have no more validity than the stereotypes of Indians we are trying to banish." Placing the ethnic studies in broad perspective, she suggested that we were "just beginning a search for a new definition of American nationality" that can help the nation overcome the prospect of "accelerating intergroup hostilities and conflicts."[9]

The NCSS Racism Clinics. During the early 1970s, NCSS sponsored a series of racism clinics for teachers, which were held under a variety of titles and in various cities. Material on the Racism Clinics offers an interesting window on the changes under way in American schools and communities. Ostensibly intended to improve the teaching of ethnic studies and to further antiracist education, the clinics were also part of a membership program aimed at recruiting more members from urban areas. Moreover, one of the clinics, titled "Changing Racism and Social Injustice," had the explicit purpose to "help participants clarify and focus specific changes that are needed in their school community to lessen racism and social injustice." The clinics themselves engaged teachers in a variety of activities or "modules," including "Black and White Mask Role Playing," the "Assumption and Behavior Chart," and a focus on "Defining Racism in Teacher Behavior" through a variety of small-group and large-group simulation, role-playing, and discussion activities. Another clinic included use of the powerful "Starpower" simulation, in which participants replicate a hierarchical class society as a springboard for deeper examination of issues of race and class.[10]

Another NCSS Racism Clinic used a problem-solving approach in which participants were asked to describe problems they had experienced in their "current situation" regarding race relations in schools, by writing about the problem on index cards. Many of the participants' responses were revealing, suggesting the depth and intractability of the problem. One reported "increasing tensions between white and black students in a system with approximately 10% black. Lack of movement on the part of administration and community and most teachers to deal with tensions in any way." Another participant who worked at an "uptight suburban school" reported that the school had established a "Human Relations Committee" but that its work had been "watered down" and suggested that there was a great deal of "resistance" to the topic from virtually all members of the community. Another participant brought up the larger problem of "tracking" or ability grouping and suggested that concerned professionals could "collect and disseminate well written materials which attack tracking" and provide in-service training to better prepare teachers for a heterogeneously grouped classroom.[11]

A participant from a southwestern city described "a well-oiled very Anglo centered, power machine which completely dominates the city" and suggested that while minorities made up the majority of residents, "their enjoyment of solid community respect, economic and political power and a fair press and educational opportunity is minimal." A participant from a southern state wrote that "students—both black and white—have rejected court ordered de-segregation. What does the community now do to comply with the law? Black racism and White racism seem to be polarizing the inner city more each year." A participant, from a community "with almost no minority groups," reported that the problem was apathy. Another, from a northern city, suggested that behind the problem of racism was "a selfish desire to remain in this privileged position."

A somewhat different NCSS Racism Clinic focused on changing "teacher behavior" in the classroom, school, and community, as well as developing and using new curricula. The two-day session was open to those serving as department chairs or supervisors and to those "who wish to play a leadership role in facilitating change in their school." Participants in the clinic devoted some attention to teaching social issues and development of curriculum materials. Although the clinic had a broad focus, much of the content aimed at addressing the problem of "subconscious manifestations of racism in teacher behavior." The ensuing modules were an effort to "provide participants...with a heightened awareness of the many subtle and not-so-subtle manifestations of racism in the teacher's interactions with students and parents...(with a) focus on alternative strategies to employ in identifying and changing racist behavior" in teachers, students, individuals, and institutions. This clinic employed a variety of techniques, including problem solving of specific situations raised by participants; discussion of a list of specific behaviors described as "covert or overt acts of discrimination"; and a thorny case study involving a teacher who received parental complaints about use of a simulation game called "Sunshine: A Simulation of Current Racial Problems in a Typical American City," in a unit on "Minority Groups in U.S. History," an administrative order to stop teaching the unit, and nonrenewal of the teacher's contract. Evaluation data from participants in one of the clinics indicated that while the clinic was generally well received, there was something of a mixed response, as might be expected for serious discussion of such contentious topics.[12] Despite the probable mixed results, from the available evidence, the clinics appear to have been well intentioned and generally helpful.

The New-Wave Critique of Schooling

During the late 1960s and early 1970s, the rhetoric of social redemption through schooling experienced a brief revival. Emphasis on the dilemmas of American society had an implicit social reconstructionist orientation. The social reconstructionist camp had been moribund for some time, though a few scholars, notably Theodore Brameld, kept the tradition alive. By the late 1960s, the time was ripe for a revival of social reconstructionism in social studies. In a 1968 article entitled "The Year of the Non-Curriculum: A Proposal," Gerald Leinwand proposed a poststructuralist focus on social issues, a recommendation which appeared prophetic for a time. In his article, Leinwand suggested that a "noncurriculum" conference would focus on teachers and teaching, and on media and materials, all with "the view toward making the social studies relevant to the needs of our time." He called for a social studies curriculum that would "reflect and anticipate the domestic and foreign revolutions of the next decade" and help students and teachers interpret and participate. Deriding both the new social studies and traditional practice, Leinwand seemed to blame the lack of improvement in classrooms on "the fact that there is such a thing as a social studies curriculum." He charged that curriculum bulletins "tend to inhibit creative thinking" and were "the cause and not the cure for what still appears to be a social studies program in straightjacket." He wrote,

> I am convinced that curriculum making seems to be an embalming process in which the life blood is drained from the heart of the social studies and its pulse beat becomes muted and slack...Social evil lives on but remains outside the concerns of curriculum bulletins, and, therefore social studies teachers and teaching. Because the good only seems to be interred in curriculum bulletins, students learn a distorted, rather euphoric lesson in national and world events and emerge ill-equipped to wrestle with the evils that do exist and with which the revolutions of our day are involved. The school in general and the social studies in particular, therefore, remain detached and aloof, perhaps even alienated, from the throbbing events of our time as the curriculum bulletin decrees one thing but events show something quite different.[13]

Leinwand then proposed an NCSS conference focused on his notion of a "noncurriculum" with meetings devoted to each of the "major problems of our time" and emphasis on how teachers should teach and "what students should know how to do if they are to function effectively as intelligent members of a society in revolution." He then nominated eleven problem topics as the focus for the meeting. His list included many of the burning issues of the late 1960s: air and water pollution, traffic and transit, urban and rural slums, adult crime and juvenile delinquency, civil rights and civil liberties, the Negro in the city, urban and rural poverty, Black Power, protest (violent and nonviolent), the draft, and war and peace.

The article concluded with the recommendation that the conference could "prepare the stage by which the thrust of the social studies for students and teachers alike could be altered from that of detachment to that of militancy, from that of sideline observers to that of dynamic participants, from rear-guard action to vanguard action." Leinwand cited Brameld's similar call, almost two decades earlier, for schools to become active participants in the affairs of mankind and envisioned social studies and school programs that would "ameliorate the problems of the seventies and...restructure the social order."[14] Leinwand later published a paperback series, *Problems of American Society*, which seemed ubiquitous for a time and may have been a contributing factor in the ferment for teaching social issues.[15]

Also, in 1970, Frank Simon published *A Reconstructive Approach to Problem-Solving*, which was plainly a revival of the social reconstructionist tradition. In this "Handbook for Inquiry and Post-Inquiry," Simon called for an approach to problem-solving with a strong social action focus, substantially different from the typical problems approach. He suggested a requirement that students formulate a hypothesis on "the desirability and feasibility of taking action on the problem," thus beginning study with a much different orientation. Students would also be asked to identify proposals for a course of action, study the desirability and feasibility of taking overt group action, and, in the event of a positive decision, engage in the agreed-upon action. This was, the author wrote, a process component for inquiry and postinquiry activity on "the should question," asking students to take and act on a value position. One interesting sidelight, Simon also suggested that each student "examine his position further—by himself" as a way to minimize defensiveness and tuning out.[16]

New-Wave Literature. The development that I am labeling the newer social studies coincided with an outburst of interest in education and a new wave of analysis that rivaled the 1950s critique of progressivism, though it was from a much different direction. A slew of bestsellers called attention to the problems of the schools and proposed reform, revolution, or some other alternative. Included among the new-wave books critical of educational practice, and of "ghetto-school" education in particular, were Nat Hentoff's *Our Children Are Dying*, James Herndon's *The Way It Spozed to Be*, John Holt's *How Children Fail* and *How Children Learn*, and Jonathan Kozol's *Death at an Early Age*.[17] Each author, with the exception of Hentoff, was writing about his own experience as a teacher. As a group, they advocated greater concern with affective aspects of schooling than academic excellence; they called for humanizing teaching and the school bureaucracy; and recommended a return to some of the best aspects of progressivism. The new-wave literature was critical of schools as institutions that frequently stifled creative teaching, a curriculum that was outmoded and dysfunctional, and testing that was often counterproductive. It was also critical of teachers who behaved in an ignorant or even destructive manner toward children.

The new wave was accompanied by a host of additional titles in a similar but more radical vein, sharing, but repeatedly going beyond the new-wave critique. These included John Goodman's *Compulsory Miseducation*, Everett Reimer's *School Is Dead*, and Neil Postman and Charles Weingartner's *Teaching as a Subversive Activity*. At least two influential books, published earlier, became popular again, notably Paul Goodman's *Growing Up Absurd*, and A. S. Neill's *Summerhill*, the classic seminal work on open education and a predecessor of the new wave. Charles E. Silberman's *Crisis in the Classroom* attempted to capture the new impulse toward open education. A later addition was Ivan Illich's *Deschooling Society*.[18] These works shared a disdain for traditional schooling and embraced a philosophy that bore strong resemblance, in many cases, to child-centered progressivism and its Rousseauian orientation. They paralleled the social trends and critiques of the time and were written partly in response to the inadequacies of American schooling for children of color and the national atmosphere of racial unrest, student rebellion, and antiwar protest.

The critique of schools engendered by the new literature was quite devastating. According to the critics, schools were institutions of conformity that destroyed the souls of children, coerced them to sit through hours of lifeless classes, neglected the needs of individuals, and oppressed the culture and history of students of color. Schools were attached to a lifeless and irrelevant curriculum and used antiquated teaching methods that destroy student curiosity. It seemed there was no alternative but to either transform schools or abandon them.[19] The new radical perspective on schooling and the movement to create open and alternative schools epitomized the tone of the late 1960s and early 1970s and created a conducive climate for the rise of the newer social studies.

At least a few of these works might be thought of as forerunners of the new wave because they appeared in the early 1960s. Neill's *Summerhill* came out in 1960, just as the government backed structure of the disciplines reforms were beginning to take hold on policy makers. *Summerhill* was a largely autobiographical and anecdotal description of Neill's experiences running a nontraditional boarding school in England. Neill challenged the discipline and routine that was typical in traditional schools and believed that "the child is innately wise and realistic. If left to himself without adult suggestion of any kind, he will develop as far as he is capable of developing." At Summerhill, there were no required classes or lessons, leaving the academic side of education until the child was ready for it. Neill wrote,

> Parents are slow in realizing how unimportant the learning side of school is. Children, like adults, learn what they want to learn. All prize-giving and marks and exams sidetrack proper personality development...All that any child needs is the three R's; the rest should be tools and clay and sports and theater and paint and freedom.[20]

Though the book contained strong echoes of the Rousseauian, child-centered strain of progressive education, which had captured the imagination of many teachers and some scholars during the 1920s, it found little resonance in the United States on its initial publication in 1960. However, with the changed atmosphere of the late 1960s, the book was selling more than 200,000 copies per year. A part of the appeal may be found in Neill's criticism of traditional education, the routine, mind-numbing conformity and pedantry that characterized so many classrooms. That critique, combined with the hopefulness and ray of possibility of freedom, gave Summerhill a strong consonance with the social milieu of the late 1960s.

Another forerunner of the new wave might be seen in Paul Goodman's eloquent and impassioned writing in *Growing Up Absurd* (1960) and *Compulsory Mis-Education* (1966). In these books and a veritable deluge of essays, Goodman condemned the stifling conformity and lifelessness of middle-class American life, which had become so prevalent, and seemed the essence of normality during the decade of the 1950s. He focused upon education's often unnoticed shadow, on its destruction of curiosity and emotional and spiritual vitality. Goodman's works lay down several of the major themes of the new-wave humanist critique of schools that seemed to promise a powerful transformation of schooling. He critiqued the absurdities of life-adjustment education, but saw it as a betrayal of progressive education, rather than its logical extension. He also critiqued James B. Conant's rather narrow vision of who should be well educated in a highly differentiated system and critiqued Conant's implicit notion that schools "are, effectively, to be used as apprentice training grounds for the monopolies and armed forces."[21] Instead, he called for new forms of education that would cultivate the mind, dignify the spirit, and develop individuals with a strong sense of moral conviction and courage.

In *Compulsory Mis-Education*, Goodman suggested that reform had to begin by breaking the power of the professional educators that Arthur Bestor had railed against and that Zacharias, Bruner, Fenton, and other establishment curriculum reformers had bypassed. Goodman argued that schools were held in the grip of "school-monks: the administrators, professors, academic sociologists, and licensees with diplomas who have proliferated into an invested intellectual class." However, he rejected the notion that scholars from the disciplines would do any better, describing them as deeply implicated in creating and sustaining an increasingly technocratic and heartless society. In addition, imposing increasingly rigorous academic standards, another goal of 1950s critics and the subsequent curriculum reformers, would only produce greater anger and alienation among students. Instead, Goodman argued that compulsory schooling itself was at the heart of the nation's educational dilemmas, particularly during the postwar years when, it seemed to him, "an important function of the schools began to be baby-sitting and policing," or essentially, to "warehouse" adolescents. He argued that prolonged schooling for adolescents was "psychologically, politically, and professionally damaging," that adolescents were "herded into" schools where they were bribed, pressured, subdued, regimented, and essentially "brainwashed" to serve the system. He believed that the only reform that could improve the situation would be some form of "deschooling" by which compulsory high school education would be replaced by various decentralized alternatives, including apprenticeships and other real-life activities through which young people could discover themselves, develop a livelihood, and begin to make their way in the world.[22]

As the 1960s wore on, and as the civil rights movement, the growing counterculture, and the escalating protests against the war in Vietnam multiplied exponentially, an increasing number of Americans came to view the schools as complicit in the nation's problems. Schools were seen as an institution of oppression furthering the will of the establishment and fomenting many of the nation's problems, including racism, sexism, militarism, and the glorification of both technology and technocracy.

By the mid- to late 1960s, other works in a similar vein began to appear. In 1967, Kozol's *Death at an Early Age* and Herbert Kohl's *36 Children* told of the personal experiences of two young elementary teachers, one in Boston and the other in New York. Kozol's work, which won the prestigious National Book Award, described his year at a school in which children's self-esteem and educational chances are compromised by uncaring, cruel, and racist teachers and a school system that condoned them. Kohl told of a year of teaching during which he replaced the prescribed curriculum and encouraged his students learning through the vehicle of creative writing.[23]

As the new-wave literature multiplied and began to reach its peak in the late 1960s and early 1970s, several minigenres emerged, largely reflecting themes established earlier. Nat Hentoff's *Our Children Are Dying* told of a public school principal struggling to provide quality education for Black children; James Herndon's *The Way It Spozed to Be* and *How to Survive in Your Native Land* conveyed the story of a young teacher struggling to survive in the system and learning to treat his students humanely, as thoughtful young people; Holt's *Why Children Fail* expressed the ruminations of a teacher who had come to realize that the curriculum, methods, and regimentation of the school suppress the joy of learning; and, finally, Ivan Illich's *De-Schooling Society* advocated a broad movement toward alternative forms of education and deschooling.[24]

In the new-wave literature, critics offered a damning assessment of the school as an institution and its social, emotional, psychological, and spiritual impact on children. The school coerced unwilling youth to sit through stultifying classes, producing docile servants of the industrial, technocratic machine. The school and its teachers and staff neglected the needs of individuals, imposing an irrelevant and culturally biased, one-size-fits-all curriculum on children with diverse backgrounds, needs, and interests. It chastened or repelled creative teachers and rewarded sycophants. For those who agreed with the new-wave indictment, there was no good alternative other than to engage in serious reform or burn down the schools and start over.

The new-wave literature is of some importance to the history of social studies in schools because it captured and reflected the spirit of the times. Moreover, during the late 1960s and early 1970s, the new-wave literature and their dramatic titles seemed ubiquitous, prominently displayed in bookstores and storefront windows across the nation. For social studies, the implications were immense, in terms of both pedagogy and curriculum. All of this touched social studies partly because the critiques of irrelevance and cultural bias pointedly hit their mark in history and social science topics and courses. Yet, only a few works of the new-wave literature had a special focus on social studies. One in particular deserves some discussion. *Teaching as a Subversive Activity* by Postman and Weingartner appeared in 1969. The book's cover depicted an apple, that staid standby of the teacher's desk, with a fuse where the stem would normally be, and the fuse was ready for lighting. Because of their long association with the "authoritarian" school, the traditional academic subjects received especially sharp criticism. Earlier critics of schooling during the cold war era had presented them as vital to national security. To new-wave critics, mathematics, science, foreign languages, and the social sciences were seen as complicit by affiliation in the establishment's war machine. So it was not too surprising to see Postman and Weingartner's call to "dissolve all subjects, 'courses,' and especially 'course requirements'" and require "every teacher who thinks he knows his 'subject'" to write a book on it so that he will no longer have "the necessity of inflicting his knowledge on students." While many items in their list of sixteen proposals were fanciful, others embodied the essence of reflective teaching practice. One proposal called for the teacher to limit her or his speech to "three declarative sentences per class, and 15 interrogatives" and included an admonition to "declare a five-year moratorium on the use of all textbooks." The essence of the authors' argument revolved around inspiring students to question, doubt, and challenge their society, as shown in the following passage from their first chapter:

> We believe that schools must serve as the principal medium for developing in youth the attitudes and skills of social, political, and cultural criticism. No. That is not emphatic enough. Try this: In the early 1960s an interviewer was trying to get Ernest Hemingway to identify the characteristics required for a person to be a "great writer." As the interviewer offered a list of various possibilities, Hemingway disparaged each in sequence. Finally, frustrated, the interviewer asked, "Isn't there any one essential ingredient that you can identify?" Hemingway replied, "Yes, there is. In order to be a great writer a person must have a built-in, shockproof crap detector."[25]

They went on to explain that Hemingway had identified an essential function for schools, "a new education that would set out to cultivate...experts at 'crap detecting,'" that would help to undermine "misconceptions, faulty assumptions, superstitions, and even outright lies" that are sometimes held as fond beliefs. The book also contained an excellent and still helpful chapter on "the inquiry method" and thoughtful commentary on "pursuing relevance" and "what's worth knowing." "Relevance," one of the watchwords of the newer social studies meant, "unless an inquiry is perceived as relevant by the learner, no significant learning will take place." Thus, the student must perceive "whatever is to-be-learned as worth learning." The topic of learning might be suggested by the teacher, the student, or even the curriculum, but regardless of the source, it must connect to reality and to student interest. Describing their approach as a "warmed-over 'progressive education,'" they suggest that the curriculum should focus a good deal of attention on relevant problems in society, and a variety of resources as determined by students' questions, and suggested by a set of provocative questions they list in a chapter titled "What's Worth Knowing?"[26] Despite a tendency toward overstatement and a sense of romantic adventurism, *Teaching as a Subversive Activity* remains a treatise of the new-wave critique, with many direct applications to learning to teach thoughtfully.[27]

Gradually, the new-wave writers and critics developed a fairly consistent list of changes that they believed would lead to the transformation of American schooling. The essence of the list was captured by Ronald Gross in 1971:

1. Students, not teachers must be at the center of education.
2. Teaching and learning should start and stay with students' real concerns, rather than the artificial disciplines, bureaucratic requirements, or adults' rigid ideas about what children need to learn.
3. The paraphernalia of standard classroom practice should be abolished: mechanical order, silence, tests, grades, lesson plans, hierarchical supervision and administration, homework, and compulsory attendance.
4. Most existing textbooks should be thrown out.[28]

Rather than being new and truly revolutionary, the core ideas of new-wave critics were a warmed-over, sometimes romanticized version of at least two strains of progressive education, combining variations on child-centered progressivism and social reconstructionism with emphasis on overturning the dominant racist, sexist, and militaristic interests of the day. The new-wave humanistic educators of the 1960s and 1970s reapplied and sharpened the critique of schools first given voice by the social reconstructionists of the 1930s, dissolving the facade of neutrality and cosmetic democracy that usually obscured the real functioning of schools, to sort students into subservient roles that would benefit the ruling elite and perpetuate capitalist institutions and all that accompanied them. Theodore Roszak, one of the intellectual leaders of the counterculture that lay behind the new-wave critique of schools, observed, "We call it 'education,' the 'life of the mind,' the 'pursuit of truth,' but it is a matter of machine-tooling the young to the needs of our various baroque bureaucracies: corporate, governmental, military, trade union, educational."[29] Moreover, in lively rhetoric that frequently surpassed that of the social reconstructionists, many new-wave critics believed that the revolution could begin in the schools. Unlike the reconstructionists, however, many saw variations on child-centered education, including open schooling, free-schooling, and deschooling as both the ultimate incubator of revolutionary thought and the best venue for educational experimentation.

The 1971 NCSS Guidelines. For its part in the revolution, NCSS did what such organizations often do when things get stirred up. They appointed a task force to make curriculum recommendations. The recommendations made in the 1971 NCSS curriculum guidelines fully embodied the essence of the era, proposing an issues-centered approach to social studies. The guidelines, developed by an NCSS task force composed of Gary Manson, Gerald Marker, Anna Ochoa, and Jan Tucker, began with a basic rationale, postulating a twofold purpose: "Enhancement of human dignity through learning and commitment to rational processes as the principal means of attaining that end." The task force defined human dignity as including "equal access...due process...social and economic justice, democratic decision making, free speech, and religious freedom." They went on to suggest that students of social studies "should apply their knowledge, abilities, and commitments toward the improvement of the human condition," a meliorist and reconstructionist goal. The task force statement included passages on knowledge, abilities (skills), valuing, and social participation, offering a rationale and theoretical framework for social studies that was clearly within the meliorist tradition.[30]

The guidelines themselves included nine major statements each supported by subguidelines. The nine guiding principles included recommendations that social studies should be directly related to concerns of students, focus on the real social world, draw from the social sciences, provide clear objectives and engaging and active learning experiences, draw on a variety of learning resources, and include systematic evaluation. The second section postulated that "the Social Studies Program Should Deal with the Real Social World." This section included a number of important subguidelines or "shoulds," including

- focus on the social world as it is, its flaws, its ideals, its strengths, its dangers, and its promise.

- emphasize pervasive and enduring social issues.
- include analysis and attempts to formulate potential resolutions of present and controversial problems such as racism, poverty, war, and population.
- provide intensive and recurrent study of cultural, racial, religious, and ethnic groups.
- meet, discuss, study, and work with members of racial and ethnic groups other than their own.
- build upon the realities of the immediate school community.
- participation in the real social world...a part of the social studies.[31]

The next passage stated that "enduring or pervasive social issues such as economic injustice, conflict, racism, social disorder, and environmental imbalance are appropriate content for the social studies curriculum."

The third guideline sounded a new social studies orientation and emphasized "currently valid concepts, principles, and theories in the social sciences" as well as "proficiency in methods of inquiry in the social sciences." However, the operative word was "draw," as in "the program should draw upon all of the social sciences." With a focus on pervasive social issues and problems, they suggested that "basic questions in students' lives can be helpful in deciding upon what to draw from the disciplines" and hinted that a melding of the power of the scholarly disciplines and social issues might be possible and "deserve[s] staunch support." Though the authors did not offer a revised scope and sequence for social studies courses, they did call for "a fresh look at the conventional pattern of subjects and formal course offerings." They suggested that "schools ought to encourage mini-courses, independent study, small group interest sections, specially planned days or weeks focused on social problems, alternative courses of study proposed by students, or other innovative plans for unfreezing the frigid school year."[32]

The extent to which the guidelines were utilized is difficult to assess, though there were a few indications. According to one non-representative attempt to evaluate their dissemination conducted in 1974, the guidelines were utilized in many school districts to revise curricula or to serve as a basic reference in evaluating materials, writing objectives, and developing exemplary models for social studies programs. In districts where they were used, "the preponderant opinion is that the Guidelines have provided the basis for fundamental, systematic, and innovative change." Unfortunately, the authors reported, though many school districts were using the guidelines, "many more are not." Apparently, the guidelines were not used or even known in "some large urban centers and in some states."[33]

New Trends in Social Studies

The minicourse explosion may also provide an indication of the possible impact of the NCSS guidelines, though there were unquestionably many influences contributing to this trend of the late 1960s and 1970s. In the April 1973 issue of *The Clearing House*, a proposal was presented for the restructuring of traditional-length courses into a series of minicourses that would be more accommodating to student interests and needs. Accompanying the proposal was a survey of minicourse offerings in schools, an indication that the trend was already well under way by that time. One survey conducted in the mid-1970s indicated that 31 percent of the public high schools in Kansas had developed minicourse programs in social studies, most commonly in American history and government. The most regularly offered minicourses in American history were focused on the Civil War, recent American history, the American west, and the colonies. The most frequently offered government courses were State and Local Government, the Presidency, the Constitution, and Youth and the Law.[34]

Origins of the Minicourse. The origins of the minicourse curriculum are somewhat difficult to establish with certainty. Several trends growing out of the 1960s seemed to point toward the development. Early in the decade there was a surge of interest in "ungraded" or "nongraded" schools at the elementary level, which began to spread to secondary schools.[35] Moreover, the new-wave and humanistic literature led to a great deal of interest among teachers and administrators in infusing the schools with a more humane spirit and atmosphere, relaxing regulations, cutting the number of required classes, giving students greater curricular choice and flexibility with their time, and, in a few places, radically restructuring the curriculum. Along with these broader institutional trends came a much greater focus on appealing to student interests. If schools were the dreary and lockstep institutions depicted in the new-wave critique, perhaps an answer could be found in offering students more curricular choice, through minicourses, and through what was called flexible modular scheduling, in which it was possible to offer class periods of varying length.[36]

The idea for minicourses had developed in English education earlier in the 1960s. Robert Carlsen, professor of English and education at the University of Iowa and head of the university lab school English department, and his colleagues developed a reorganization of the traditional high school English program's year-long general courses into a series of ten one-semester courses. They developed a "college type" catalog allowing student choice: each student was required to elect one literature course, one composition course, and one speech course and was required to take at least one additional course. Based on a conviction that students were not receiving enough individualization and were disaffected in school, the revision led to a change in attitude among students because "they came to their courses knowing in advance what kind of activity would take place...[and] they had some choice in the matter...[and] evinced a spirit of enthusiasm." Carlsen's revised curriculum became the prototype for many subsequent minicourse programs. Key features included the following: student choice of short, self-contained courses; nongraded or mixed age classes; and nonsequencing of the curriculum.[37] Perhaps the single most powerful project to disseminate information on the formulation of elective programs was the federally funded Project APEX in Trenton, Michigan, in 1966. APEX served as a pattern and added a new feature, the concept of phasing, indicating the level of course difficulty.

By 1968, educational journals, especially in English, were filled with articles about the creation of elective curricula. The surge of excitement was partially a result of the zeitgeist of the times: the civil rights movement, the antiwar movement, and the growing counterculture, along with the growing influence and popularity of books by the new-wave critics of the school. In the late 1960s and early 1970s, the elective curriculum caught on, expanding across the nation, a grassroots movement providing a new and welcome alternative to the traditional academic model.

Rationale. Strongly reminiscent of progressive education, which had been so heavily criticized in the 1950s, critics of the minicourse movement insisted that it lacked a rationale. Though advocates of the minicourse curriculum seldom pointed to the progressive educators of an earlier day, the movement seemed to adhere to a four-part philosophy. The curriculum's first and most important philosophical base was student interest, providing choice among topics and courses. The thinking was that if a student was interested in a particular course, then learning and teaching would be improved. A second philosophical concern centered on change and variety in the curriculum. What emerged was a range of course lengths, from a few weeks to a semester, and a veering away from the dominant hard-cover textbook. A third philosophical base was the rejection of the core curriculum, the requirement that all students should learn the same essential content, though this varied in application. A fourth key philosophical plank was devotion to the concept of relevance. "Relevance" could mean directly related to present life interests, or it could mean related to enduring social issues, but it definitely meant that the new courses would come up with content, topics, and titles that would seemingly have a stronger interest and appeal to high-school-age youth than the traditional curriculum.

The minicourse experiment seemed to enter the social studies field by osmosis, seeping over from English and becoming a fairly strong general trend. School administrators were key players in the shift that occurred in many schools. A survey of principals conducted in the early 1970s in Kansas found that minicourses were offered for reasons reflecting many of the rationales discussed earlier, including giving students more variety and flexibility, allowing teachers to teach in areas of their greatest interest, appealing to student interest and eliminating apathy, developing contemporaneousness, comprehensiveness, depth and relevancy, revitalizing interest "in a particular subject area—usually language arts and social studies," to reduce teacher-student conflict, and to take advantage of new materials and encourage use of a thematic approach.[38]

Although most schools incorporated standard features of "curriculum-electing," including nongrading, nonsequencing, and phasing, other schools developed variations, including modular scheduling, team teaching, more elaborate phasing, some sequencing within the social studies electives, and requirements to take a few specific courses. Permutations on the theme of choice versus control varied widely, resulting in chaos and dissatisfaction in some cases.[39]

A fairly early list illustrative of minicourse offerings in Kansas high schools collected by survey in the fall of 1972 included the following:

A Nation is Torn, Roaring 20s and Dirty 30s, Doves and Hawks, Witchcraft to Statecraft, ISMS, Rise of the City, Candidates and Elections, Prejudice and Discrimination, The U.S. Farmer, Crusade and Disillusion—1918–1933, History of Western Political Thought, Revolution, That Mysterious Dollar, Who Am I? Who Are You?, Red, White, Black, and Yellow, Standing Room Only, Cold War—Hot Bomb, Making Your First Million.[40]

It appears that there was quite a bit of variation from state to state and school to school. Moreover, the elective curriculum, at least in some cases, may have led to an infusion of inquiry and interactive approaches to teaching incorporating materials from the era of the new social studies and other contemporary materials, greater depth of study, and a focus on themes and issues, at least as reflected on paper. A catalog from the Anchorage, Alaska, school district describing their "Survey-Elective Social Studies Program" listed forty-seven elective high school social studies offerings. The stated philosophy of the program was "to recognize the basic worth of the individual and to help each student reach his potential." The curriculum emphasized "inquiry skills, attitudes, values, and knowledge," and each course listed an impressive array of objectives and resource materials, including books, media, and simulation games, and frequently including inquiry-oriented textbooks such as the Fenton series. Each course outline also included a specific list of discussions that would be held as part of each course, and electives were graded as to their difficulty.

The one-semester survey in US history took a thematic approach and included the following unit titles:

> Emerging Nation, Rise of Industrialism, Reform, The Emergence of America as a World Power, American Mind and Cultural Development, Civil Liberties, and Challenges of the 70s.

Course outlines for electives illustrated a similarly thoughtful issues-oriented approach, and many included specific questions that would be the focus of study and discussion. A course entitled "The Question of Extremism" offers a strong illustration. The course used *Extremism—USA* by John Carpenter as a basic text along with a long list of interesting books and articles ranging from those on the left, the SDS and Black Panthers, to the Ku Klux Klan and the John Birch Society on the right. Questions included the following:

> What place does dissent have in a democratic society?
> When does dissent become civil disobedience?
> Why is dissent so prevalent today?[41]

Another example from the eastern seaboard was the Yale–New Haven History Education Project, which began in the spring of 1970. Thirty Yale professors, including several well-known Yale historians and outside consultants, notably Richard Brown, worked with a comparable number of high school teachers to create approximately eighty "minicourses" in US history replacing the required survey course. Funded by the United States Office of Education (USOE) and private groups and sponsored by the American Historical Association (AHA), the group developed a wide-ranging list of courses, including "The Puritans as People," "The American Revolution," "Harlem Renaissance," "F. D. Roosevelt and the New Deal," "Minorities in America," and "Alienation in America."[42]

Major "selling points" for the high school teachers included the fact that it was "student-oriented" and "teacher-tailored," offering the teacher and student the opportunity to develop their own curriculum, thus "making history more personal and interesting to both," and affording teachers the opportunity for professional growth. Participants were enthusiastic about the program and reported very positive results. First, many seniors were voluntarily enrolling in a second year of minicourses, "living proof that history can be interesting." Second, fewer students were failing as compared to the year-long survey course in US history, a fact attributed to a "higher level of motivation, relevant course offerings, the opportunity to have new teachers and new learning environments each quarter, and new approaches in methods and teaching techniques." Third, students preferred changing classes quarterly, not only giving them the opportunity to retain a teacher they prefer, but also allowing them to have a greater variety of teachers. Fourth, students seemed motivated to work at a higher level if the material is inherently interesting. Finally, the selection process (a conscious choice of courses) "tends to force him [the student] to be more responsible for the work done since he is in the course of his own choosing."[43]

The main thrust of the program was to "turn kids on" to history by breaking down "an unmanageable amount of material into manageable blocks," by allowing "choice and movement" within a required course of study (US history was required for graduation), and by using "methods and teaching techniques that place a premium on maximum student participation." The inquiry method was cast as "the crux of the mini-course approach," with the understanding that it would be used in conjunction with development of basic skills, logical thinking, written and visual material, and a "more viable relationship" between student and teacher.[44]

A listing of social studies course offerings from Tamalpais High School in Marin County, California, 1976–1977, provides another good example of a minicourse curriculum. The school offered forty-four social studies courses, in domains labeled American Studies, World Studies, and General Studies, with one year of study required in each area. Most courses were one-semester, though a few were quarter-length. The list included numerous topical courses emphasizing appeals to student interest such as "Bread and Roses," "Minorities in American History," "Revolutionary Movements," "Is War Necessary?" and "Human Sexuality," as well as the more traditional survey courses.[45] This kind of rich array of alternatives to the usual social studies curriculum persisted in some school districts into the early or mid-1980s.

Research. Despite its relatively widespread adoption, there were few research studies conducted on minicourse curricula, but the few that were completed tended to temper the claims of the staunchest advocates yet offered modest support for continued experimentation with the format. One study suggested significant gains for minicourse students on evaluation of arguments and more positive attitudes toward teachers, but no difference in learning outcomes, motivation, or attitudes toward school. Another study, which found that 36 percent of responding high schools in Kansas, Missouri, and Nebraska had minicourse programs, suggested that minicourses could help schools develop "a more humanistic program" and offered schools "a greater chance of meeting the goals of a humanistic curriculum." A study in Kansas mentioned earlier found that 31 percent of high schools in the state offered minicourses in social studies, that minicourses were focused primarily in the traditionally required subject areas of American history and government, and that in schools with the new program the number of social studies offerings averaged 24.4 courses and ranged from a low of 2 to a high of 66 courses.[46]

On the whole it seems that there was some evidence that both students and teachers liked the elective curriculum and that it offered potential advantages for reaching humanistic, issues-centered, or inquiry-oriented goals. The minicourse option seemed to be used most frequently within the framework of specific subject matter offerings in which students would be required to take a certain number of minicourses to meet their requirement for one Carnegie Unit of American history or government. Though it appears that only about one-third of schools experimented with the new innovation, among schools that did use the minicourses, it was most prevalent in English (83 percent of the experimenting schools) and second most prevalent in social studies (45 percent of experimenting schools).[47] As illustrated by the Yale–New Haven collaboration, and as suggested in several other reports, it offered enhanced opportunity for depth, choice, and inquiry. Despite this potential, there was nothing inherent in the restructuring of courses that guaranteed use of innovative teaching techniques, improved student attitudes, or greater learning gains in any way. Nonetheless, the enthusiasm generated by the minicourse curriculum and the limited successes reported suggest that its potential was being realized in a few places and that it deserved further experimentation and consideration. Though it had long had opponents and would soon reap a whirlwind of criticism, the impulse behind the progressive new-wave focus on interest, relevance, experimentation, and variety in a field as diverse, rich, and multifaceted as social studies seems unlikely to ever disappear.

The Quest for Relevancy. "Relevance" was perhaps the key watchword of the new-wave literature and the newer social studies, and rightfully so, for it captured the essence of the era's critique of traditional forms of education, and its insistent call for an education that would make a difference in addressing the persistent problems that confronted the nation and the world. For too long, education in social studies had exemplified Harold Rugg's 1923 critique of the field as a curriculum focused on "reading and answering teachers' questions," emphasizing a great deal of "minutiae" of the past without an effort to "treat adequately the pressing industrial, social, and political problems of the day." As Rugg wrote in 1932, "The world is on fire, and the youth of the world must be equipped to combat the conflagration."[48]

Though the term "relevance" was trumpeted far and wide during the late 1960s and early 1970s, its meaning and implications for teaching social studies was perhaps best expressed in a book published as a bulletin of the NCSS in 1974 and edited by Allan O. Kownslar entitled *Teaching American History: The Quest for Relevancy*. In the book's first chapter, Kownslar described the old ways of teaching history in the pre-Sputnik era, during which it was "often regarded...as nothing more than...memorizing and quickly forgetting dates, events, and names of people. It was a learning process which embodied little if any relevance to the present or preparation for the future." "In such a sterile atmosphere," he wrote, students failed to grasp the implications of history, the way it can "enlarge life experiences" or teach "the inevitability of change." The goal, instead, was "accumulation of data strictly for knowledge's sake" focused on learning "the story."[49]

Resistance appeared from students who were discontented with their passive role and asked, "What good's this gonna do me?" The new social studies seemed to move students beyond "the story" and toward relating their own experiences to the topics they studied, but focused primarily on cognitive processes embodied in "modes of inquiry," needed if students were to become "educated critical thinkers." Much of the work done during the 1960s' new social studies had focused primarily on helping students understand abstract ideas, helping them acquire a mode of inquiry, and in history, helping them learn to think like a historian. The new social studies, Kownslar argued, provided a cognitive foundation whereby history and social studies could be made more relevant.[50]

With the influence of the new-wave critique and its emphasis on relevance, Kownslar suggested that there was an important shift of emphasis from the cognitive to the affective processes, which "seek to stimulate or affect some kind of response which directly involves the student" in their "efforts to cope with contemporary life." It involved a renewed emphasis on affective-type goals, including various ways of empathizing with people of the past; values clarification, which meant "an attempt to have students carefully re-examine, explain, and justify whatever it is they cherish, and why," along with considering the logical consequences of their beliefs; and greater use of Socratic dialogue. Kownslar recommended a cyclical approach to values clarification by going from "a present-day emotional problem to a parallel issue in the past," and back, thus bridging the gap by "relating a contemporary problem to one in the past" and described it as "another form of teaching history 'backwards' whereby a class can"

1. begin with a contemporary issue of special concern,
2. trace causes for the emergence of that problem or examine similar instances of that problem in the past, and
3. then compare them to reasons for concern today.[51]

In making a case for what he described as "the 'New' New Social Studies," Kownslar cited several new-wave writers, including Alvin Toffler, author of *Future Shock*, who theorized that our society often prepared people for survival in a system that was changing so rapidly that their knowledge and skills would soon be outdated; Holt, who likewise emphasized how quickly knowledge changes and how much of what students were learning in schools would quickly become irrelevant; Silberman, who argued that "nothing could be more wildly impractical" than education for "the world as it is"; and Postman and Weingartner, who argued strongly for relevance in education and suggested a literacy that allows "a high degree of competence in analyzing...propositions, evaluating them and correlating them with reality." Rather than abolish history courses because of their "irrelevance," which a few scholars had actually recommended, Kownslar argued for an alteration in the ways history classes have been taught. He wrote, "Students must be led to understand how and why a study of the past does have meaning and practical application as they face a difficult present and uncertain future." He recommended "history taught as a quest for relevancy, incorporating the best qualities of the Old, the New, and the 'New' New Social Studies" whereby history could serve as

> a vehicle by which students can acquire an applicable mode of inquiry, develop useful concepts, successfully empathize with the past, continue to clarify values, learn to recognize and to cope with suspected myths and stereotypes, and to ask critical questions about the past, present, and future. If our goal, then, is to effectively teach American history as a quest for relevancy, students should never need ask: "What good's all this gonna do me?" They'll already know.[52]

The edited volume contained rich sample lessons demonstrating use of modes of inquiry, raising pertinent questions from past and present for values clarification, and coping with future issues. In essence, Kownslar, steeped in the new social studies as a protégé of Ted Fenton, had produced a volume that adapted the new history of the 1960s to the era of student questioning, doubt, and relevance of the 1970s. At the time, it seemed a step in the right direction.

Values Clarification. Values, values clarification, and the role of values in a process of decision making or inquiry had received a great deal of attention from social studies scholars during the preceding decade, from Shirley Engle, Donald Oliver, Ted Fenton, and others. During the period of the newer social studies, values education received a new shot of enthusiasm, scholarship, and classroom application from the work of Louis E. Raths, Sidney B. Simon, and others. In *Values and Teaching* (1966), Raths and colleagues developed a theory of values and an approach to values clarification in the classroom. Drawing on John Dewey, this work aimed at offering "concrete and effective aid to teachers" with several chapters on method, including "The Clarifying Response," which gave examples of thirty clarifying responses: that is, "Is this something that you prize?," "How did you feel when that happened?," "Did you consider any alternatives?," and "How do you know it's right?" The book also described other practical applications such as "The Value Sheet," in which students would be presented with a value-laden dilemma in the form of a brief story with a choice to be made, followed by penetrating questions for discussion. Rather than imposing a set of traditional values through moralizing, the intent was to ask students to reflect upon and choose their own values.

A later work, *Values Clarification* (1972), popularized many practical strategies for teachers interested in applying the approach to creating a more humane classroom atmosphere, many of which had application to teaching of subject matter. Examples of values clarification activities included "values voting," "rank order," "forced choice," and the "public interview," all variations of the theory of values explicated earlier and applied to classroom teaching in a very practical handbook, which was to become one of the most popular applications of the humanistic turn.[53]

The Kohlberg Bandwagon. Closely related to the work on values clarification was an emergent focus on moral education and moral reasoning centering on the work of Harvard educator and social psychologist Lawrence Kohlberg. Built on the work of Dewey and cognitive psychologist Jean Piaget, Kohlberg developed a theory of moral stages that had broad implications and applications in a variety of fields. In a manner somewhat similar to values clarification and other new applications of values-oriented teaching, Kohlberg's theory of moral stages was applied to social studies and became, at least for a few adherents, something of a panacea. For others, it had become a "bandwagon." A special issue of *Social Education*, edited by Ted Fenton and appearing in 1976, was devoted to the topic. Both Fenton and Jack Fraenkel, perhaps the chief critic of the "Kohlberg bandwagon," were new social studies reformers who had become involved in values education in social studies. Fenton proposed that Kohlberg's six moral stages from the "preconventional" level, based on punishment and reward, to the highest level, based on "universal ethical principles" could be readily applied to the social studies classroom, and changes in stages could be facilitated by programs focused on the use of moral dilemmas. Fraenkel expressed serious reservations about Kohlberg's theory and its application in social studies. Far from a panacea, he challenged some of Kohlberg's central assumptions and the applicability of the model in the classroom. Urging teachers to critically examine all approaches to values education, Fraenkel suggested, "What is lacking at present is any sort of educational theory which integrates psychological notions about both intellectual and emotional development, together with a philosophical consideration of what values education should be about."[54]

Other Problems and Methods. In addition to minicourses, values clarification, and moral dilemmas, teachers of the period witnessed what must have seemed a dizzying array of new topics and methods. For one thing, there was a new emphasis on the social problems or "crises" of the times, reflecting a forward looking and social reconstructionist, even revolutionary sensibility. A range of "new" topics aimed at teachers appeared in the social studies literature and on bookstore shelves. Most of these embodied a recapitulation of topics long a part of social studies offerings such as Problems of Democracy, but often with a new framing and certainly with a new urgency and sense of timeliness. New and emerging topics included urbanization, environmentalism, consumerism, population, poverty, futurism, racism, minorities, women's studies, and area studies, particularly focused on Africa and Asia, previously all but ignored. And, the focus on new topics was accompanied by a rash of topical courses, including those focused on citizenship education, law-related education (LRE), global education, consumer education, career education, political education, energy education, pollution and the environment, ecology, and population. Some of the newer topics had a self-esteem focus or accompanied formation of encounter groups or sensitivity training. Many of the new topics were also addressed by new social studies materials, some of which were just beginning to reach the market in the late 1960s and early 1970s, which probably added to the sense of change and excitement for those teachers and students caught up in the newer trends.

Another new emphasis was methodological or procedural. Although there was a range of emphasis, from a focus on behavioral objectives to open education, many new-wave authors focused on ways to humanize schooling with values-clarification and moral education representing perhaps the epitome of the trend. Within the official subject-centered curriculum, there was increasing emphasis on inquiry, concepts, games, simulations, and decision making, approaches that had been embraced by the new social studies and were part of the newer social studies and the spirit of innovation inspired by the new-wave critique.

There were other trends to be sure, some of which may have had a more dominant influence on most schools and in most classrooms, though it is difficult to say with any certainty. According to educational historians David Angus and Jeffrey Mirel, curriculum differentiation remained the overriding characteristic of the high school, even though tracking and other forms of ability grouping had been severely criticized by new-wave critics and were no longer considered politically correct. As evidence they cite what they describe as a "neo-efficiency or accountability" movement that ran concurrently with the new-wave or humanistic trend but captured less attention from most scholars and the media. "Under the accountability umbrella," they wrote, "was a conglomerate of old and new reform ideas: programmed instruction, individualized instruction, differentiated staffing, behavioral or performance objectives, competency-based instruction, teaching machines, instructional systems, computer-managed instruction, team teaching, behavioral modification, performance contracting, and career education." Ironically, as they point out, many of these innovations, most of which were plainly at odds with the new wave, were rooted in the "education for social efficiency" championed by administrative progressives of an earlier era.[55]

Conclusion

Despite its impermanence, the newer social studies and the burst of innovation, reflection, and critique that emerged during the 1960s and early 1970s offers a fascinating glimpse of something like what a free-wheeling progressive approach to the field might look like. The civil rights movement, free speech movement, antiwar movement, and new-wave critique of schooling all contributed to an innovative explosion of interest in making schools a place in which studies were relevant, in which students asked value questions, and teachers and avante-garde materials inspired activism for social justice. Ethnic studies, antiracist education, the "noncurriculum" focused on social issues, a renewal of social reconstructionism, the minicourse explosion, the quest for relevancy, values clarification, and moral education were all embodiments of a new ethos that raised questions about societal institutions, social injustice, and the role of schooling in a democracy. The newer social studies serves as a fitting embodiment and reflection of 1960s issues and turmoil, as if the counterculture had entered the school.

In some respects, the newer social studies serves as a model for innovation, albeit a bit wild, unfinished, and rough around the edges, but with a laserlike focus on timely issues and topics that matter. The focus was not just current events, but deeper persistent issues that cut across time. For many teachers and curriculum developers, it was an exciting and entrepreneurial time driven by concerns over social justice and a host of issues and problems. One can imagine a curriculum thoughtfully combining elements of the new and newer social studies in an innovative and engaging approach to education for democracy. Though it was exciting while it lasted, the focus on issues, values-clarification, and social activism that emerged in the late 1960s and continued through the 1970s was a brief flash of innovation, an anomaly in the larger pattern of schools continuing to do what they had always done: staying focused on textbooks, curriculum guides, tests, and assignments; meting out discipline and punishment; and indoctrinating youth into the patterns of American culture.

3

Larger Trends in Schools

Many trends of the late 1960s and early 1970s were broader in scope, went beyond the new and newer social studies, ran concurrently, and influenced schooling at all levels. A few suggested the possibility that exciting changes were afoot, changes that could potentially transform schooling from the work-a-day routines of the past to a new, avant-garde, and innovative future. Among the larger trends that influenced schools during the period of the late 1960s and early 1970s were the open school movement, a rebirth of Rousseauian child-centered education spurred by Summerhill and the British Infant School; the movement for ethnic studies and multiculturalism, a direct outgrowth of the civil rights movement; and, critical pedagogy, a new variant on education for social reconstructionism embodying strong influences from European critical theory. What emerged in the late 1960s and early 1970s was an era of innovation and change that had broad but largely temporary influence on the climate in schools. For many teachers, and in many school districts, it was an exciting time to be alive.

Moreover, many of the new wave trends in secondary school social studies had their counterparts in other subject areas and lower-grade levels, as if the changes proposed by advocates of a new education arose in unison, in rebellion against the oppressive traditional school in which coerced youth sat through a boring, irrelevant curriculum dominated by antiquated methods that obliterated the student's innate curiosity. The movement for "open education" was on the cutting edge of the trend for change for a significant number of years in the late 1960s and early 1970s. Often running parallel to several of the trends of the newer social studies, the open schools movement had something of a life of its own, but it would simultaneously influence a variety of school subjects, including social studies, and spin off several variations, including "free schools," "alternative schools," and a largely rhetorical movement for "deschooling."

Open Education

Interest in open schools grew naturally out of the critiques offered by new wave authors such as Paul Goodman, John Holt, and Jonathan Kozol, but received a strong catalyst in a series of articles by Joseph Featherstone that appeared in *New Republic* in 1967. Featherstone extolled the virtues of the British model of infant education, which he described as "a profound and sweeping revolution in English primary education, involving new ways of thinking about how young children learn, classroom organization, the curriculum, and the role of the teacher," and he discussed the findings of Britain's Plowden Commission, which enthusiastically supported the new approach.[1] As reprints of Featherstone's articles spread, more and more American educators began to see the British model as a revolutionary innovation, and as a possible answer to the condemnations of schooling by critics. If the schools were inhumane, irrelevant, and harmful, perhaps the answer could be found in freedom and in a "new" form of instruction. Many American educators, who had cut their teeth on the progressivism of John Dewey, Harold O. Rugg, and William H. Kilpatrick found in the British "integrated day" a recapitulation of their favored and familiar theories. Many young teachers, after reading Kozol or Herndon, undoubtedly viewed the British approach as a way to bring a humane and democratic spirit to the classroom.

As the movement for open schooling gained momentum, it received its greatest boost from Charles Silberman's bestseller, *Crisis in the Classroom* (1970), which gave open education a new level of exposure as perhaps the most important of cutting edge educational innovations. Silberman described an American society gripped by crisis and turmoil, schools that were producing "dissent and alienation" that were "grim and joyless places...intellectually sterile and esthetically barren." Schools, he wrote, were preoccupied with "order and control" and were producing "docility and conformity" through a curriculum that emphasized "banality and triviality." The central problem with American schools was a pervasive sense of "mindlessness," resulting from the fact that few educators thought "seriously or deeply about the purposes or consequences" of schooling. The solution to the crisis, Silberman seemed to suggest, could be found in the British primary schools. He described the activities of American exponents of the infant school model such as Lillian Weber of New York and Vito Perrone of North Dakota. Silberman extended the same principles to the high school, which, he believed, needed a similar rethinking emphasizing a move toward greater freedom, flexibility, and curricular choice for students.[2] The influence of Silberman's work served to universalize open education, applying it to a wide range of educational institutions and suggesting its elevation into an ideology about children, learning, and schooling that seemed intended to revitalize society and the quality of life in America.

The years that followed witnessed a proliferation of books and articles describing the theory and practice of open education. As with progressive education, its advocates tended to define it negatively, by clearly demarcating what it was not: it was not traditional, nor was it simply about removing walls, nor was it another name for nongraded classes. Roland S. Barth, a well-known advocate, developed a list of twenty-nine assumptions that open educators shared: children are innately curious; full involvement and fun in a school activity meant learning is taking place; measurements of performance may have a negative effect; the child's experience is the curriculum; and educators should focus on "the quality and meaning" of the experiences for students.[3]

Though these ideas found fertile ground among many educators, applications often ran into trouble and seemed strongly dependent upon the aptitudes and attitudes of teachers, students, and community. As with progressive education, many attempts to apply open education led to children given freedom to run amok, which was far from what the original advocates had suggested. The open education movement took a variety of forms, including free schools, alternative public schools, and deschooling. Free schools were the educational version of counterculture alternative organizations that had sprouted up in the 1960s and included free clinics, legal collectives, and food co-ops. They were a "rejection of authority as a valid principle for organizing group life" and were often an expression of political or cultural radicalism aimed to "create a new sort of human being and a new model of cooperative social life." Many public school districts responded with the formation of alternative schools that embodied most of the same principles and gave students who were unsuccessful or who did not fit the regular classroom a separate institution and a new opportunity.[4]

Despite its meteoric rise to prominence, critics of open education soon emerged. Just as Dewey became a critic of progressive education, and Jerome Bruner became a critic of the discipline-based reforms, so too many advocates of open education became quite critical of its application to American classrooms. Featherstone reported after visiting many open classrooms, "The best are as good as anything I've seen in England; the worst are a shambles." Barth wrote an article entitled "Should We Forget about Open Education?" in which he argued that the movement had become a new orthodoxy. By 1974, Donald A. Myers, who had studied open education extensively in New York state, wrote an article suggesting that open education had "died" partly because it was poorly defined; because teachers misunderstood the need for an individualized structure for each child as was present in the British model; because it required exceptional teachers, of which there were too few; and because it failed to "come to grips with fundamental factors in American education and American society," that made such radical reform unlikely to last without "a more financially equal society." As Amitai Etzioni had written in his review of Silberman's book, "There is very little reason to believe that America is headed toward either a humane or a just society or could be so transformed by any educational reforms the present system would tolerate. Why then design an educational system to serve such a transformed society?"[5]

The spirit of innovation encapsulated in open education spread to other trends and innovations, particularly those that embraced greater freedom for teachers and students and a role for students in selecting or developing their own activities. These innovations often took the form of student-designed and student-taught courses; the relaxation of high school graduation requirements; minicourses, and expansion of the number of courses available; flexible scheduling; deemphasis upon alternatives to letter grades; heterogeneous or mixed-age grouping of students instead of tracking or ability grouping; and credit for life experiences or community involvement.

Open education did have some direct influence in social studies. Vito Perrone, Dean of the New School for Behavioral Studies at the University of North Dakota and one of the prime innovators, coauthored an article on social studies in the open classroom for *Social Education* in which he explained the meaning of open education for social studies. Perrone and his coauthor listed eleven characteristics of the process of instruction in the open classroom that included such humanistic goals as "mutual trust and respect," the "teacher as a guide, advisor, observer, provisioner, and catalyst," use of a "a wise assortment of materials," a focus on "learning through play, games, simulations," the role of "interest" in a setting with multiple activities occurring simultaneously, "few barriers between subject matter areas," a "minimum of restrictions determined by the clock," learning marked by "cooperation" and "conversation," "older children assisting younger children," and emphasis on the "expressive and creative arts." They emphasized that social studies was "not looked upon as a discrete area separate from reading" and the other subjects and described an organic and dynamic curriculum in which the most "meaningful classroom experiences may grow organically" out of a particular field trip, a discussion, a conversation, or an object. They described a group of students in North Dakota who turned a story they read into a house-building project. Children grew so excited that they gathered building materials, tools, and expertise that eventually resulted in a clubhouse for younger children to use during recess.[6]

In March 1974, Robert D. Barr, Mario Fantini, and others published a special section and series of articles on social studies in alternative schools for *Social Education* in which they described a wide array of options. These included open schools, free schools, continuation schools and schools without walls, learning centers, multicultural schools, and schools within schools. It seems that many of the new wave trends found expression in an exploding variety of schools. Fantini thoughtfully described the main themes of alternative schools and humanistic education, including the trend toward smaller schools, a focus on legitimizing affective content, greater integration of the cognitive and affective, and developing "the individual's sense of potency" and ability to "control his own destiny." He also included the aim of "valuing...the dignity and worth of each human being" by doing away with the "dysfunctional...labeling problem" through which learners are classified and placed "on a continuum from winners to losers." The process, he wrote, results in a psychology of institutional expectations that has a "negative effect on...promoting individual worth." Finally, he noted that "humanistic educators point to the *change process* itself as being dehumanizing" and call for a change strategy that is not imposed by an external "change agent" or its representative. Other articles described five alternatives in social studies ranging from the open school to an educational park.[7]

There were other entries in the literature on social studies for open education, notably a book by Shirley H. Engle and Wilma S. Longstreet titled *A Design for Social Education in the Open Curriculum*, published in 1972. Engle and Longstreet built on themes of relevance and openness, combined with action-concepts and decision making to offer an argument for a topical curriculum design in social studies. Another entry was a practical guide titled *Social Studies in the Open Classroom* (1973) in which Evelyn Berger and Bonnie A. Winters described applications of the open classroom in elementary social studies, including "task cards," baskets of materials containing individual and group activities, audiovisual activities, research skills, map study, language arts and communication skills (media, poetry, drama, games, etc.), art cart activities, problem solving, and expanding horizons (current events, field trips, ecology, cultural diversity, etc.).[8] These forays into open education in the social studies field illustrate the broad reach of the idea, and notably, the variety of applications that sometimes diffused its meaning.

Multicultural Education

Another larger trend in educational rhetoric and practice and an important influence on social studies and schooling growing out of the 1960s came in the form of discourse over multicultural education. An outgrowth of the civil rights movement, multicultural education became a major focus for growth and development in universities and schools of teacher education as well as in the public schools. The multicultural education of the late twentieth century was the culmination of a long trend reflecting the civil rights movement: from intercultural education during World War II, to early multicultural education in the 1960s and 1970s, to the 1990s *Handbook of Research on Multicultural Education*, national concern over political correctness, and debate over the place of Western culture in the curriculum. There were, to be sure, new players in the curriculum game. Groups that had long been excluded were now among the power brokers struggling over the curriculum.

Articles on multiculturalism had gained space in *Social Education* since the late 1960s. NCSS endorsed a multicultural focus in the curriculum with publication of its "Curriculum Guidelines for Multicultural Education" in 1976, calling for a strong component of ethnic studies in the curriculum from preschool to twelfth grade and beyond. By the late 1980s and early 1990s, controversy over multiculturalism reached new heights. On one side were the long-term advocates of a multicultural curriculum and a revised canon, including scholars in education and ethnic studies led by James A. Banks, Henry Louis Gates, Cornel West, Molefi K. Asante, and Gloria Ladson-Billings. On the other side were neoconservative scholars such as Diane Ravitch, Arthur M. Schlesinger, William J. Bennett, and Thomas Sowell who wanted schools and universities to include multicultural materials, but to continue emphasizing the common culture.

Supporters of multicultural education asserted that the perspectives of persons of color, women, and the working class had been excluded from the study of history, literature, and the humanities, leading students to conclude that civilization was the product of European males and their culture. They maintained that mainstream ignorance of multicultural groups, of both their contributions and their historical oppression intensified intolerance and contributed to bigotry. Multicultural education was based on the premise that the purposeful inclusion of the stories, literature, and historical perspectives of diverse groups in school curricula and textbooks could help students attain a broader perspective and contribute to creation of a more equitable society. According to James Banks, multicultural education "helps students transcend their cultural boundaries and acquire the knowledge, attitudes, and skills needed to engage in public discourse with people who differ from themselves and to participate in the creation of a civic culture."[9]

Critics of multicultural education, on the other hand, argued that multicultural education was divisive because it deemphasized our common heritage and culture and placed undue emphasis on conflicts and differences related to race, class, and gender. They argued that it would Balkanize the nation, result in shallow exposure to multicultural topics, and led to an unfortunate deemphasis on significant content related to the development of Western culture and general cultural literacy. Moreover, some critics asserted that multiculturalism often functioned as a means to indoctrinate students to leftist political ideologies. According to one observer, "The call for diversity in education too often...is a red herring for a radical agenda."[10]

Diane Ravitch, maven of the neoconservative cause and Assistant Secretary of Education in the George H. W. Bush administration, authored a number of articles critical of multiculturalists. She charged that in the name of multiculturalism, ethnocentric "particularists" were undermining the national culture and sacrificing "unum" in the name of "pluribus." Preferring the image of a "mosaic" of ethnic groups, Ravitch maintained that particularists neglect "the bonds of mutuality" among groups and "encourage children to seek their primary identity in the cultures and homelands of their ancestors." She argued that the United States has a "common culture that is multicultural" and that this insight was behind the evolution of a "wisely and intelligently designed...multicultural curriculum." Ravitch called for an education that "promotes pluralism, not particularism" and offered the California History-Social Science Framework as a model emphasizing the common culture and "a nation that unites as one people the descendants of many cultures, races, religions, and ethnic groups." She offered the New York State report, "A Curriculum of Inclusion," as a "Europhobic" counterexample. The "particularist" approach, she wrote, "teaches children to see history as a story of victims and oppressors, and it endorses the principle of collective guilt." This approach, she lamented, "encourages a sense of rage and victimization" and "rekindles ancient hatreds in the present." Behind "A Curriculum of Inclusion," she charged, lay a dubious pedagogical theory that changes in the curriculum would "raise the self-esteem" of children of color and enhance their academic performance. Ravitch questioned whether history should be used as a mechanism for instilling self-esteem and filiopietism.[11] On the other hand, Ravitch's assertion that multiculturalism was filiopietistic was especially ironic, given her support for what many critics labeled a white self-esteem curriculum.

In his book, *The Disuniting of America*, historian Arthur M. Schlesinger, Jr., sounded many of the same themes. Schlesinger charged that "a cult of ethnicity" had arisen to attack the common American identity, and to replace the goals of integration and assimilation with fragmentation and separatism, with the end result being "resegregation, and tribalization of American life." Multiculturalists, he wrote, viewed European civilization as the root of all evil, as inherently racist, sexist, classist, hegemonic, and irredeemably oppressive. Like Ravitch, he called on a return to a "balance between *unum* and *pluribus*." Schlesinger also endorsed a return to teaching history "for its own sake—as part of the intellectual equipment of civilized persons—and not to degrade history by allowing its contents to be dictated by pressure groups." "Above all," he went on, "history can give a sense of national identity" and can teach us that our values "are worth living by and worth dying for." Schlesinger argued that history had given us our values "anchored in our national experience, in our great national documents, in our national heroes, in our folkways, traditions, and standards...Here individuals of all nations are melted into a new race of men."[12]

Both Schlesinger and Ravitch inspired a great deal of criticism from advocates of multiculturalism, none more pointed than the comments of Gloria Ladson-Billings, who suggested that the crux of the debate centered on Schlesinger's assertion that we were once "united" as a nation. She argued that Americans were far from united, and that our disunity had a great deal to do with economics and opportunity. She criticized Schlesinger for clouding his arguments with personal attacks, distortions, decontextualizations, and defamation. She wrote that Schlesinger wanted to see all Americans unified around a set of ideals, but failed to recognize that the underlying cause of disunity could be found in "the widening economic gap between blacks and whites." She also made note of the fact that Schlesinger, like Ravitch, all but ignored the long history of scholarship and research on multiculturalism. In closing, she charged that Schlesinger's attack on multiculturalism fed into "a growing climate of intolerance."[13]

There were many similar exchanges during the peak years of debate over multiculturalism between advocates and defenders of the multicultural education movement. By the late 1980s, the popular press had gotten wind of developments in both multiculturalism and critical theory, and conservative opponents had made an issue of political correctness on campus. *Time* and *Newsweek* ran cover stories. An article entitled "Thought Police" was representative. Soon, a slew of books and magazine articles made a cottage industry out of the growing controversy. Dinesh D'Souza's *Illiberal Education* charged that revolutionaries and nihilists in the form of critical theorists, deconstructionists, and multiculturalists were transforming college campuses into institutions of politically correct conformity, debunking hierarchical and Euro-centric institutions, and turning their backs on the need for a broad liberal education. Roger Kimball in *Tenured Radicals* charged that the same crowd, some of whom had been activists during the upheavals of the 1960s, were now in positions of power as tenured professors and were transforming universities into bastions of radical activism.

Although there may have been some truth to the charges, universities have long had a liberal atmosphere, the vast majority of academics were relatively untouched by the new criticism, which had achieved its greatest gains in literary criticism. Though critical theory was wielding some influence in other fields, it was far from dominant in most. On the other hand, some aspect of multiculturalism touched almost everyone. *Debating P.C.* and other similar collections chronicled the arguments of multiculturalists and their more traditionalist opponents. A few leading scholars who had come under attack in the political correctness wars had their say in Mark Edmundson's,

Wild Orchids and Trotsky. Debates raged over course requirements and curriculum revisions on many campuses across the nation, a public spectacle before galleries. Similar debates emerged over curriculum reform in the schools and textbook adoptions in New York, California, and a host of other states. Unfortunately, it seemed during much of the 1980s and 1990s educators were busy shouting past each other from entrenched camps.[14]

Critical Pedagogy

The educational dialogues of recent decades have included multiple voices from many different perspectives. Charges of "political correctness" were, in fact, a reaction to two trends in the academy: the increasing influence of critical theory and the growing mandate for multicultural education. Though they were ostensibly separate movements, the two had much in common, shared many insights, and held a similar orientation toward using education as one avenue for social transformation.

Critical theorists in education were far from a monolithic group and included scholars specializing in reconceptualist curricular theory, cultural studies, feminist scholarship, and other forms. Critical scholarship in the United States was strongly influenced by European theoretical perspectives, including the critical theorists of the Frankfurt School, neo-Marxist social theory, structuralism, and more recent developments in postmodernism and poststructuralism. Many observers saw in the growing influence of critical theory a delayed impact of the civil rights and human potential movements of the 1960s. It was true that campus radicals had aged and many now held tenured positions at major universities. Moreover, critical theory was gaining broader influence in academia as well as in schools of education.

In the United States, critical pedagogy retained a strong connection to the work of Dewey and forged some direct links to social reconstructionist theory. Frequently, critical pedagogues drew on the works of European theorists, including Hans-Georg Gadamer, Antonio Gramsci, Jürgen Habermas, Michel Foucault, and Jacques Derrida. Their agenda was similar in ultimate goals to the social reconstructionists, but their work seemed to focus on building a community of scholars critical of mainstream educational practice, conversant in critical theory, cognizant of the systemic and interwoven nature of educational, political, and social systems, and committed to resisting the dominant interests that control the bulk of wealth and power in America.

Among the earliest and most influential critical pedagogues was the Brazilian educational theorist Paulo Freire. In his seminal work, *Pedagogy of the Oppressed* (1970), Freire drew a distinction between traditional forms of education built around the banking theory, in which knowledge is bestowed upon ignorant students by knowledge-able teachers, mirroring the oppression of capitalist society, and problem-posing education, which breaks this hierarchical pattern. "Education," he wrote, "is suffering from narration sickness." The narration at the heart of traditional educational practices "turns students into 'containers,' into 'receptacles' to be 'filled' by the teacher." Education then becomes "an act of depositing, in which the students are the depositories and the teacher is the depositor." Instead of communicating, the teacher "issues communiqués" and makes "deposits" that students patiently receive, memorize, and repeat. Banking education maintains this dehumanizing hold "through...attitudes and practices, which mirror oppressive society as a whole." Problem-posing education, on the other hand, creates a dialogue of teacher-student with student-teacher through which both teacher and student teach and learn simultaneously. It is an approach through which "they become jointly responsible for a process in which all grow." This was not simply literacy education, but a process of liberation or conscientization that would provide students with the means to challenge an oppressive social order—to transform oppressive social relations.[15]

Several other important works contributed to the growth of critical perspectives on education. One of the most important was *Schooling in Capitalist America* by Samuel Bowles and Herbert Gintis, published in 1976. Bowles and Gintis asserted that far from being the great equalizer, public schooling fostered and reproduced social-class based distinctions. They introduced the terms "reproduction" and "correspondence theory" to an emerging generation of radical educators. The central propositions of the book included, first, the idea that schools prepare students for adult work roles by socializing them to function well in the hierarchical structure of the modern corporation or institution and did this by replicating the environment of the workplace. Second, that parental social class and other aspects of economic status are passed on by means of unequal educational opportunity. And, third, that the evolution of schooling in America was best explained by a series of class conflicts arising through the social transformation of work. They argued, in essence:

> The educational system serves—through the correspondence of its social relations with those of economic life—to reproduce economic inequality and to distort personal development, thus under corporate capitalism, the objectives of liberal educational reform are contradictory: it is precisely because of its role as producer of an alienated and stratified labor force that the educational system has developed its repressive and unequal structure.[16]

The work of Bowles and Gintis was very influential on the development of critical pedagogy. To varying degrees, critical pedagogues shared an affinity for reproduction and correspondence theories, often extending them to argue that not only school structures, but their hidden and overt curricula tend to mirror and reproduce the dominant social hierarchy, imposing different kinds of knowledge on diverse groups in accordance with their place in a stratified social order. Through intellectual and moral influence as well as direct coercion, dominant groups (the economic, political, and cultural elite) maintain the hegemony of the dominant culture and retain power over marginalized groups (women, the poor, and persons of color). Somewhat more recently, resistance theorists accepted most of the insights of reproduction theory but were more optimistic regarding the potential for education to challenge the dominant interests. From this perspective, schools can best be understood as "contested terrain" and school curricula as "complex discourse that simultaneously serves the interests of domination while also providing possibilities for opposition and emancipations."[17]

Another path-breaking work was *Ideology and Curriculum* by Michael Apple, published in 1979. Among the first to establish a link between the curriculum and its implicit political ideology, Apple noted that not only the school as an institution, but the curriculum itself served as a means of reproducing the social, cultural, and economic patterns of society. Thus, schools were engaged in preserving and distributing the symbolic property of cultural capital. He argued that we needed a better understanding of "why and how particular aspects of the collective culture are presented in school as objective, factual knowledge. How, concretely, may official knowledge represent ideological configurations of the dominant interests in a society? How do schools legitimate these limited and partial standards of knowing as unquestioned truths?"[18] Apple's book was significant both for its insights, and for the fact that it marked the beginning of an emerging dialogue among educational theorists, a critical discourse reminiscent of exchanges in *The Social Frontier* during the 1930s.

Other major contributors to the discourse that has extended from the 1970s up to the present included William F. Pinar, Henry Giroux, Jean Anyon, Peter McLaren, Carmen Luke, Elizabeth Ellsworth, and others. Though critical pedagogy and social reconstructionism differ in many ways, and developed independently and at different times, they shared many of the same methods, concerns, and perspectives. As mentioned earlier, critical pedagogy was strongly influenced by European theoretical perspectives, including critical theory, neo-Marxism, structuralism, phenomenology, postmodernism, poststructuralism, and by more recent developments such as feminist thought and scholarship. Moreover, while social reconstructionism was largely part of modernist discourse, critical pedagogy developed more recently, in what some have called the postmodern era.

Among the key propositions of the critical perspective on education are the following ideas:

1. Emancipation from domination by others should be the central aim of education. (domination could be economic, political, sexual, and intellectual)
2. Knowledge itself is socially constructed and usually serves to support, legitimate, and maintain dominant interests.
3. If the quest for knowledge is addressed to understanding the significance of dominant interests, schooling can offer the possibility of emancipation.
4. Mastery of analytical skills and the tools required for reading, writing, and computation should be inspired by a commitment to work for a collectively emancipated world.
5. Teaching must be guided by a continuous examination of fundamental beliefs, experiences, and knowledge, a critical discourse.[19]

These ideas had practical implications for the teaching of social studies, including a focus on discourse analysis and the examination of language and content to determine bias. They promoted awareness of the ways language may be shaped by dominant interests, and a focus on the study of ideology, the ways of domination, and the means of emancipation. Thus, in the study of history, for example, critical pedagogy implied concentration on understanding the influence of dominant interests on the development of social institutions and an emphasis on the means of emancipation, on the struggles of the oppressed to obtain their own liberation.

In social studies, critical theory made a brief appearance in *Social Education* in a special issue that appeared in 1985 titled "The New Criticism: Alternative Views of Social Education." The issue included articles by leading advocates of a critical perspective. It included Henry Giroux's "Teachers as Transformative Intellectuals" and contributions from Michael W. Apple, William B. Stanley, Cleo Cherryholmes, Jack L. Nelson, and others.[20] At the time, it seemed the dawn of a new period in which critical perspectives might play a prominent role in social studies theory and practice. By the mid-1990s, critical perspectives were a common feature of *Theory and Research in Social Education*, but made only infrequent forays into the practitioner-oriented journals. Elsewhere, Bill Bigelow contributed to a growing understanding of what a critical approach might look like in schools through articles in *Rethinking Schools* and other publications. Moreover, Amy Gutman's *Democratic Education* gave voice to a thoughtful approach to schooling built around a democratic theory of education. Despite increasing rhetorical support, others wondered whether critical theory was having much real impact in schools.[21]

Given its political stance, critical theory was not without opponents. Many scholars asserted that it was unrealistic, naïve, or unreasonable to expect schools and teachers to act as agents of social transformation. The majority of teachers and school administrators were mainstream in their thinking and reflected the general populace. Others charged that social reconstructionism had the potential to lead toward indoctrination of students, toward proselytizing, and propaganda. In addition, a number of feminist scholars, who shared a critical orientation, accused critical theorists of being gender-blind and ignoring feminist scholarship. They accused critical pedagogues of framing their work within epistemologies that are essentially masculinist and patriarchal, thus privileging logic and rationality at the expense of emotional, intuitive, and moral ways of knowing. Though these developments grew, in part, out of and in reaction to events of the 1960s and 1970s, as we have seen, they have continued to develop and draw both critical commentary and defense in the years since.

Behind the Newer Social Studies

As discussed earlier, the late 1960s burst of issues-oriented materials and concerns, reflecting issues in the society, had been simmering for some time. The origins of the newer social studies may be found in the burning issues of the era, and in the culmination of much of the educational thought and criticism of the 1960s. The issues focus was foreshadowed by the work of theorists such as Engle, Hunt and Metcalf, and Oliver and Shaver. However, it is difficult to assess the degree to which their work may have influenced the turn of events. They did not appear to be leaders of the newer trend. In hindsight, leaders were difficult to discern. There was no Saint Jerome, nor was there a new "Mr. Social Studies." Instead leadership seemed quite diffuse and included new wave educational critics, multiculturalists, critical theorists, and a host of others together offering a penetrating critique of American schools and society and pointing the way toward a more humanistic and progressive future. Perhaps most poignantly, the true leadership of the newer social studies could be found among those who had lived the quest for social justice: the civil rights leaders and Black Power advocates, the student rebels and free speech advocates, the antiwar groups, the leaders of the women's movement, gay rights movement, and the quest for environmental and ecological health. Leadership was spread widely among those engaged in the struggle to lift shackles of oppression and to reform the schools that had for so long reproduced it.

There were several influences at work behind the explosion of interest in the newer social studies. First, the tradition of issues-centered education was strong in the educational rhetoric of the times, as mentioned. The works of Oliver and Shaver, Hunt and Metcalf, Massialas and Cox, Newmann and Engle were current and may have had some influence on the thinking in schools. These scholars tended to support attention to current issues as well as a deeper issues-centered approach to the social studies subjects. Moreover, the approach had been simmering in the background for some time and reflected 1960s issues and the alternative educational culture. The progressive, meliorist and reconstructionist traditions had always been present, were often studied in schools of education and were favored again for a time, if only briefly. The approach had its roots in questioning of the system. In the 1960s, with the civil rights and antiwar movements there was a palpable sense of revolution in the air.

So, it seems reasonable to assert that a confluence of educational ideas and societal trends led to the burst of energy favoring questioning and issues-oriented teaching. In any event, the new approach captured the attention and imagination of many teachers and citizens. Its strong appeal and meteoric rise reflected the concerns of the times. It was a hopeful approach at a time when the counterculture was in vogue. In short, issues-centered teaching became something of a fad. It was fashionable, like bell-bottom trousers, long hair, and marijuana. But the word "fashion" does not do justice to the teachers, writers, scholars, and students who were part of the newer trend because it belies the sincerity of their efforts, yearnings, and dreams.

Above all this was a hopeful, forward-looking trend brought on by a groundswell of new ideas and a spirit of revolution. Though new wave critics and advocates of the new humanist social studies instigated numerous practical and topical reforms in schools and curricula (minicourses; flexible scheduling; relevance, inquiry, and valuing; and openness and social criticism) their crusade was, at root, a romantic quest driven by utopian visions. Naïve at times, the topical and methodological shift was, it seemed, more easily and more flexibly applied at some meaningful level in the classroom than was the new social studies and its focus on discipline-based inquiry. Though the newer movement borrowed concepts, ideas, methods, and even manpower from the new social studies, it was less meticulous in its application and seemed to be applied broadly, sometimes grafted on to what teachers were already doing and sometimes replacing it.

The new wave humanists and newer social studies also seemed to embrace several key underlying assumptions, with varying degrees of earnestness. First, it seemed to many humanist critics that there was little in the schools worth preserving; second, the critics and advocates seemed at times to favor change and innovation for its own sake; third, many seemed to suggest that the pathological institutional patterns of schooling were so pernicious that the only change worth attempting was of the fundamental, institutional, or systemic kind; and finally, it seemed that the way to overcome war, racism, and various forms of oppression was to change, abandon, or transform the schools.[22] If these assumptions led, at times, to overly pessimistic perspectives, and at other times, to overly optimistic and naïve reforms, it was understandable. Such, it seems, is the nature of progressive school reform as it proceeds in tension with countervailing forces and institutional momentum that can be deeply entrenched and very powerful.

Behind the newer social studies and humanist new wave was an important set of questions about schools and learning that cut deeply into ultimate purposes, to questions of what kind of society we should have and whose interests schools should serve. For teachers and students, there were questions of freedom versus control; the role of interest in the classroom; the extent to which student interest should govern choice of topic and teaching methods; the question of relevance, its meaning and implications; and questions about the role of teachers and students in determining both the curriculum and the rules governing schooling. And, behind this, there were persistent questions about the functioning of schools as an institution. Was school to serve as the great equalizer and as a force for social justice, or did schools in fact serve as an arm of an oppressive culture, sorting students into wage slaves or servitude in other forms? These were difficult and sometime divisive issues that had no easy resolution. Perhaps the most remarkable aspect of the newer social studies was that these issues were raised at all. That fact suggests the possibility that many of the issues highlighted during the era of the newer, humanist social studies will continue to be addressed by generations to come.

Influence in Schools

The level of influence of the newer social studies is difficult to assess with any certainty. Yet there is evidence suggesting that it had at least as much influence on schools and classrooms as did the new social studies, and perhaps more. Given the attention high schools received during the period and the enthusiasm and passion expressed over various reform proposals, one would expect substantial change in the curriculum.

National trend data suggest that the minicourse trend may have had significant influence by the 1972–1973 school year, perhaps at a level similar to what the research reported earlier suggests. The curriculum as a whole was marked by stability, despite the rhetoric and dramatic changes suggested by protest movements, new wave critics, and educational reformers, and despite an explosion of new courses, programs, and reform initiatives during the late 1960s and early 1970s. Partially in an effort to provide curricular differentiation, researchers noted "considerable experimentation in course offerings and the introduction of many new courses" along with a "drift away from the basic courses" in most subject areas. They also suggested that "new methods of instruction were experimented with" and that "core courses, minicourses and interdisciplinary approaches were introduced in an increasing number of schools" at the same time as "graduation requirements were relaxed" in many schools and "elective courses became more prominent."[23] Statistical evidence on the ratio of enrollment in year-long courses compared to semester-long or shorter courses supports a significant shift, especially in English and social studies, and belies the characterization of stability. In a 1960–1961 survey, shorter social studies offerings made up only 19 percent of enrollments in the field, while 81 percent of enrollments were in year-long courses that had long made up the standard sequence. By 1972–1973, shorter course offerings of one-semester or less suddenly accounted for 42 percent of enrollments, more than double the 1961 figure. This suggests that the data reported earlier may be accurate. The finding that by the mid-1970s more than one-third of high schools in three midwestern states had chosen to develop minicourses and an elective-curriculum likely reflects a broader national trend.[24]

Though offering little numerical evidence, a number of studies on the high school curriculum written during the early to mid-1980s suggest that the trend toward an elective curriculum may have had an even more widespread influence, although it seems to have varied widely by district. Critics complained that school knowledge had become "fragmented and incoherent" and that the concept of a "core" curriculum had "receded or been abandoned." Researchers and critics charged that specialized, narrow, and trivial electives had proliferated, and that course content was often determined by teachers "in isolation" who developed classes based on "personal predilections, and hobbies" in hopes of "attracting students in a competitive market" with course titles and descriptions designed to appeal to an "adolescent's definitions of 'knowledge' and 'relevance.'"[25]

Criticisms Emerge. Critics suggested that curricular fragmentation represented a culmination of several trends. Among these were the influence of federal and state policies combined with pressure from interest groups that led to mandated instruction in nonacademic areas such as sex education, consumer education, drug and alcohol education, and environmental education. More significantly, they suggested that the content of the basic disciplines had become increasingly fragmented because high school teachers were developing specialized courses that resembled the courses they had taken in college. As a result, courses focused on narrow topics or themes began to appear in increasingly voluminous high school course catalogs. At the height of the humanist trend, it was not uncommon for diverse, comprehensive high school course catalogs to resemble the college version and to offer dozens of electives in each subject. A typical school might offer 35 different English classes and 30 separate courses in social studies. The superintendent of the Dallas, Texas, school district noted in 1983, that the typical high school in his district offered 320 different courses, and that "magnet" or alternative programs offered another 230, pushing the total to 550.[26]

Other critics charged that an elective-curriculum contained too few requirements and allowed students to select the easy route, that it frequently minimized a focus on academic skills, that it narrowed the curriculum around "relevant" topics at the expense of a broader knowledge and understanding, and that it ended up grouping students by ability and social class, thus condemning poorer students to a second-rate education. Fueled by the back-to-basics movement, criticism of the elective curriculum grew dramatically in the late 1970s and early 1980s. Additional critics charged that schools were abdicating their professional responsibility to define academic content and argued that narrow, specialized electives left students unfamiliar with their cultural heritage and limited students' opportunity to master basic academic knowledge. Still others charged that the "stampede" to introduce electives in place of year-long required courses in basic disciplines, a trend that reflected the effort to meet student demands for "relevance," had degenerated into a tendency to let student interest define elective subject matter, leading to even further fragmentation.[27]

Some were especially concerned about the trends in social studies. One administrator in Denton, Texas, named James M. Benjamin, charged in *Social Education* that it was becoming "increasingly difficult to defend the social studies before a questioning public." He listed complaints about several aspects of the newer social studies including the following:

- The emphasis on conflict as a societal change agent in social studies is unrealistic and misleading to the intellectually immature student.
- The emphasis upon the supremacy of individual rights is unreasonable.
- There is an undue emphasis upon the "current" and the "immediate" in the social studies. When we consistently consider the present without a sure grasp of its historical roots, we are more likely to make mistakes.
- There is excessive emphasis upon "humanizing" historical figures.
- There is an excessive emphasis upon the inadequacies of American society throughout our history.
- There is an underlying theme … that all opinion is valid if openly arrived at and strongly held.
- Social studies methodology seems filled with gimmicks … A disproportionate amount of time seems spent on student activities, plays, role-playing, gamesmanship, and juvenile political participation.

He concluded by suggesting a focus on helping young persons gain "the knowledge and skills necessary to understand and appreciate our own society...and gain a feel of the real hope of democracy."[28] There is little doubt that Benjamin gave voice to complaints and criticisms held by many parents and citizens, and probably even a few teachers.

Benjamin's critique was countered in the same issue by Allan O. Kownslar, an advocate of the newer approaches, who argued, point-by-point:

- Conflict had sometimes served to provide the basis for our democratic society.
- Value clarification can play a vital role in conflict issues.
- The rationale for the new social studies places emphasis on current events and issues without ignoring their relationship to the past.
- The "humanizing" of historical figures is best suited for more mature secondary students.
- Our nation's history is one in which we have labored diligently to overcome inadequacies.
- An underlying theme in New Social Studies materials and methodology maintains that all opinion is worth consideration if it is *objectively* (not openly) arrived at and *validly* (not strongly) held.
- Use of audiovisual materials, role-playing, simulations, and political, economic, or social participation that rewards *rational thinking* will be more useful than wasteful and ineffective memory work.[29]

Kownslar offered a logical and very reasonable defense of the new and newer social studies and probably represented the response that most scholars in the field would have made, if given the opportunity. However, the times were changing and the pulse of the nation seemed to beat out a rhythm closer to Benjamin's position.

By the 1980s, several researchers were offering critical assessments on the status of the comprehensive high school. One book described it as a "shopping mall high school" that offered students a "consumption experience" with teachers as "salespeople" providing students a wide array of choices from which to buy or not buy and failing to challenge the majority of students to reach their potential and a high level of learning. Another charged that "electiveness" and "curricular enlargement" that had students choosing from myriad electives had led to limitations on many students' intellectual growth and undermined the "egalitarian ideal."[30] A later critic described the new humanism as part of the "feel-good curriculum" with its emphasis on progressive child-centeredness, student interest, and a culture of therapy, and charged that it had led to the "dumbing-down" of American students. By that time in our nation's educational history, the mid-1980s, critics of the humanist impulse and its embodiment in schools were beginning to have a strong influence on the direction of reform.

Conclusion

What happened to this new movement for relevance and social activism? Why was it short lived? Several factors weighed against an issues-centered approach having major and lasting impact. The long-term trends in curriculum of the time were discipline-based, and by the mid-1970s, toward a back-to-basics approach. The war in Vietnam ended. Optimism was replaced by cynicism, with Watergate, the perceived American failure overseas, and the specter of nuclear holocaust. All denied the possibility of social improvement. Moreover, there were other and countervailing trends at work in schools. The neoefficiency movement that spawned a new emphasis on career education, minimum competency testing, and accountability was ultimately more compatible with the schools' organizational structure and more consonant with the power structure in the society. After all, business, the military, schools, colleges, and other mainstream institutions needed a steady supply of human capital to continue functioning. Traditional social studies was a better fit with these institutional structures, and the traditional subject-centered curriculum had long ago proven its resiliency.

The issues-oriented approach, as it became fashionable in the late 1960s and early 1970s, was frequently flawed and poorly conceptualized. In too many cases it became a hodgepodge of topics, addressed helter-skelter. That kind of freedom may have exceeded the public's zone of toleration. The newer social studies, in many iterations, reflected something closer to a simple-minded presentism than a thoughtful issues-centered approach to teaching. In much of the literature of the newer social studies and the new wave, it appeared that history and the social sciences were too often an afterthought, left behind in the rush to concern over today. In some cases, it was the established disciplines themselves that were plainly the enemy. Finally, and perhaps most tellingly, both the new and newer social studies led to attacks on teachers, textbooks, and curricular programs. Those attacks, especially when combined with a trend toward more traditional forms of schooling, may have marked the beginning of the end of a remarkable era.

Yet, the period that I have labeled the newer social studies was in many ways a beautiful time of romantic and progressive reform during which anything seemed possible. There is little doubt that the period still resonates for many social studies professionals who lived through it or participated in it. It was an exciting time. First, the topical focus on social issues brought many troubling topics to the fore that deserved, and still deserve, extensive attention in schools. Many of the "closed areas" of American life that Hunt and Metcalf had first suggested needed to be explored in schools were suddenly open to study.[31]

Second, it was a pedagogically progressive era during which experimentation and freedom were prized. Both the new and newer social studies encouraged a new and broader mix of pedagogical innovations, including issues-centered discussion, simulation, panel discussion, open forums, and debate that could, when well conceived and thoughtfully applied, lead to higher levels of classroom thoughtfulness. Third, at its root, the challenge to authority and order represented by the newer social studies centered around basic, enduring dilemmas of a society built on greed and ambition, steeped in oppression and exploitation. To those who supported the reform, it offered a glimpse of possibility.

The social science critique of American industrial and capitalist society that emerged in the 1960s and 1970s may help explain both the rise and the subsequent dissipation of the newer social studies and many of the larger trends that accompanied it. Anthropologist Jules Henry in *Culture Against Man* (1963) described the drivenness of American culture, the preoccupation with amassing wealth, and the role of schooling in "drilling children in cultural orientations." Critical theorist Herbert Marcuse in *One Dimensional Man* (1964) decried the overarching influence of technology in modern life and the limitations on freedom that it imposed, of which the school was but one expression. Philosopher Michel Foucault in *Discipline and Punish* (1975) described the control and surveillance conducted in the prison, a metaphor for the subtle ways in which modern institutions, including schools, controlled, directed, and oppressed the population.[32]

The new wave critique, the new humanism, and the newer social studies all were an expression of rebellion, a cry in the wilderness against the oppression of modernist American culture and the drivenness, technocratic unfreedom, and shackles it had created. But in the end, as we shall see in the remaining chapters, other elements of the culture, even the system itself, would strike back at the rebel.

II

Reaction

4

Aftermath: "We Face a National Conspiracy"

In the late 1960s and early 1970s, along with the emergence of issues-oriented approaches in the newer social studies came growing concerns over academic freedom. National Council for the Social Studies (NCSS) issued policy statements supporting preservation of academic freedom and began to play a more activist role by getting directly involved in several local disputes that emerged by mid-decade. A number of academic freedom cases of the period signaled a significant negative reaction to the new curricular approaches and likely had a chilling effect on attempts at reform. Textbook controversies recurred, often instigated by a single parent and stirred by conservative activists. A special issue of *Social Education* was devoted to academic freedom concerns in April 1975. Ironically, the special issue appeared just as the battle over MACOS reached its zenith. The MACOS conflict proved a major blow to the survival of the social studies reform movement.

Though most controversies involved multiple participants from various perspectives, as it emerged it seemed that there were two sides in the academic freedom controversies of the 1970s. On one side were teachers, school administrators, and scholars who were engaged in the reform and improvement of schooling, trying to make the curriculum more interesting and up-to-date with inquiry, decision making, and valuing exercises and trying to make the schooling a more humanistic experience for children. On the other side were groups of parents and conservative activists, interest groups, and foundations many with deep pockets, who were concerned that the American way of life was being undermined by the new turn in the school curriculum spurred by the reform movements of the past decade or two and dedicated to undoing the social, racial, environmental, and sexual revolutions of the 1960s.

Academic Freedom Cases

There were a number of academic freedom cases involving individual teachers decided during the period. In a 1970 case related to social studies, English teacher Luke Callaway was dismissed from his position at a suburban Atlanta high school after implementing an open-ended curriculum designed at a Georgia college that called for study of modern writers and recommended films, including the surrealist film classic *An Andalusian Dog* written and directed by Salvador Dali and Luis Bunuel. The film depicted an eyeball being slit with a razor, putrefied carcasses of two donkeys, and ants crawling from a hole in a man's hand. Callaway was chastened for using a film to illustrate surrealism, for failing to follow the prescribed curriculum, for using an article from *Playboy*, and for including *Black Voices*, an anthology of black literature on his reading list. He was subsequently dismissed, but his firing was later ruled illegal by a federal jury.[1]

Thompson. Another case from 1969 involved history teacher Bennie G. Thompson, a young African American teacher in Madison, Mississippi and centered on the charge that Thompson was negative in his approach, and that he led discussion and assigned written work on issues that were not popular with the County School Board and other members of the White power structure in Mississippi. Thompson had also been criticized for his activities as a city council member in a nearby county, and his involvement in voter registration drives and other efforts to extend services to the poor. The federal suit filed on his behalf alleged that his contract was not renewed because he had exercised his rights to free speech.[2]

Sterzing. Keith Sterzing, a high school political science and economics teacher in Sugarland, Texas, frequently stressed current issues and debate and often played devil's advocate. Sterzing taught a six-day unit on race and prejudice during the 1967–1968 school year during which he presented films and supplementary articles by Dr. Benjamin Spock and B'nai B'rith. Sterzing often used controversial methods to stimulate discussion, such as saying his grandmother was a Black woman. Following a complaint by a parent, he was brought before the school board and told to avoid controversial subjects, to which he said it would be impossible. He was also told not to advocate sensational ideas to stimulate student thinking. After complaints by two additional parents in February, 1968, Sterzing was abruptly dismissed. After a seven and one-half year fight in federal court, Sterzing received a $40,000 out of court settlement. The case was hailed as "precedential" for giving teachers wider latitude in dealing with controversial issues. However, Sterzing never returned to teaching and was effectively silenced. In Sterzing's court hearing, a young O. L. Davis, professor of social studies education at the University of Texas at Austin, submitted an affidavit that made a strong statement for teacher freedom to discuss controversial issues and to take a provocative stance to stimulate discussion.[3]

Ahern. Francis Ahern taught for ten years at a Grand Island, Nebraska, high school before attending a National Defense Education Act (NDEA) summer institute for teachers. Following the institute, she encouraged students to participate in planning her classes. Students chose the school system itself as the specific institution to be studied. While Ahern was attending a follow-up conference in March, 1969, a student in her third period consumer politics class was struck by the substitute teacher, who followed a traditional method of instruction and classroom management. The controversy arose after Ms. Ahern expressed her concerns about what had happened. Consequently, the school principal ordered Ms. Ahern to change her philosophy of teaching, not to discuss the incident with students, and to return to more traditional teaching methods. "Her philosophy does not fit in this school," he stated. Ms. Ahern, who refused to go along with the order and encouraged student circulation of a petition, was suspended, then dismissed. Subsequently, her contract for the following school year was rescinded.[4]

Rochester, New York. Another academic freedom case centered on a Gay Liberation speaker who appeared before a class at Schroeder High School, in suburban Rochester, New York, in October, 1973. The speaker appeared on invitation from students in a Minority Studies class, which focused on various "liberation" movements, including Black Liberation, Women's Liberation, and Gay Liberation. In compliance with school district regulations and procedures for dealing with controversy, the teacher had received approval for the speaker from the departmental chairman and the building principal. Following the speaker's appearance and a positive student reception, the immediate parent and community response was quite negative, and included twenty-five letters of protest and harassment via anonymous phone calls to the departmental chairman's home and office.

Several school board meetings were held to deal with the ensuing controversy. Substantial community support for the teachers emerged, and the school board ultimately stood behind the teachers and administrators. Though the academic freedom of teachers and administrators was upheld, and student response was positive, according to one participant, several less-positive consequences indicate the cost: dealing with the initial hostility of a minority of the community was overwhelming; the time commitment was "crushing." Although it appeared that academic freedom won the day, the indirect effects of the incident left its scars. According to the department chair, "A year later we find ourselves a bit gun-shy; that is, we reflect more frequently on what might or might not be controversial...it may represent a vacillation in the direction of censorship."[5]

Fogarty. Yet another case that occurred later in the 1970s involved an English teacher, John Fogarty, in St. Anthony, Idaho, who recommended Ken Kesey's *One Flew Over the Cuckoo's Nest* to his high school students and announced that the class would read the novel, along with six others, during the 1977–1978 school year. Parents complained to members of the school board and administrators, protesting the use of the text because of "objectionable language." The school principal ordered recall of the book from students and removal of the novel from Fogarty's classroom. Though Fogarty protested the administrators' decision, he obeyed the order. He later voiced his complaints to the media. He was subsequently placed on probation by the school administration, and renewal of his contract was put in jeopardy. According to a story in the *Los Angeles Times*, the battle over *Cuckoo's Nest* represented a small town's efforts to "shape a world of its own liking—a world with only good, pure, and happy elements."[6]

The Fenton Textbook Controversy

One of the earliest major textbook controversies of the period occurred in Georgia in 1971–1972 over a series of new social studies textbooks on American history by Edwin Fenton. The controversy began in earnest when one member of the State Board of Education attacked a single book *The Americans*, an inquiry textbook aimed at "slow learners" and edited by Fenton.[7] At its meeting on November 24, 1971, the board postponed action on the list of approved social studies books as recommended by the State Textbook Committee after board member

Kenneth Kilpatrick of Jonesboro "objected to one author" and Al Leake, an Eastern Airline pilot and chairman of the Georgia Basic Education Council circulated material asserting that books by Fenton and another writer (Nat Hentoff) violated a section of state law, which requires that the curriculum include "study of and devotion to American institutions and ideals." Leake, who had been criticizing Fenton's work since at least 1969, objected to Fenton's books "on the grounds that his works included un-American teachings."[8]

Previously, Leake had appeared at the October meeting of the Fulton County Board of Education and attacked their social studies program, which was made up largely of Fenton materials. Getting little response from the County board, he went to the October meeting of the State Board where he attacked Fulton County's use of books that "did not teach Americanism." Dr. Paul West, Superintendent, who had just retired, and Leake had to be separated in the hallway after the meeting because "their 'discussion' was about to lead to a fist fight."[9] A polemic written by Leake and distributed before the December meeting read in part, "When approving the textbook list, please exclude all books authored or edited by Ed Fenton."[10]

At the December 16th meeting of the State Board, referring specifically to one text titled *The Americans*, Kilpatrick charged that the book "injects some things that I don't think have anything to do with the subject of history" and argued that "the book would create disruption and dissension in our society. In many respects it's a biased book...I believe there is more in the book about the Vietnam War than the American Revolution...I believe that students should get both sides of every issue, but I don't think they should get only one side under the guise of getting both." He also charged that the book "promulgates and teaches a 'nothing philosophy'—a nothing philosophy about life, home, family, and country." Kilpatrick moved that the recommended list be approved, with the exception of any books authored or edited by Fenton. The State Board of Education then ruled out inclusion of the Fenton texts on the state approved list on a motion by one member, Kilpatrick.

The ten Fenton books on the list were then referred back to the Professional Textbook Committee, which had originally approved the books, for further study. The committee, which rated textbooks on a 1,000 point scale that took into account authorship, organization, general content, illustrations, and instructional aids, had previously given Fenton's books a 900 rating. Moreover, in the past the board generally accepted the recommendations of its Professional Textbook Committee. However, in 1951, a single member of the state board had convinced her colleagues to remove Magruder's American Government from the approved list because it "played up world government and played down the American government." Though the board's suspension of the book lasted only five months, it suggested that the board could be moved to act hastily on the basis of hearsay evidence.[11]

In the newspaper coverage that followed the meeting, Kilpatrick's charges against the Fenton materials were countered by an NEA spokesman who stated that "the removal of the books...raises some serious questions concerning the abridgement of academic freedom." In a story that appeared the following week, Fenton was quoted as saying: "The issue is what social studies teaching is all about. Is it simple indoctrination or should we teach student to think critically about the issues? And if we don't trust them to think for themselves, then why don't we, since we live in a democracy?"[12]

During the month of December, 1971, as the controversy seemed to be reaching a peak, Fenton received some interesting letters. One letter, from a teacher, stated that

> I still think it is rather flattering that social studies materials and teachers could cause societies problems—frankly I can't even get the students to do their homework...Hooray for stupidity—I think I'll smuggle your materials into my classroom because once the kids know they have been banned they'll love them—a real boom for motivation. More power to you![13]

Another, from a citizen sympathetic with the critics, gave voice to the anger and disillusionment behind what was becoming a nationwide crusade, and read,

> So you don't like your textbook on history being rejected in Georgia...You probably went to college to evade the draft, like so many others did, but you didn't absorb any useful knowledge. Teachers like you are a dime a dozen...Militant students are making diploma mills out of our colleges, where the faculty and administrators are afraid. We need professors like Hayakawa, who are honest and strong for our country and morals are in a process of decay like Rome was...Why don't you try to peddle your book in Russia?[14]

Following the December meeting of the State Board, Fenton addressed a letter to the editor of the *Atlanta Constitution*, which appeared in the January 4, 1972 edition. In his letter, Fenton provided an explication and strong defense of inquiry learning as a "vital ingredient" of "Americanism," and asked,

> Should the schools help students learn how to think carefully about basic problems of democratic society? Or should they instead require boys and girls to memorize one author's interpretations? This issue lies at the heart of the controversy about the use of my books in Georgia's schools.[15]

In a letter updating Fenton the next month, Vernon Anderson, Director of Marketing for Holt, wrote to Fenton. At the time, Fenton was in Israel on consultation, but had offered to return to meet with the Georgia State Board. The letter read, in part:

> Then at the meeting on January 19, in an emotional meeting, the board heard a 3 hour and 45 minute presentation from the publisher's representative "to explain what inquiry teaching is about" and "what we were trying to accomplish by the inquiry method...[then] took each book and went through it giving page references, specific lessons, etc."[16]

Following the presentation, and a lengthy statement from the book's critics, the State Board voted 5–4 to add the 10 Fenton texts to the state approved list. On the previous day, the board had received a report from the State Textbook Committee reaffirming its earlier approval of the books.

Following the January reversal, Leake, Kilpatrick and other critics of the texts did not give up in what proved to be a relentless campaign. At some point early in the year, Kilpatrick vowed to bring the matter to a vote every time the board met until the books were dropped, and agitation against the Fenton texts continued into the spring. Kilpatrick requested three additional copies of *The Americans* from the publisher, and on February 17, Leake showed up at the Holt, Rinehart, and Winston offices asking for a copy of *The Americans*. J. H. Summers, who was handling the series, described what happened next:

> I looked up from my desk and Al Leake was standing at the door. Frankly, I got as nervous as a cat on a hot stove. He wanted a copy of THE AMERICANS. I sold him one at full list price. Also, I gave him

a teacher's guide and pointed out the necessity of looking at the total program and not just the textbook. Also, I made it clear to him that the book is designed for the non-achiever who reads poorly at best. We talked for at least 30 minutes. He has some rather traditional ideas on education as one would expect. Also, he threw in a comment about some senator wanting to review the book. God only knows what will happen next.

We have not had any great repercussions from this mess in the field. There is one large county superintendent which has asked his supervisors to be extremely careful in adopting any Fenton materials. Gene and I will see him next week and I think we can work out this matter. We may have to sacrifice THE AMERICANS to win the others.

I am about fed up with this entire matter and felt like letting Al Leake have one right in the smacker![17]

At its meeting on May 18, in what was described as a "stormy session," the State Board voted 5–4 to remove the Fenton series from the state approved list of textbooks. The reversal occurred in part because one member of the board, who agreed with Kilpatrick, was hospitalized and had missed the January meeting. The board's ruling meant that no state funds, which typically paid for 80 percent of the costs, could be used to purchase the books. However, several board members emphasized that a local district could still purchase the texts with nonstate funds. Thus, they suggested, the book had not been "banned" from public schools.[18] Despite their claim, few districts would choose to go it alone to buy the books. In an internal memorandum an employee of the publisher wrote, "There is nothing we can do to get the books approved... We must simply absorb the loss... [of] approximately $100,000 in forecasted sales." The memo closed with, "I do not believe there is anything else to add to what has been a long period of anxiety with a sad ending."[19]

At the June meeting of the state board, following the recommendation of an ad hoc committee composed of three members who had opposed the Fenton texts, the board agreed to prescribe a mandated course of study for eleventh and twelfth grade history and government, and to restrict use of state funds for the purchase of textbooks for American history to only four noninquiry chronological history textbooks they had selected from the state adopted list. Despite protests from educators and an attempt to limit the state board's power by changing state law, the board retained "undiminished power to override professional evaluations" and the power to effectively censor selected volumes.[20]

In his own reflections on the episode, Fenton wrote that some of the complaints against his texts stemmed from "a misunderstanding of the nature of history...as a collection of facts about the past," the assumption that social studies and history courses "should teach only knowledge," ignoring values, skills, and attitudes, and from the belief that students and teachers "cannot be trusted to make their own decisions." A couple of years later, Fenton noted that when he first learned of the criticisms in 1969, he "did not take Mr. Leake's article seriously" because his charges "seemed so absurd and inaccurate" that he "could not imagine any responsible person giving credence to them." However, after the conflict had more fully developed, and after the John Birch Society had effectively fanned the flames of controversy via its network of bookstores, news of the disagreement spread widely through the media. Fenton soon found himself flying around the country to defend the textbooks and the new social studies, including making an appearance on the "Today" show. Recalling those days in a recent interview, Fenton said, "It [the controversy] was all over the Pittsburgh papers...It bothered my kids."[21] After the dust had settled and his books were effectively eliminated from further adoption in Georgia schools, he framed the episode, and the larger growing controversy, in broad perspective and wrote:

> The attack on inquiry learning in the social studies has been mounting in several states, particularly in Arizona. We face a national conspiracy. A handful of people has [sic] spearheaded a well-planned drive to undermine your freedom and mine. In the process, they have eroded the strength of our democratic political institutions, and they are robbing the children we teach of the right to learn from the social studies materials we know are best for them.[22]

The Kanawha County War

Perhaps the most well-known localized textbook controversy of the 1970s was the battle that occurred in Kanawha County, West Virginia, in 1974. The battle was perhaps the most violent of any textbook dispute in the history of the nation, involving stormy meetings and several individual acts of violence and intimidation, including dynamite used against school property and bullets shot at student-less school buses.

The controversy began in spring, 1974, when Charleston School Board Member Alice Moore made a motion to delay adoption of 325 language arts textbooks for its K-12 curriculum until they could be examined more thoroughly. The wife of a local fundamentalist minister, Moore had been elected to the board in 1970 after leading opposition to a United States Office of Education (USOE) sponsored sex education program, which she claimed was anti-Christian and anti-American, and which purportedly indoctrinated an atheistic and relativistic view of morality. Later, the National Education Association (NEA) asserted that she received support from MOTOREDE, the "Movement to Restore Decency," which was affiliated with the John Birch Society. Following her election, the health and family program was rewritten, and sex education was eliminated.[23]

After perusing the books at home, and being appalled at their contents, Moore contacted Mel and Norma Gabler, the ultraconservative Longview, Texas, couple who reviewed textbooks from their home. The Gablers airmailed reviews of some of the books that were also up for adoption in Texas. The Kanawha County School Board held a meeting on May 16th at which the teachers committee that had originally selected the books defended its choices on the grounds that American society is made up of diverse groups and that students needed textbooks that exposed them to different points-of-view and that challenged them to think. Mrs. Moore questioned the teachers' philosophy and argued that the books contained material that was "disrespectful of authority and religion, destructive of social and cultural values, obscene, pornographic, unpatriotic, or in violation of individual and familial rights of privacy."[24]

Mrs. Moore and others objections to the books were based on the fact that they contained profanity; the writings of controversial persons such as Malcolm X, Eldridge Cleaver, and Charles Manson; and activities in which younger children were asked to imagine that they were God or to decide solutions to open-ended situations.[25]

Moore believed that there was a worrisome connection between reading and behavior, that reading profanity would spur its use, that reading about atheists would produce atheists, and that, on the other hand, reading "good clean literature" would produce "good clean people." In her view, schools in recent years had taken up the aim of social change and were trying to undermine or alter traditional American values. "I know that state law says our books must reflect multiracial, multiethnic, and multicultural viewpoints, but that's no excuse for teaching or even legitimizing nonstandard English...or for including book selections that paint Christianity in a bad or hypo-critical light."[26]

The controversy escalated after Mrs. Moore launched a vigorous campaign against the books in fundamentalist churches and in the media, exhibiting passages from the books at churches and commu-nity centers. Various groups entered the fray. The Parent Teachers Association (PTA) voiced opposition to several of the main book series, while the local National Association for the Advancement of Colored People (NAACP), the Young Women's Christian Association (YWCA), and the West Virginia Human Rights Commission sup-ported the choice of books. Much of the controversy it seemed, centered on "the explicit character of some of the writings deal-ing with Blacks." Thirteen students polled by the *Charleston Daily Mail* opposed censoring books for junior or senior high, and most of them felt that the issue was whether they would be allowed to read Black authors.

Although the local media, *The Charleston Gazette*, the *Charleston Daily Mail*, and WCHS Television endorsed the book adoptions, media coverage of the growing controversy, including a series of six editorials aired by WCHS in early June, served to fan the flames. On June 24, ten ministers from mainline religious denominations gave support to the books. One of those was Reverend James Lewis, min-ister of one of Charleston's Episcopal Churches, who stated, "The books in question are creative books, written with the intention of helping our children discover the truths...these books open up a world of opinion and insight. They're not un-American or ungodly." The problem, according to Lewis, was that

> this country is experiencing a religious crusade as fierce as any out of the Middle Ages. Our children are being sacrificed because of the fanatical zeal of our fundamentalist brothers who claim to be hearing the deep, resonant voice of God.[27]

On June 26, another coalition of twenty-seven ministers from fun-damentalist churches, organized by a Baptist minister, endorsed a statement that while there was much that was good in the textbooks, "there is also much that is immoral and indecent" and thus objected to their use.[28]

The next day, at a meeting attended by more than 1,000 people, with the crowd overflowing into the hallways and out into the rain, and after nearly three hours of stormy testimony, the school board voted to purchase all the books, with the exception of eight of the most controversial. Moore and other protesters were not satisfied with the attempted compromise. Throughout the summer months the protesters organized, caucused, and continued the campaign against "the books." Among the organizations joining the cause were Christian-American Parents and the Concerned Citizens of Kanawha County. For the most part, the controversy was stoked by newspaper advertisements that took many of the objectionable materials out of context, and which struck a chord with the sincere religious fundamentalism of many protesters. However, during late summer rallies new fliers appeared that contained purported excerpts from the textbooks, but that were actually drawn from other sources such as Kate Millet's *Sexual Politics* and another titled *Facts About Sex for Today's Youth.* The fliers contained "blatantly sexual material that had nothing to do with the language arts textbooks" and served to fuel the flames of the controversy. From that point, for many of those involved, "the books" became "the dirty books."[29]

At a Labor Day rally that drew more than 8,000, the Reverend Marvin Horan called on the crowd to boycott the schools when they opened the next day. During the first week of September, textbook protesters kept an average of 9,000 of the districts 45,000 students out of school. In the Upper Valley, absenteeism at some schools ran as high as 80 to 90 percent. In sympathy with the protesters, and unwilling to cross pickets, thousands of mine workers staged wildcat strikes, and picketers closed bus stations, grocery stores, and construction sites. The strong feelings erupted in violence. After several incidents of bombings and shootings, including gunfire that blew out windows in the Board of Education headquarters building, the School Board announced on September 11 that it had withdrawn the textbooks from the schools and that they would undergo a thirty day review period by a citizens committee. The next day, high school students staged a walkout in protest over removal of the books. Despite the board's apparent concession, protesters led by several fundamentalist ministers continued to stir citizens against the books. Rev. Charles Quigley, one of the fundamentalist ministers leading protests, shocked many county residents by saying, "I am asking Christian people to pray that God will kill the giants [the three board members who voted for the books] who have mocked and made fun of dumb fundamentalists."[30]

In the midst of the growing violence, one high school student remarked during the walkout, "They're shooting people because they don't want people to see violence in the books," pointing out the irony of Christian protesters engaging in exactly the kinds of behavior they so frequently repudiated. Violence escalated during the second week of school, and the number of striking miners grew to between 8,000 and 10,000. Two men were badly wounded and another beaten; a CBS television crew was roughed up; car windows were smashed; and threats were leveled against the school superintendent and some parents. By September 13, the safety of the community was so endangered that Superintendent Kenneth Underwood ordered all 121 schools in the district closed for a four-day weekend and cancelled football games and extracurricular activities. The superintendent and several board members slipped out of town to avoid threats, as did Alice Moore, who remarked, "I never dreamed it would come to this."[31]

The textbook review committee began its deliberations after appointments were made on September 24, in a charged atmosphere filled with rallies, pickets, boycotts, and unlawful damaging of school buildings. And additional groups emerged to influence the outcome, including a pro-book group called the Kanawha County Coalition for Quality Education, the Kanawha County Association of Classroom Teachers, and an antibook group called the Business and Professional People's Alliance for Better Textbooks led by Elmer Fike, who published antibook ads and pamphlets and served as a liaison to the Heritage Foundation, a new conservative think tank, and who hoped to "give a better image to the protest movement." Meanwhile, the Gablers visited the county and spoke to parents groups throughout the region.[32]

While the review committee was doing its work, an elementary school was dynamited and another fire-bombed; other schools were targets of gunfire, fire-bombs, and vandalism; rocks were thrown at the homes of parents defying the boycott and at school buses. For his own personal safety, Superintendent Underwood lived in hiding, Alice Moore was threatened by phone and gunshots, and both were protected by guards.[33]

Meeting at noon on November 8 amid strong security measures, with a few representatives of the Ku Klux Klan picketing outside, the board voted to return all of the controversial books to the schools with the exception of the two most controversial series, which were placed in school libraries to be used only with parental approval. At the end of November, the board adopted new textbook selection guidelines similar to a list the Gablers had sent, with Mrs. Moore forcing a point-by-point vote, though the guidelines were later opposed by an NEA inquiry panel appointed to review the controversy after a request by the local teachers association. The NEA inquiry concluded that the guidelines could lead to grave violations of first amendment freedoms and could so narrow the field of choice "as to make a mockery of the selection process."[34]

Though the controversy was apparently over, protests led by fundamentalist ministers continued until April 1975, when the diehard leader, Rev. Marvin Horan, was tried and sentenced to three years in prison for conspiracy to bomb schools. Two other ministers were sentenced to brief jail sentences for defying a court injunction. The NEA inquiry panel held hearings from December 9 to 11, 1974, at which they heard testimony from groups on both sides. After reviewing all the evidence it had collected, the NEA report identified key issues in the conflict: What are the rights of parents and community members in selecting textbooks? What are the responsibilities of educators? The report concluded that parents and community members have a right to serve as advisors but that educators must make the decisions. The NEA report also identified several causes for the conflict. The citizens of Kanawha County were deeply divided by differences in income, lifestyles, religious belief and values, and educational ideas between well-off city dwellers and poor rural families. Liberal school administrators had failed to effectively communicate with conservative farmers and miners, and the board had failed to respond swiftly to the initial protests. Moreover, the NEA suggested, the crisis was made worse by the involvement of several right-wing extremist groups, including the John Birch Society, Citizens for Decency through Law, the Heritage Foundation, National Parents League, and the Ku Klux Klan.[35]

In the larger national realm, the conflict's deeper causes might be found in a host of troubling developments of the time that one historian has labeled the "nightmare decade." "Watergate, a changing set of values, Vietnam, inflation, and a host of other confusing trends in the social order... brought about a situation in which people [were] frustrated, confused, angry and fearful. When such conditions exist...there is a desire on the part of human beings to seek simple solutions to complicated problems, react to change with hostility, and meet authority...with...lack of trust...The textbooks [became] a convenient scapegoat."[36]

Looking beyond the violence, this was, as Todd Clark wrote in *Social Education*, a "conflict over the role of an American institution," with large numbers of sincere citizens on both sides, many of whom wanted a school program "that emphasizes basic skills and patriotic indoctrination, typical of our schools in the past."[37] At issue were a host of contested principles, values, and beliefs, and legal issues centering on the parents right to protect their children from unwanted influences, in tension with the student's right to know. Though the conflict in Kanawha County was extreme, it was an expression of an emerging national mood that would have a profound impact on the new and newer social studies. Throughout the 1970s evidence would continue to mount to support Ted Fenton's charge of an emerging "national conspiracy."

Conclusion

The controversies described in this chapter served as a prelude, foreshadowing what was to come, including a significant shift in the national climate of opinion regarding the status, function, and purposes of schooling. Individual academic freedom cases literally put innovation in the classroom on trial and signaled a limit to the public's zone of toleration for change. The Fenton textbook controversy in Georgia raised the stakes considerably as a major innovative textbook from the era of the new social studies, which also embodied many of the newer progressive trends focused on issues and values, came under attack. The Kanawha County textbook controversy was a major local confrontation that soon became a central rallying cry for the new right. Alice Moore became a featured speaker of the Christian Crusade, "secular humanism" became the new evil conspiracy, replacing communism, and the Heritage Foundation emerged as a clearing house for new right protest, forming the Congress for Educational Excellence to coordinate the activities of roughly 200 textbook protesting organizations nationwide.[38] So, the academic freedom controversies of the 1970s served as a catalyst to continued action by the new right and an emerging coalition of groups who were troubled by the fragmentation and dislocation of school curricular reforms. They wanted to restore order and reassert their vision of the American way.[39] This was especially true for the Kanawha County conflagration, which, because of the media coverage and outside interest it inspired, has been described in recent years as one of the "first shots" in the culture wars, a conflict of "liberal v. conservative, religious v. secular, wealthy v. poor, black v. white, scholarly elite

v. working class pragmatists."[40] Moreover, according to at least one observer, the Kanawha County controversy had at least three tangible impacts: Bob Dornan was elected to Congress as a champion of Christian fundamentalism, the "virtually unknown" Heritage Foundation was able to find its voice and mission, and the textbook publishing industry "has never been the same."[41]

Man:
A Course
of Study

Seminars
for
Teachers

Figure 1 Jerome S. Bruner (Photo courtesy of Education Development Center, Inc.).

Figure 2 Edwin P. Fenton (Photo courtesy of Carnegie Mellon University Archives).

RE-ELECT
ALICE MOORE
FOR
BOARD of EDUCATION

Dear Friends,

The schools belong to the people who pay for them, not Washington Bureaucrats, not School Administrators, not National Education Organizations.

Nationally, education is costing us more than **61 billion dollars a year**, more than is spent on education by all the rest of the world combined. This is a **1000 percent increase** in 20 years while enrollment has barely doubled. Yet, almost **one third** of our high school graduates cannot pass college placement exams and this number increases annually.

Are your children getting the education you want for them? I am convinced most parents expect the schools, for which we pay and for which we provide the children, to:

- Offer the best academic education possible with emphasis on basic skills.

- Respect family privacy and our right as parents to rear our children according to **our own moral, ethical** and **religious beliefs** without interference.

- Provide a disciplined and morally up-lifting educational climate for the safety and peace of mind for both students and teachers. **Stop coddling the class trouble-makers at the expense of serious minded students.**

- Operate the schools as efficiently as private enterprise.

As a board member, I have tried to represent the **public interest**, not an Educational Bureaucracy. This is the kind of education I want for my five children. If this is what you want, please give me your vote and contact your friends on my behalf.

Sincerely yours,

(Mrs.) Alice Moore

The **final** board vote is at the May 11 primary. Democrats, Republicans and Independents can vote for me, for this non-partisan position.

Figure 3   Alice Moore Reelection Poster (Photo courtesy of West Virginia State Archives).

Figure 4 Mel and Norma Gabler (Photo © 2010 by Danny Turner. All rights reserved).

Figure 5 Robert Welch, founder of the John Birch Society (Photo courtesy of Oregon Historical Society, Or Hi 104938).

Figure 6 Peter B. Dow (Photo by Annaliese Garver, courtesy of Peter Dow).

Figure 7 Jigging for lake trout (From Netsilik photos by Asen Balikci, courtesy of Peter Dow).

Figure 8 John Steinbacher (Photo courtesy of Pacific University and John Steinbacher).

Figure 9 Congressman John B. Conlan (Courtesy of Arizona State Library Historical Archives, photo no. 97-8035).

Figure 10 Legislative aide George H. Archibald, with Vice President Gerald R. Ford, at a 1973 fundraiser for Congressman Conlan (Photo courtesy of George H. Archibald).

Figure 11 Ed Feulner introducing President Ronald Reagan at a Heritage Foundation dinner, November 30, 1987 (Ronald Reagan Presidential Library and Museum, no. C 43865-15).

Figure 12 Joseph Coors and President Ronald Reagan shaking hands while attending a dinner for the board of governors of the Ronald Reagan Library Foundation at the Ritz-Carlton Hotel in Washington, DC, December 14, 1985 (Ronald Reagan Presidential Library and Museum, no. C 32550-22).

Figure 13 George C. Wallace announces he is a presidential candidate, February 8, 1968 (Library of Congress, Prints and Photographs Division [reproduction number: LC-U9–18605–18A]).

Figure 14 William J. Bennett, Secretary of Education, 1985–1988 (George Bush Presidential Library and Museum).

Figure 15   Diane Ravitch, with Barbara Bush (George Bush Presidential Library and Museum).

The MACOS Controversy and Beyond

The academic freedom battles of the 1970s reached a climax in the MACOS controversy that signaled the virtual end of the funding period for new social studies projects. Many conservatives and traditionalists who wanted the schools to transmit the "American way" perceived MACOS as a threat. MACOS, or Man: A Course of Study, was originally the brainchild of Harvard Anthropologists Douglas Oliver and Irven DeVore for a K-6 historical and evolutionary sequence of "The Human Past." When the project was taken over by Jerome Bruner and the Harvard ESI staff in 1964, it limited its focus to the middle grades (4–6) and focused on the question, "What is human about human beings?" Reflecting DeVore's influence, four organizing themes emerged, designed to help children understand culture: social organization, language, mythology, and technology. The themes were to dictate where postholes would be dug. In addition, "contrasts and models" were adopted as pedagogical approaches. Contrast was to come from exercises comparing the life cycles of fish and animals with the social behavior of humans, in this case, the Netsilik Eskimos. Dramatic and graphic scenes of Netsilik life were included, among them materials depicting senilicide and other taboos of mainstream US society. Bruner and colleagues were aware that the inclusion of graphic materials could precipitate controversy, but believed that the materials provided students with the opportunity for a powerful learning experience. Following field tests and much revision of the initial plans by a large and well-financed staff, the final package of materials included ninety-five teacher guides, thirty children's booklets, sixteen records, five filmstrips, three games, fifty-four artifact cards, and various odds and ends. The package received numerous awards for its creativity and quality.[1]

Despite the accolades, commercial publishers resisted such a logistically complex package, and the Education Development Center (EDC, formerly ESI) at Harvard funded its continued development and promotion using a total of $6.5 million in National Science Foundation (NSF) funds. By 1968, 6,000 students in 200 classrooms were using the program, and by late 1969, more than 1,000 classrooms were on board, success that led to a publishing contract with Curriculum Development Associates (CDA). Unfortunately, the program's unbridled success was short-lived. MACOS was soon embroiled in a series of controversies that began not long after the published materials began to enter schools on a widespread basis.

Initial Confrontations

Lake City, Florida. The earliest local controversy over MACOS began in the fall of 1970 after a parent and fundamentalist minister in Lake City, Florida, whose daughter was using MACOS in a sixth grade class, requested a copy of the materials. After examining the materials, the minister denounced MACOS as "hippie-yippie philosophy" that was "sensual in philosophy" and linked it to "humanism, socialism, gun control, and evolution."[2] In Lake City, a rural north central Florida town of about 10,000, the charges resonated.

Shortly after the start of school in September 1970, Rev. Don Glenn of Montrose Baptist Church in Lake City requested and received copies of MACOS materials from his sixth-grade daughter's social studies teacher at Niblack Elementary School. He subsequently discussed the course with teachers, learned that it was not on the state adopted list, and then proceeded to form a "study" group of "concerned citizens." Glenn and his group, which allied itself with a group called Citizens for Moral Education (CME), began circulating petitions demanding that the course be dropped. Glenn, president of the local unit, charged that the course presented a "leftist, Godless approach that de bases traditional values." At the school's first PTA meeting of the year on November 4, Glenn rose and stated the group's objections:

- The basic philosophy is humanistic. It leaves God out of it.
- It teaches evolution as a fact.
- It has a socialistic and sensual philosophy throughout its content.[3]

The three teachers who were teaching the course vigorously denied Glenn's charges and stood at the meeting and challenged Rev. Glenn. John Millis, a teacher who was also the pastor of a small Baptist church in Lake City and respected as a man of impeccable integrity, informed the gathering that the purpose of the course was to teach children what makes man unique and urged parents to come to the school to see how the course was taught. He argued that discussion of sex was "no more frequent than in other texts dealing with man" and objected strongly to Glenn's suggestion that there were "no moral guidelines" for discussion. A second teacher, Quintilla Lynch, claimed that critics were spreading deliberate lies about the course, and the third, Joyce Tunsil, with twenty-five years experience in the district, defended the course and recommended that it be retained. Perhaps the most powerful testimony of the evening came in the form of comments that Millis had asked his students to write regarding their understanding of the course. One student wrote, "In social studies we are studying how man is different from animals. We are not studying that man came from ape[s]." Another wrote, "All the course is trying to teach us is how proud we should be that we can do things we want to do, and animals can't."[4]

Glenn and CME found passages in the teachers' manuals for the course that he and his group interpreted as advocacy for sex education, evolution, the hippie-yippie philosophy, pornography, and communism. Excerpts of the passages were circulated along with a petition they distributed to enlist membership in the organization.

With sponsorship from a local hardware store, Glenn purchased airtime on a local radio station and presented four one-hour programs criticizing MACOS. On the programs, Glenn read the passages cited on the petition and interpreted them as "heinous signals" of the impending doom of democracy, Christianity, and parental control in America. For example, on one program he stated,

> If you can tell me how you can teach the process of reproduction without teaching sex education I'd like to know how it's done...Now parents and concerned friends, may I say that reproduction information with specific, detailed description can not be disseminated or taught without teaching sex education. We're not against sex education, per se, but we are against sex education without moral guidelines...We, as Christians, subscribe to the moral values of the Bible, God's word, which have been ruled out of the schools and classroom by virtue of the Supreme Court.[5]

During the radio broadcasts, Glenn urged his listeners to attend a meeting of the CME where the executive secretary at the state level, Elizabeth Piazza, would speak. An estimated 700 people attended the meeting, where charges against MACOS were repeated, and Mrs. Piazza embellished them with descriptions of "pornographic activities" that had allegedly occurred in the Orlando, Florida schools. Mrs. Piazza and CME brought national attention to Orlando with their challenge to SIECUS (Sexuality Information and Education Council of the United States) materials some eight months earlier.

At the school board meeting on November 12, Glenn and CME filed its formal appeal for the removal of MACOS from the local school. At the tense and heavily attended meeting, Glenn spoke for fifteen minutes, repeating his previous charges. Six parents spoke spontaneously, in defense of the course. The board then appointed an eight member panel made up of four educators and four laypersons to review the materials, hold a closed hearing at which each side could make its case, and make a recommendation to the board.

Behind the scenes, Robert Harrison, a professor and administrator at Florida State University and regional director for dissemination of MACOS, met in his motel room with the three teachers, the superintendent, and the chairman of the school board and pledged assistance from "higher levels" in an effort to bolster the confidence of those accused. Despite their support for the course, the superintendent, Silas Pittman, who was a personal friend of Rev. Glenn, remained publicly noncommittal, though he pledged to abide by the board's decision. However, he did seek influential laypeople who would defend the course on its merits. In a press interview sometime later, he remained equivocal, stating, "The people are divided on the course. Some say children find this their most exciting course. Others want it removed." On the question of evolution, he made a similarly obtuse comment. The principal of Niblack School never made any public comment on the course during the entire controversy.[6]

When the review committee met on November 17, it heard two hours of testimony from each side. Harrison induced both Peter Dow and John Gentry, the course publisher, to travel to Lake City to speak at the review committee hearing. Five parents of students enrolled in the course, and Rev. Phillip Lykes, pastor of The First Baptist Church of Lake City, along with Harrison and John Lunstrum of Florida State University spoke in favor of the course and addressed the implications of permitting "arbitrary censorship of materials" in a public school.[7] Dow described his experience before the review committee:

> It was a tense occasion. I had spoken about MACOS innumerable times but always before friendly audiences, and I was unprepared for the hostility that pervaded the hearing room. I began by recounting the intellectual history that had inspired the course...then discussed each unit and its intended purpose in some detail. I stressed our commitment to the development of cross cultural understanding and pointed out that we had done very little with the concept of evolution.
>
> When I had finished, Reverend Glenn looked me hard in the eye, thrust his open palm in my direction, and inquired, "Mr. Dow, do you believe that the human hand is a product of evolution?" I was startled, at first, by the question, suddenly realizing that Glenn was far more concerned about how the developers of the course thought than about what the materials said...He wanted his fellow panel members to believe that the course had been put together by atheists and communists who were out to undermine the religious faith of the young...He wanted me to admit, to a room full of Southern Baptists, that I was a committed evolutionist and thus an enemy of fundamentalist Christianity. I had never been faced with such an interrogation before, and I struggled for a response...Taking refuge in the scientific data, I stuck to the known biological facts and avoided being drawn into a discussion of my beliefs.[8]

Dow's testimony was aired on the radio the next evening, following a request by Harrison for equal time. The next night the radio station held a two-hour question-and-answer forum that allowed the public to pose questions to a panel with two respondents on each side of the issue, with Rev. Lykes and Rev. Glenn on opposite sides.

The same day as the radio forum, Harrison phoned the *Florida Times-Union* and complained that CME was resorting to "smear tactics" in their press and radio criticism and stressed that the university and NSF were squarely behind the course. In his rebuttal, printed the next day, Glenn again stated his opposition: "The entire course is predicated on the philosophy of humanism. Humanism in turn is based on the evolutionary concept of man...We feel this course furthers the aims of the communists in this country." He added that communists will attach themselves to "any vehicle that will in some way compromise the basic precepts" upon which the nation was founded.[9]

Meeting in special session in the auditorium of Lake City High School on Tuesday night, November 24, the chairman of the Columbia

County School Board called the meeting to order and asked Rev. Glenn to lead the group in prayer. Glenn's homily was temperate, calling for trust and understanding, and for healing the divisive feelings regardless of the board's decision. Frank King, pastor of the First Presbyterian Church, presented the review committee's report and its recommendation, that MACOS "be continued, and that after the end of this school year (1970–71) the course be made an elective and a state adopted course be offered." The members of the board sat in silence, temporarily immobilized by ambivalence. Eventually, a motion was made to accept the committee recommendation. It died for lack of a second. Finally, another motion was made: keep the course, but make it elective as of tomorrow, and offer students both MACOS and the traditional course. The motion was seconded and passed.

Besides the review committee's report, the board also received two minority reports. One from Rev. Glenn restated his group's objections to the course and added, "It is purely amoral in that free discussion of our culture, our society, our family unit, sex and laws are made without reference to any God or constant law—The student decides for himself at age 10 what is best of several cultures, societies, sex habits, etc."

Glenn then made a recommendation: "I therefore recommend that the Board tonight discontinue the use of 'MAN: A COURSE OF STUDY' in our public schools. If this is not the pleasure of the Board, then as an alternative, I recommend that this course be made an elective now and be discontinued at the end of the year." At the close of his statement, he starkly noted the importance of the decision, which he stated had "the potential to destroy a Nation as well as the minds of our young people or produce a heritage that will be a standard of Freedom and Prosperity to the world."[10]

Glenn's statement was followed by a dissenting opinion by Robert E. Marks, a local dentist, who objected to the critics' case on the grounds that "some of the published objections were incorrect and inflammatory to a degree which could create undue alarm." His disagreement with the committee's vote rested primarily on his belief that the precedent established "could be detrimental to future, and other present, courses of study."[11]

The faculty at Niblack School saw the decision as an invasion of their academic freedom, and twenty-one teachers, two-thirds of the faculty, signed a letter of protest presented at the next school board meeting on December 3. Citing the precedent set by the decision, the letter argued that such disruptions to the curriculum "may endanger the educational atmosphere for both students and faculty" and called for maintenance of MACOS as a required course for all sixth-grade students. Though their protest was remarkably daring, it was to little avail.[12]

In the end, Rev. Glenn and the CME had their way, parents were given a choice of courses for the remainder of the school year, and the materials were ousted from the school entirely after the one-year trial. Following the incident at Lake City, Dow sent questionnaires to school districts nationwide that were using MACOS. Of 134 replies, the vast majority rated the materials excellent, and only 14 reported complaints about the materials, that is, the switch from American history and explicitness about Netsilik life. However, the minister had apparently touched a nerve and a growing avalanche of hostile criticism would eventually be unleashed.

After the board's decision was made, Robert Harrison, presciently, proposed a gathering of regional directors and representatives of CDA, EDC, and NSF, the key groups behind MACOS, for the following January with the specific aim of establishing guidelines for local districts faced with similar extremist charges. He wrote, "While my proposal may be construed as the alarm of someone who has recently undergone an extremist attack, some very sober reflections regarding the potential destruction these groups could evoke and the nature of present political feelings nationwide indicate such a meeting may be in the best, long run interest [of] all of us involved with MACOS."[13]

Dow, in a reflective mood after the controversy had more or less ended, wrote to a colleague who asked about his reflections on what had been a tense confrontation with Rev. Glenn. Glenn was really asking, he wrote, "Where do you stand, Dow?" Agreeing with Glenn that teachers and curriculum developers are not really neutral, he ruminated, "All of our courses take a value position on human questions even though it is primarily an intellectual one. We say in effect that knowledge rather than blind faith is our best hope, that mankind has a chance, and that in particular an intelligent understanding of his condition and his origins will improve his chances." Where the school's functions end and the church's begins was less clear, Dow wrote, "a very complicated matter which I don't begin to understand myself."[14]

Montgomery County, Maryland. As the next school year approached, another controversy over MACOS erupted in a larger district, one that had a reputation for excellence and commitment to innovation. This controversy occurred during the same school year as the Fenton textbook controversy in Georgia, which was discussed earlier. The Montgomery County system's elementary schools had pilot-tested MACOS in 1970 and planned to expand the program to more schools in the fall of 1971. Then, in August, an article entitled "What Educators Are Doing With Your Federal Taxes" appeared in *Human Events*, a tabloid-size national conservative newspaper distributed by the John Birch Society and others. The masthead for the tabloid clearly stated that it was "not impartial" and that it looked at events "through eyes that are biased in favor of limited" government, "private enterprise and individual freedom." The article, originally a letter sent to 80 US Senators and some 300 members of the House of Representatives, was written by Dr. Onalee S. McGraw, a Montgomery County resident who signed the article as curriculum director for a group called Citizens United for Responsible Education (CURE). The central claim of the article was that federal tax dollars were being used "to support educational philosophies and theories to which [many parents] are unalterably opposed." McGraw described an "almost monolithic" education establishment controlled by the National Education Association (NEA) aimed at socializing the child and shaping students to the "social attitudes and values which the educators believe are most desirable." This meant that the home would play a subservient role; that all questions, values, and moral issues were " 'open' and relative"; and it implied decreased emphasis on academic learning focused on development of "intellect and basic skills."[15]

McGraw cited MACOS as a prime example of a federal education program revealing the ideological biases of the "elitist social scientist turned educator" and noted that "M:ACOS [*sic*] replaces history in the social studies curriculum" though as we have seen, grade level varied somewhat by district. She was especially critical of the program's treatment of the Netsilik Eskimos and wrote, "The problem is that the Netsilik Eskimo study as presented instills in the children the concept that all values are relative and culturally determined," because the children were asked to "compare the religious myths of the Netsilik Eskimo with the Judeo-Christian 'myths' of their own culture," but with little opportunity to study their own culture in any depth. She cited specific materials from the teachers' guide and argued that "the concept of the soul and man's spiritual life are absent from the author's definition of 'humanness,' " and argued that Bruner defined humanness in terms of five characteristics, including the "desire to explain his world through science or myth."

McGraw charged that the aims of the course were "*philosophical* rather than factual," and that the course aimed to "shape the attitudes and values of the student." She then posed the question at the heart of her critique: "Is it the legitimate function of the federal government to subsidize certain philosophies and value systems at the expense of others under the guise of 'the scientific presentation of facts using the methods of the behavioral sciences.'" She suggested that the reader would "search in vain" for any similar program using federal funds to describe the "development of Christian culture."[16]

Though MACOS was cited as the most dramatic example of federal funding gone awry, McGraw argued that the programs she cited were not isolated instances, but were typical of federal projects that aimed at the "psychosocial formation of the child" as opposed to development of basic skills and intellect. In conclusion, she recommended (1) strict guidelines to ensure that education grants "require philosophical and political neutrality...do not violate the sanctity of the home and the privacy of the child...and preclude the manipulation of teachers and student," and (2) vouchers for parents who do not want their children subjected to such "manipulative education." She closed by stating her belief that "young minds" were at stake, with nothing less than "the future course of our nation" hanging in the balance.[17]

Following the appearance of the McGraw article, which was circulated throughout Montgomery County, the school board asked superintendent James M. Reusswig to investigate the course. Reusswig conducted a national survey of 167 school districts that were using MACOS. One hundred of the 134 superintendents responding described the course as "excellent," twenty-eight as "good," and none as "fair" or "poor." Fourteen districts reported complaints, with objections focused upon the switch from American history, sex education, teaching evolution, too much depth, and explicitness about Eskimo life. After learning that CURE had a membership of only twelve to fifteen in Montgomery County, Reusswig and the board approved plans to continue implementation of MACOS in the district.[18]

Though the battle to continue MACOS was won, temporarily, the arguments made by McGraw gained increased circulation among conservative activists, serving as a building block for future disputes over the course and over the new social studies and the humanist school curriculum generally.

Phoenix, Arizona. Probably the most widely publicized local controversy over MACOS erupted in the Madison Park School District of Phoenix after Mrs. Phyllis Musselman, a local parent who did not have a child in the course but had enrolled her son in kindergarten, wrote an article that appeared in Arizona's *Weekly American News*, a conservative newspaper devoted to right-wing causes. Titled, "MACOS Social? Study?," the article began, "While high school sophomores supposedly cannot survive without sex education, elementary students will be learning this fall that violence, youth and power are necessary for survival." Later, it read, "Teachers are instructed to concentrate on examples of cannibalism, infanticide, genocide and senilicide until these acts of violence are acceptable and understandable to the children." They "play act leaving grandmothers to die as they were too old to be useful" and are asked "to decide whether they would rather live in a human society with laws and regulations or in a baboon group-gang 'where you can see and do everything.'"[19]

Musselman's article generated so many parent calls to the newspaper that they asked Mrs. Musselman to write a series on the course. She wrote a total of four additional articles, which ran in the *Weekly American News* from September through early October, detailing and criticizing additional "facts" from the course, including its depiction of evolution, its portrayal of man as "just another animal," its mythical stories of "stabbing, wife stealing, animal beating and bloodletting" and cannibalism, and its description of Netsilik "creation myths" that led children to "begin thinking that Genesis is just another 'myth' about creation."[20] Another article in the series alleged that the course aimed at "changing behavior" rather than the traditional goals of learning basic skills and assimilating knowledge. Musselman alleged that the course was subtly conditioning children "to accept violence" and "situation ethics" that will be remembered and acted upon in times of stress.[21]

Following Musselman's initial story, school superintendent M. E. Hatter reacted by sending a memorandum to assistant superintendent Dow Rhoton and principal Marvin Cornell requesting more information about the program. He wrote,

> If some of the innuendos and statements are true, I would join with our conservative friends' viewpoints about the dangers of such a program...I would like to know what the program actually does [and] if it's true that children are not led to the development of values based upon Judeo-Christian ethics...We need to be able to answer charges such as those.[22]

Rhoton and Cornell responded by calling parent's meetings at which several teachers tried to explain the course, which was being used with 106 sixth- and seventh-grade students as part of a two-year pilot. At one of the meetings, Mrs. Musselman rose to address the parents attending: "I am Phyllis Rae Musselman and I speak on behalf of Madison Park parents who love their children enough to have read the MACOS materials. We are amazed at the way this board expects us to placidly accept such dull, useless, violent material for our children. We are stunned that you would overestimate our apathy as taxpayers...and insult our intelligence in this way. This course is an insult."[23]

Then, after one of the meetings, when parents returned to their cars they found an unsigned handbill on their windshields that urged parents to contact the school board and to attend the special board meeting on October 28. The flyer read, in part:

WHO DO WE EAT?

Kill useless old grandma, eat the wife's flesh and save the bones. Murder baby girls, exchange wives, learn to think like a baboon, and study animal mating. Simulated hunts and role playing...[make] lasting impressions on children's minds as they pretend...A steady diet of blood-letting and promiscuity is presented...and [the] impressionable child is thereby induced to believe that man is only an advanced animal.[24]

The flyer also charged that Bruner was "an expert on psychological warfare in World War II" and suggested that he was applying similar techniques to shaping children's values and behavior. It was true that Bruner had been involved in psychological warfare, as he later admitted to Dow prior to Dow's trip to defend MACOS before the Phoenix board. It was also true that Bruner had been involved in other "secret" projects during World War II and the cold war, that he employed "systems thinking" as an overarching frame for his work in schools, and that he had once compared the teaching system to a weapons system, though it seemed quite a stretch to suggest that he was deliberately trying to manipulate the minds of children for ulterior purposes. The aims of MACOS were clearly spelled out, and most observers, indeed most parents found them unobjectionable.

As tension in the controversy continued to build, at least two local church ministers got involved. Richard Jackson of North Phoenix Baptist Church, who had personally examined the materials, wrote a letter suggesting that the course "can add nothing" to the education of young people. Another, Richard W. Cain of First United Methodist

Church of Phoenix helped organize a public forum for discussion of the curriculum.

Musselman and other opponents of the curriculum collected ninety-eight signatures on a petition presented to the board that was accompanied by letters from respected members of the community. One was from physician Dr. James Severance. Another, from Burton S. Barr, Majority Leader of the Arizona House of Representatives, stated that the mood of the legislature was "to get back to basic education in Arizona." Moreover, Weldon Shofstall, Commissioner of Education for the state, banned all future purchases of the course and urged opponents to file a lawsuit charging that the course was unconstitutional because, "teaching that man is an animal and nothing more is teaching about the existence of God and religion."[25] Another letter directed to the school board from F. J. MacDonald of Phoenix offered a blistering attack on the course then charged that the board "either was ignorant of the contents of the course...or is guilty of careless experimentation with the lives of children...The only other conclusion that could be drawn is that the Board is guilty of being drawn into the web of Socialism and Communism which is attempting to undermine this country."[26]

One parent, who believed that most of the opposition was coming from people who did not have children taking the course, conducted a telephone survey of 137 parents with 159 children in sixth or seventh grades. Her poll revealed that 71 parents wanted their children to take the course, 51 expressed no opinion because they knew too little about it, 5 parents were not happy but did not request an alternative program, and 10 were against the program and wanted an alternative course.[27]

The controversy in Phoenix came to a head at a school board meeting on October 28th held in a large auditorium with 700 people attending, along with local media. The five school board members sat on a stage. A podium and microphone were provided for testimony. The evening began with dispassionate statements from course supporters from the Madison Park staff who spoke about the benefits of the program. Several teachers strongly endorsed the program, one gave an overview of the materials, and another described her use of the materials in class and read student comments from an evaluation survey. Principal Marvin Cornell reported the results of a questionnaire sent to the parents of the 106 children in the MACOS program. When parents were asked about their child's reaction to the course thus far, 61 were favorable, 7 unfavorable, and 5 had no reaction.

Fifty-nine parents responded that they wanted their child to complete the MACOS program. Cornell proposed that his school be allowed to continue the program.[28]

In his presentation, Dow described the program, the intentions of its creators, and the results of field-testing and evaluation. He urged that parents be given freedom of choice and closed with a short film illustrating the program being used in a fifth-grade classroom and providing some indication of the independent thinking they hoped to inspire.

A short time later, Earl Zarbin, a newly appointed board member, took the floor and critiqued the course as a deliberate attempt to mold the children's behavior, to shape children in the image of course developers, and to perpetuate the Godless philosophy of "humanism." Following Zarbin, a parent named Thomas Doeller presented a list of signatures from fifty-two parents of children in the course indicating that they would like their child to continue. Another parent urged that MACOS be continued, noting that an alternative course based on the textbook, *The Free and the Brave*, had already been provided for those who requested. Mrs. Musselman spoke in opposition to MACOS and proposed formation of a textbook committee through which parents "could choose a basic, concrete social studies program of worth and educational value if the board would drop MACOS." She intimated that her proposed alternative would be preferable to a state legislative investigation. The last scheduled speaker, Frank Lewis, a parent, presented statements from more than 350 people supporting the Madison School Board in its initial decision to pilot MACOS and urged the board to "not give in to the pressure of a small percentage of people to abandon or change its original decision in midstream."[29]

The meeting was then devoted to two-minute speeches by members of the audience who had requested a chance to express their views, and who had each indicated their preference for or against MACOS on cards collected at the start of the meeting, allowing equal time for each side. A Boy Scout leader stated that his wife was home sick "because of this program," and that parents were losing control of their children because of "Skinner, Bruner, and the rest of these jokers from out of state." A "born again" Christian stated his support for the course, arguing that moral values are "caught" in the home rather than taught at school. A mother and former teacher read a passage from one of the teachers' guides:

> "Neither the eye of the camera nor the knife of the surgeon can distinguish the man from the seal." [Brandishing the teachers' guide in the

air] This is MACOS. The man indistinguishable from the seal...With a view to human overpopulation and a reminder that the seal is in a diminishing existence, let's be glib. Let's keep our humor. Listen to the expert, Jerome Bruner, and take a seal to bed![30]

After the time allotted for comment had expired, Jeanne S. Chisholm, the board president, brought the session to an end. After a short recess, board member Rev. Sam J. Lindamood moved that "the MACOS program be continued for the remainder of the year with the option being given to parents for their children to be enrolled in an alternate social studies course" if so desired. The motion was seconded and passed on a 3–1 vote. Zarbin abstained because he came "on the board with a preconceived notion of what he believed."[31]

The next day, October 29th, Dow, Mrs. Musselman, and another parent, Mrs. Anna Day, appeared on a talk show with host Logan Stuart on Phoenix radio station KRUX. Though he was wary of facing off against Mrs. Musselman whom he later described as a "mistress of half-truth and innuendo," Dow accepted the invitation in the hope of bringing an alternative and informed view. The debate proved to be thought provoking and inspired a good deal of reflection, in Dow's words:

> Although serious dialogue was impossible, since my opponents were close-minded and fanatically rigid in their views, I admired their perseverance and their devotion to what they believed. Their objections to exposing children to the darker side of Netsilik life—birth control through infanticide, the vulnerability of old people, or the necessity of killing to survive—made me pause to wonder why we had chosen to include so many of the harsh realities of Arctic life, and in particular, what purpose we had served by dwelling on one Netsilik's decision to abandon his aging mother-in-law...Why had we left ourselves open to such easy criticism?[32]

Musselman and Day wanted to know the rationale for including the study of animals and the basis for animal-human comparisons. Was the course suggesting that humans were "just 'evolved' animals?" Then moderator Stuart, abandoning any attempt at neutrality, suggested that by introducing students to the values of another culture, the course was undermining the moral foundations of American society. When Dow protested, Stuart blurted out: "What I am trying to extract from you Mr. Dow, is an admission that the most important thing to teach a child is faith!"

Dow's reply crystallized the essence of a controversy that centered on competing notions of the purposes of schooling:

> Not in the public schools. In Sunday school, of course we teach children what we want them to believe; but as for the rest of the week, the proper purpose of schooling is to cultivate doubt, to raise questions, to help our children see the world from another point of view.[33]

Schooling, Dow was suggesting, should be concerned with the growth of the mind rather than the transmission of belief. Dow's exchange with Stuart helped crystallize a fundamental issue separating the supporters of MACOS from its critics. The MACOS program, like most of the materials of the new and newer social studies, centered on asking children to question and to explore the meaning of being "human" through a process of inquiry that would both respect their intelligence and help them learn to think for themselves. On the other hand, opponents of the course, and most of the ultraconservative critics of the new and newer social studies, viewed MACOS as anathema to their purposes. They wanted an approach that would promote traditional American values. They did not believe that children should be encouraged to question. Instead, they should be told what to believe by their parents, teachers, textbooks, and other sources of authority. Any social studies program that sought to cultivate a questioning attitude in students was dangerous because it failed to impose absolutes, and because it did not encourage unquestioning acceptance of traditional, conservative American values.

Though the immediate outcome of the controversy in Phoenix was a modest victory for the proponents of the course, it was a pyrrhic victory. Of the 110 students in the program, 22 were eventually placed in another course. After the two-year trial period, MACOS was quietly dropped. The school board had become more conservative and was increasingly taken up with performance objectives, minimal competency standards, and other indicators of the back-to-basics mood of the day. Given the shift in priorities, it seemed that alternative and innovative programs did not make sense, at least not in Phoenix. Sometime after the controversy had been settled, and MACOS removed from the school, Rhoton suggested in an interview, "We felt that right now the proponents of the three 'Rs' are so strongly in the saddle as far as the Madison District is concerned, and so far as the State of Arizona is concerned, that people ought to be well warned ahead of time before they take on a program such as MACOS."[34]

Nationwide Controversy

In the ensuing years controversies sprang up in communities from coast to coast, spurred in part by a growing nationwide network of conservative activists. Dow and others who were developers of the MACOS program seemed reluctant to believe that there was any kind of systematic, national campaign against MACOS. However, there were growing indications that such was the case. In Lake City, on the day of the committee hearings, the president of the school board had received a telegram from the "coordinator of the National Coalition on the Crisis in Education" warning that "parents across the country are watching the Columbia County School Board." And in Phoenix, Mrs. Musselman, the key instigator of the controversy, was an active member of the John Birch Society who spoke to a reporter while she helped "man" the John Birch Society booth at the Arizona State Fair in early November, near the peak of the controversy.[35] Though I do not have a great deal of evidence from inside the John Birch Society, it is well known that members of the group kept each other informed through a monthly magazine, a newsletter, and other informal means, and that they distributed materials and sought recruits via a network of American Opinion Bookstores. Moreover, it is very likely that McGraw's article criticizing MACOS and other federal social studies programs that had appeared in *Human Events* was circulated widely among conservative activists and may have caught the attention of a local activist like Mrs. Musselman.

Another controversy over MACOS occurred in April 1972, in an innovative school district in Bellevue, Washington. The official complaint, lodged by two parents, Mrs. Rosanne McCaughey and Mrs. Richard O'Hara, included many of the same charges that were made in Phoenix and cited many of the same quotations from student and teacher materials. Following consultation with Dow at EDC, Art Ware, social studies coordinator for the district, discovered that the opposition to the course was coming from only a few persons, and that the course was enthusiastically supported by the largely liberal and middle-class community. The controversy in Bellevue ended without the extensive investigations and the emotionally charged public meetings that had transpired a Lake City and Phoenix. However, the incident proved "worrisome" for Dow because it raised questions of outside influence. It showed that controversy was possible even in a relatively liberal community, and seemed to suggest the possibility of a growing nationwide controversy.[36]

Another limited controversy occurred in Houston, Texas, beginning in February 1973, when a group called Parents in Action led by Nadine Winterhalter launched a letter writing campaign and filed a petition with forty-eight signatures asking that "MACOS be withdrawn from use in any public school in the state of Texas." The letter contained many of the same charges as in Phoenix with quotes taken out of context. It included reference to the series of articles by Musselman from the *Weekly American News*, and her assertion that Bruner worked in Psychological Warfare during World War II and had employed similar techniques to influence children through the MACOS materials. Edward Martin of EDC responded to Peggy Chausse, the district consultant who was handling the complaint in Houston, with a packet of materials for defense of MACOS: a film, "Innovations Perils" that documented the Phoenix controversy; a transcript of an interview between Dow and Bruner; and advice on handling the situation.[37]

Despite continuing controversies, sales of the course continued, achieving modest growth from 1971 through 1974, along with proper training to ensure that materials were used in ways that the developers intended. For a few years, at least, it seemed that careful implementation along with intense teacher training were contributing to growing success and allowing EDC to weather the storm of controversy. But, in the fall of 1973, the course came under renewed attack in Burlington, Vermont, from a group that called itself, "Citizens for Quality Textbooks" (CQT), organized under the leadership of Donald Davie, a South Burlington engineer. The controversy over MACOS came to the attention of Davie and other Vermonters after Mrs. Norma Gabler was invited to visit and spoke in Burlington in late September 1973:

> A short, chubby, Longview, Tex., housewife…emptied a suitcase full of textbooks onto a display table at the Ramada Inn in South Burlington. These textbooks, said Mrs. Norma Gabler, Texas' most powerful influence on the state committee authorizing textbooks for public school use, typify what she calls the kind of scum she is managing to sweep out or keep out of Texas classrooms because it breeds moral corruption and anti-Americanism.[38]

Mrs. Gabler's display included selections from MACOS and other textbooks. The Gablers had been informed about MACOS by parents in Arizona, most likely Mrs. Musselman. To the Gablers, who

by this time had developed a powerful reputation as textbook critics, MACOS was "the perfect example of a closed system of government indoctrination for neutralizing the values taught by church and
home." As Mrs. Gabler told one civic group:

> After looking at textbooks for 11 years I thought I was unshockable.
> But this wins the prize for being the worst. Fifth-grade children, at an
> age when they are most impressionable and curious, are led to "dis-
> cover" the life-style of the Netsilik Eskimo tribe of Canada. And what
> do the Netsilik's practice? Cannibalism, infanticide, murder of grand-
> parents, wife swapping, mating with animals—the most degrading
> things you can imagine. And what is the teacher to say about all this?
> She is not to make a value judgment. The children must decide with the
> clear implication that if the Netsiliks want to live this way, then these
> crimes against God and nature are all right. The whole idea is that
> one culture is as good as another and that the values of no culture are
> absolute.[39]

The uproar over MACOS spread into Vermont immediately after
Mrs. Gabler's talk at the Ramada Inn in South Burlington. Unhappy
parents in Morristown, an hour east of Burlington, who were previously unaware of the presence of MACOS in their schools, began
urging the school board to remove it from the classroom.

Following Mrs. Gabler's visit to Burlington, the group invited
John Steinbacher to speak in Burlington on two separate occasions.
Steinbacher, a reporter for the *Anaheim Bulletin*, a California Daily,
was the author of two books, *The Child Seducers* and *The Conspirators:
Men Against God*, critical of new programs in the schools, which he
opposed, including sex education and those he viewed as embodiments of secular humanism. For Steinbacher, MACOS was "one more
illustration of Deweyism, pragmatism, Behaviorism, psychic manipulation, and, above all, Humanism." He viewed the "tax supported
school system" as "the leading vehicle for transporting Marxist revolution" into American society and believed that the schools were
"destroying the souls of an entire generation of America's young."
Steinbacher appealed to parental fears of "being impotent in the
lives of their children," of children being "weaned from the truths
of God and Christianity by humanistic behavioral scientists" who
transferred clinical methodologies from the mental institutions to the
school system. He described schools as a "vast mental hospital for
the psychic manipulation of the young." According to Steinbacher,
the behavioral scientists were bent on taking over children's minds

and preparing them to accept "the concept of a socialized One World totalitarian state."[40]

For Steinbacher, MACOS represented part of a conspiracy to destroy American civilization. In an interview with a reporter from the *Burlington Free Press*, he stated that "the MACOS program has a basic philosophy...that attacks most of the civilizing influences in our society. During the fifth grade, U.S. history is thrown out. Instead they concentrate on one civilization. You'd think they'd pick one that contributed something. Instead they pick a totally obscure Eskimo tribe which...has a lifestyle diametrically opposed to ours."[41]

In Steinbacher's view, "A roving band of degenerate men and women were out to seduce the souls and bodies of America's children" by undermining the Christian values taught in the home. Thus, the world and the schools were seen as "a battleground between the forces of Christ and the forces of Satan." Steinbacher, like many other school critics of the time, wanted to turn back the clock toward the traditional educational system of the past, lionizing "the great church related schools of early America...[with their] Judeo-Christian philosophical underpinnings." He argued for a return to the traditional disciplines and a focus on teaching the basics, including traditional history focused on the greatness of the American heritage.[42]

Davie, the central figure in the Vermont controversy, believed that the course "teaches atheism based upon evolution which will lead to the downfall of the United States." Davie, who claimed that he had thoroughly researched the subject, argued that MACOS was developed by humanists who believe that love of God and country must be "erased" in children so that they can accept the humanist idea of one world in which all are "world citizens." MACOS, according to Davie, was "one of 1,000 instruments aimed toward this goal." Moreover, he said, he "unquestionably" believes that programs such as MACOS are linked to communism or could easily fall prey to it, because they break down the moral fiber of American youth, "stripping them of their will to resist Communist indoctrination."[43]

In the end, the controversy in Vermont led to removal of two particularly controversial texts from the MACOS series being used in Morristown. After being pressured by parents and CQT, in a compromise the board voted 4–1 to remove two books, but to continue using the rest of the program.[44]

Though other localized controversies occurred in a variety of locations over the next year, the controversy still had not reached full force. In Corinth, New York, in January 1974, a group of parents disrupted classes at the Springbrook School in a working-class community. It seems that a classroom discussion of evolution had turned into an argument, and some of the children had returned to school brandishing religious tracts that denounced the theory of evolution. Soon, parents were demanding that the school give equal time to the teaching of religious beliefs if it was going to "preach" evolution. The principal attempted a compromise by offering an alternative program for the children of objecting parents, but to no avail. In April, the school discontinued the MACOS program.[45]

During 1974 and early 1975, opposition to MACOS continued to spread, apparently led by a loosely organized group of ultraconservative critics who were steadfastly opposed to the MACOS course and other materials that they viewed as undermining traditional education. Among the chief critics of MACOS were The Gablers, McGraw's National Coalition for Children, John Steinbacher, the Heritage Foundation, the Council for Basic Education, the John Birch Society, and George Wallace's American Party.

A sign that the controversy might be headed for a higher national profile occurred when the Leadership Foundation of New Jersey hosted a morning seminar and luncheon under the title "GOOD EDUCATION OR MIND CONTROL" in South Orange, New Jersey, on January 31, 1975. The seminar was led by Susan Tovey, former president of the group, who spoke on the topic of "Value Training" and John E. Patton who addressed "Transcendental Meditation in Our Schools." It featured a luncheon address by George Archibald, legislative aid to Congressman John B. Conlan of Arizona. Archibald, a former staff writer for the *Arizona Republic*, had previously served on an Arizona commission to develop guidelines for social studies textbooks for the Arizona State Board of Education. He had set a personal goal to "get schools out of the business of social engineering and indoctrination...Schools exist for people, not for gurus" and was familiar with the materials.[46] Archibald's speech was titled "MACOS, A National Controversy," and the meeting, it was suggested, would be "overwhelmingly Anti-MACOS." An EDC contact in the vicinity who forwarded a flyer announcing the event, suggested that "if many school board members attend...a major controversy could develop" and reported that several area communities "have already abruptly dropped MACOS, almost without discussion."[47]

By the following month, a controversy had developed in Boise, Idaho, in which critics centered their concerns on what they saw as the devious psychological manipulation of children. Principal Daniel

Burns of Owyhee Elementary School reported that a group of anti-MACOS people were "drawing a link between Jerome Bruner's past work as an experimental psychologist in the area of cognition, subconscious learning, and subliminal messages to the MACOS program," arguing that he would not have let such an opportunity to incorporate his life's work in schools pass him by. They were "concerned about the control over young people's minds with such a program" and linked Bruner to behaviorist B. F. Skinner, who was also a Harvard psychologist. Dow wrote back with a supportive letter distinguishing between Skinner and Bruner and noting, "Bruner's work is largely based upon observing children... [and] deriving hypotheses about their thinking processes." Moreover, Dow wrote, cognitive psychologists like Bruner believed that cultivating growth in children was similar to growing a beautiful flower, "the capacity for growth is within the organism itself," and that the role of the educator is to provide a stimulating environment and materials. Dow also noted that a congressional committee, the Committee on Science and Technology that authorizes the NSF budget, was investigating MACOS, and that conservative members of congress, influenced by a letter-writing campaign conducted by a small group of "agitators," had organized themselves in opposition to the course and were seeking to cut off funding.[48]

Who Were the Critics?

Critics of MACOS included an array of conservative and ultraconservative groups who gained considerable momentum during the 1960s and 1970s, including the John Birch Society, the Heritage Foundation, McGraw, textbook reviewers Mel and Norma Gabler, conservative columnist James J. Kilpatrick, and the CBE, which was, ironically, an early supporter of new social studies reform.[49] A few deserve more extensive treatment.

Mel and Norma Gabler. The Gablers seemed to be involved in virtually all of the academic freedom controversies of the period. They were a common thread running from one local conflict to another and a critical element in the glue that held the protest movement together. Mel and Norma Gabler were an east Texas couple active in "Bible-believing" churches who had become the nation's leading textbook critics. Mel, who had served in the Army Air Corps during World War II was employed as a clerk by Esso Oil until his retirement in 1974. Norma was a housewife, mother, and superintendent of the youth department at their church. Their activities in textbook analysis and criticism began in the fall of 1961 after their oldest son, Jim, 16, complained that something was wrong with his textbook. Mel examined the book, *Our Nation's Story*, published by Laidlaw Brothers, and read passages that enumerated the powers of the federal government, but failed to include discussion of any limitations on federal power, or the powers reserved to the states and the people. "This set Mel on fire." On further examination, the couple did not find any mention of familiar stories and sayings of patriots, such as Nathan Hale's "I only regret that I have but one life to lose for my country," and Patrick Henry's "Give me liberty or give me death." The book's emphasis appeared to be on modern history, the benevolence of the government in Washington, and world government through the United Nations (UN). They later compared the book to older textbooks published in 1885 and 1921 and reached the "startling conclusion" that the publishers had misrepresented history.[50]

On a first-name basis with school officials, they asked the local superintendent how books were selected, and who selected them, and were told that each year in Austin a State Textbook Committee chose two to five books for certain subjects and grades on a rotating basis. "We're bound to their list," he said. "If you want to have an impact, go to Austin." They followed his advice, and within a few years had developed a textbook analysis operation of national reach operating out of their home. By the late 1970s, they had house full of books, a staff of eight, 2,000 square feet of rented warehouse space for extra storage, and with a mailing list of 10,000 names, had built a network of like-minded contacts throughout the country. Over more than four decades, the Gablers railed against textbooks that promoted humanism, evolution, values clarification, problem-solving, sex education, relevance, critical perspectives on the American past, and anything that they believed intruded on parental rights. They joined the fight against MACOS, convinced that it was the vanguard of a "new" social studies designed "to promote a humanistic world view" financed with tax dollars. They viewed MACOS and many of the other innovative and inquiry materials of the time as forms of "mental child abuse" designed to undermine religion and the family. They stated sometime later:

> We favor honest inquiry when children are given sufficient information on all sides and allowed to develop their own conclusions. We want sound education. The new educational change agents want

indoctrination on their terms with resource material cleverly introduced to manipulate students toward humanistic conclusions. This
they falsely call "inquiry."[51]

Though they operated on a relatively small budget, the Gablers, and
their nonprofit organization, Educational Research Analysts, received
support and funding from a variety of conservative groups and organizations, including the Heritage Foundation and, later, the Castle
Rock Foundation, a Coors family source of funding for conservative
activism.[52] The Gablers and other textbook watchdog groups used the
support of many local organizations that formed to monitor schools,
some of which were branches of the John Birch Society.[53]

John Steinbacher. Another figure of some influence through his writing was John Steinbacher. A reporter for the *Anaheim Bulletin*, a former
teacher, and author of books critical of the new approaches in schools,
Steinbacher was a contributor to a nationally distributed ultraconservative monthly newspaper, *The Educator*, and author of a "School and
Family" column that appeared in the *Anaheim Bulletin*. His book, *The
Child Seducers*, 1970, criticized sex education programs, the SIECUS
(Sexuality Information and Education Council of the United States),
sensitivity training, secular humanism, and progressive social studies,
much of which was traced to the influence of John Dewey, other pro-
gressives, and secular humanists on the schools and to the Humanist
Manifesto that Dewey signed in 1933.[54]

Dr. Onalee McGraw. Another influential figure, mostly through her
writing and speaking, was Onalee McGraw, who held a PhD in political science from Georgetown University. A resident of Montgomery
County, Maryland, an officer in the National Coalition for Children,
and a member of Leadership Action, Inc., of Washington, DC,
McGraw wrote one of the earliest nationally distributed articles critical of MACOS in 1971 that appeared in *Human Events*. She was also
involved in a variety of local conservative organizations and may have
been among the most intellectually astute of the critics of the new
social studies. A longtime consultant to and an analyst at the Heritage
Foundation in 1977 and 1982, she authored a key Heritage study published in 1976 entitled "Secular Humanism and the Schools: An Issue
Whose Time Has Come," which provided "a case study of the growth
of humanistic teaching in the public schools and the efforts of local
parent groups to stymie the humanistic trend." The influential thirty-
page pamphlet quickly went into a second printing and became one
of the Heritage Foundation's most popular early publications.[55] She

would later serve as a member of the National Council on Educational Research, an appointed position requiring senate confirmation, and on the professional staff of the House Committee on Children, Youth, and Families during the Reagan administration.[56] Other individuals, already introduced, who made key contributions to the growing fight over MACOS included Congressman John B. Conlan and his legislative aide, George Archibald.

The John Birch Society. Several conservative and ultraconservative organizations made key contributions to what was initially a campaign against MACOS, but was steadily becoming a larger protest movement against the new and newer social studies. One of the key organizations involved was the John Birch Society, though its role was frequently in the background, or in the guise of smaller local organizations through which its members sought to influence schools. The John Birch Society was founded in 1958 in Indianapolis, Indiana, by Robert Welch, a retired Massachusetts candy maker, and named after a US military intelligence officer and Baptist missionary who was killed by Chinese communists in 1945. Welch's investigation of communism had begun during the 1950s while he was a board member and chairman of the Educational Advisory Committee of the National Association of Manufacturers (NAM) who had a long history of involvement in textbook criticism and manipulation of schools and society through propaganda campaigns. Over the years, the John Birch Society has supported limited government based on the constitution and traditionally conservative causes such as anticommunism and individual rights. By the early 1960s, it had 25,000 members, including leading industrialists Fred Koch and Harry Bradley who would become two of the main benefactors of the conservative movement. By the 1970s, Birchers were seen by many as an extremist group, the harbinger of conspiracy theories, yet with the group's emphasis on limited government, its support for parental control of education, and its ongoing campaign against "world government" and US membership in the UN, it found itself and its members in firm alliance with the ultraconservative critics of MACOS and the new social studies. At its peak, the John Birch Society claimed between 60,000 and 100,000 members, and its main publication, *American Opinion*, reached a circulation of more than 100,000. Its policies resonated with a significant minority. Opinion polls found that more than 5 percent of Americans broadly agreed with the society. Moreover, it sponsored an extensive network of local chapters, a speakers' bureau, and an antitax committee. It also sponsored a chain of American Opinion

Bookstores that helped its members circulate an array of conservative literature and ideas, including materials that lay the groundwork for local activism against the schools.[57]

The Heritage Foundation. Significantly more mainstream than the John Birch Society, the single most influential conservative think tank to play an important role in the campaign against MACOS and the new social studies was the Heritage Foundation. The founding of the Heritage Foundation in 1973 launched what was probably the most notably important of an emerging network of conservative policy-oriented institutions. Heritage was founded by a group of conservative legislative aides, notably Paul Weyrich and Ed Feulner, to serve as a "talent bank" and nationwide communications center for Republicans. The logic was relatively simple. Liberals had dominated Washington by out-organizing conservatives. As Weyrich once explained, "If your enemy has weapons systems working and is killing you with them, you'd better have weapons systems of your own." Unlike the American Enterprise Institute (AEI) that had long supported conservative causes but focused on in-depth scholarship, Heritage decided early on to target members of Congress and their staffs and produced policy-oriented materials ranging from one-page executive summaries and twelve-page background papers to full-length books. "Paul and I decided," as Feulner recalled, "that conservatives needed an independent research institute designed to influence the policy debate as it was occurring in Congress—before decisions were made."[58]

Initial funding for the Heritage Foundation came from brewery magnate Joseph Coors, and right-wingers Richard Scaife and Edward Noble. Other large corporations, including Gulf Oil made early contributions. By the 1980s, Heritage reported that eighty-seven leading corporations were providing support. Over the next few decades, Heritage would become the single most prominent conservative think tank leading the effort against big government and promoting deregulation, "traditional family values," and a host of conservative causes. Coors, who believed that the government was undermining individual liberty through interference in the lives of citizens, and who was concerned about "atheism, liberalism, and Godless communism," had established a long history of support for right-wing causes. He and the Coors family found themselves eventually "contributing millions to undoing the social, racial, environmental and sexual revolutions of the late 20th century," even though his Coors brewery was the subject of a lengthy boycott by labor and civil rights groups.[59] In practice, the Heritage Foundation was less a traditional think tank and more of a "propaganda center" that created justification for preconceived positions that invariably confirmed the notions to which its benefactors were already committed, and then distributed its polemical materials in a format palatable to the press and politicians.[60] Heritage and a host of other conservative think tanks and political action committees became the underlying backbone of support for efforts by a broad array of ultraconservative, conservative, and neoconservative groups that sought to overturn the influence of MACOS and the new and newer social studies. Ironically, a different kind of weapons system was now being aimed against the educational "weapons system" designed by Bruner and EDC. Heritage played a role in the Kanawha County war through the influence of its liaison, Elmer Fike, and would play a key role through McGraw as the MACOS controversy came to Congress.[61]

The Council for Basic Education. Another conservative group that contributed to the attacks on MACOS and the new social studies was the CBE, which was founded in 1956 by historian and school critic Arthur Bestor and others with the aim of preserving the standards of education and countering the excesses of progressive education and the life-adjustment movement. From its inception, CBE set out to ensure "that all students without exception receive adequate instruction in the basic intellectual disciplines, especially English, mathematics, science, history, and foreign languages" as stated in its bylaws. Among its early members, directors, board members, and supporters were Mortimer Smith, Mary Bingham, Admiral Hyman Rickover, Potter Stewart, and Jacques Barzun. By 1974, its original membership of 158 had grown to 4,500, and its monthly publication, the *CBE Bulletin* had a circulation of approximately 6,700. The CBE spread its views via speeches and publications and by responding to inquiries from various persons, including congressmen, journalists, and educators. During the 1970s, it had taken an active position against some of the NSF supported curricula, especially in the social sciences.[62] The CBE's Director during the 1970s, George Weber, argued that schools should avoid controversial topics, including morality, religion, and politics, all of which he saw as permeating the NSF materials. Moreover, by promoting inquiry methods over substance (facts), Weber viewed the NSF materials as suffering the same neglect of basic skills as had characterized the progressive education movement, along with a general permissiveness and lack of teacher authority that contributed to "rampant illiteracy."[63] The CBE would later play a key role in the movement for strong national standards in education.

The American Party. Another organization that contributed to and participated in the surge of conservative interest in textbook criticism and in countering the new social studies and MACOS was the American Party. The American Party was established in 1969 as successor to the American Independent Party, which had served as a vehicle for the presidential campaign of George Wallace, governor of Alabama and an ardent conservative and segregationist. Though Wallace "did not create the conservative groundswell that transformed American politics in the 1980s, he anticipated most of its themes." Wallace gave voice to a growing white backlash in the mid-1960s, warned against the growing influence of "intellectual snobs who don't know the difference between smut and great literature," and railed against the growing influence of federal bureaucrats. His attacks on the federal government and angry rhetoric became the foundation for modern conservatism and the new ground rules for political warfare. Wallace recognized the political capital to be made in a society shaken by social upheaval. His influence helped move the conservative "politics of rage" from the "fringes of our society to center stage." The influence of Wallace and the American Party illustrate what has been called the "Americanization of Dixie and the Southernization of America." For Wallace and his followers, the greatest hope to advance their agenda was through confrontations whereby the give and take of politics became a "battleground" between Godly Republicans and the "secular anti-religious view of the left" that was embodied in the federal programs such as MACOS and the new social studies.[64]

Other small groups played a role in many local conflicts. Leadership Action, Inc., a group based in Washington, DC, devoted to "involving citizens in active government participation" promoted lay involvement in textbook selection and targeted NSF-funded courses to support its goal of a decreased federal role in schools. In the controversy over MACOS, the group mailed copies of "lurid" excerpts from MACOS to thousands of congressmen and state legislators. And, when the controversy came to Congress, it presented a display of "100 dirty textbooks" in the Capitol, mostly including MACOS materials.[65]

The growing conservative juggernaut got its message across to the public, policy makers, and a wide network of activists through newsletters, press releases, position papers, monographs, books, the tireless efforts of volunteers, donations, grants, and money from benefactors. Conservative groups also, and quite astutely, made innovative use of new media through direct mail, talk radio, Christian broadcasting, fundamentalist churches, and a network of Christian bookstores.[66] As in the Rugg controversy of the early 1940s, critics shared sources and were motivated by similar issues and values. Many of the letters published in local newspapers or sent to legislators suggested links among the protesters. The same Xeroxed articles were cited again and again. And an unsigned information sheet about MACOS was widely circulated in the spring of 1975, presenting a list of objectionable points from the course and instructing citizens to write letters to their representatives in Congress, expressing the objections in their own words. Within a few weeks, members of Congress received a flood of similar letters protesting the presentation of evolution, the disturbing portrayals and discussion of Netsilik culture, and the "atheistic philosophy" of secular humanism behind the course.[67]

Though it appears on first glance that the wealthy business leaders who helped bankroll the campaign against Rugg were absent, they were present in the 1970s campaign against the new social studies. However, they appeared to play a less-public role, preferring to offer support to conservative foundations and a multitude of national and local groups, leaving most of the protesting to local groups and the national organizations they funded.

Behind the rapid growth of the various conservative groups were a number of factors, not the least of which was the growth of conservative ministries during the 1960s and 1970s, the expansion of the ministries via radio and television, and the spread of literature through churches and a large network of Christian bookstores.[68] Much of the activity, and development of the broad infrastructure of their network, was instigated by specific issues of the time. Just as the antiwar and civil rights movements had inspired liberal and radical activism on a host of related issues, something similar happened on the conservative side, especially as the liberationist movements of the 1960s led to changes in the everyday lives of more and more Americans. Those who reacted with anger or fear organized their own movements and organizations, to counter busing, to oppose abortion, to eliminate sex education, to counter feminism, to stand up for traditional, conservative version of American patriotism, and to act as a watchdog over the schools, making sure that any materials that undermined their values and point of view were met with resistance. On this, they were relentless, and they were, ultimately, very successful.

Among protesters there were at least two or three elements: the ultraconservative evangelical Christians of the new right; the traditional conservatives—perhaps best represented in education by the

CBE; and the think tanks and conservative foundations—Heritage, AEI, and so on—which were a growing force, giving the conservative movement a formidable base of economic and political clout. Put together, these elements represented a potent political force that would soon remake the educational landscape.

Controversy in Congress

Although there had been numerous local conflicts over MACOS with varying results, and a growing nationwide resistance spurred by a network of conservative critics, it was not until the controversy came to Congress that it truly exploded. The battle received national media attention and eventually dealt a serious blow to the federal funding behind the MACOS program and support for the larger program of social studies and curricular reform. The federal funding behind MACOS inflamed the situation and led to assaults on the materials in Congress instigated by Congressman John B. Conlan of Arizona.

The controversy first found interest on Capitol Hill in 1973 when Republican representatives Marjorie Holt of Maryland and John Ashford of Ohio expressed their objections to "the usurpation by the educational system of what we used to consider parents' rights" and pointed to MACOS as one of several culprits. By late 1974, several Washington DC organizations had begun questioning the federal role in development and implementation of MACOS, including the Heritage Foundation, the CBE, and others.[69]

Conlan, a Harvard Law School graduate, Fulbright scholar, and the son of Hall-of-Fame baseball umpire Jocko Conlan, was elected to Congress in 1972. Conlan first learned of MACOS while a state senator in Arizona when citizens groups in Phoenix complained directly to him.[70] Equally important, George Archibald, one of Conlan's chief legislative aides, had been an active textbook critic for several years, had followed the development and implementation of MACOS closely for some time, and had spoken to a citizens group in New Jersey in late January, 1975, only a month before Conlan's attack.[71] It was also clear that Conlan faced a tough fight for reelection, was considering a run for the Senate, and that MACOS could be a perfect symbolic issue to give the congressman greater national visibility.

Conlan was a member of the House Committee on Science and Technology that reviewed the NSF budget and made recommendations to Congress. The proposed NSF appropriation for the next fiscal year contained a line item of $110,000, listed under the Education

Directorate, to fund "information workshops" for MACOS. Though Conlan had not mentioned MACOS during subcommittee hearings, when the bill came to the committee's usually routine "mark-up" session on March 6, 1975, Conlan attacked the course on the grounds that federal subsidies for educational materials placed the government in unfair direct competition with the textbook industry. He repeated many of the criticisms that were circulating nationally. He proposed an amendment to the NSF appropriations bill that would deny use of federal funds for the implementation or marketing of course curriculum programs unless Congress had first approved the materials. In making a case for the amendment, Conlan stated,

> MACOS is designed to mold children's social attitudes and beliefs along lines that are almost always at variance with the beliefs and moral values of their parents and local communities...based on films and stories about the baboon, chimpanzee, salmon, herring gull, other animals, and the Netsilik Eskimo...Recurring themes...include communal living, elimination of the weak and elderly in society, sexual permissiveness and promiscuity, violence, and primitive behavior. This is for ten-year-olds.
>
> Many psychological devices are used throughout the course, including role-playing, group discussions, and encounter sessions, in which students are required to openly discuss intimate aspects of their personal lives and those of their families and friends...[and] pressured to bare every emotion and all private thoughts and actions...[The] materials inculcate in children an abandonment of love and help and concern for the weak and elderly in society.
>
> I do not think this is what the taxpayers of America want to be subsidizing.[72]

He went on to describe "graphic scenes of Netsilik Eskimo hunting and fishing...including the catching, killing, [and] cleaning of Arctic game and the eating of their raw flesh and organs." He also mentioned "other lurid examples of violence and sexual promiscuity and deviation" and charged that the program "forces the children to be preoccupied with infanticide and senilicide, as well as the gory details of animal slaughter" and aimed at "making the children accepting of these practices" through "role-playing." He cited several cases of children who had developed "severe anxiety," "insomnia, school phobia," and "sexually obsessive thoughts," or who developed "anxiety and conflicts" as a result of the program. He also made note of the fact that MACOS had "caused such an uproar in my own district and in dozens of communities throughout the country" that some districts had "already dropped the course from the curriculum."[73] Though evidence on this point is slim, Dow believes that there was a mole inside NSF, feeding information to Conlan's office. Moreover, Conlan was in trouble and "may well have been looking for something to give himself more political clout."[74]

Most members of the committee were unfamiliar with MACOS. Conlan's assault took the committee by surprise and touched a deeper, ongoing congressional concern over competition between government-funded programs and commercial materials, a concern intensified with pressure from the publishing industry. The issue of federal support for school materials resulted in a lively debate with some arguing that federal support should end, and others suggesting that it was wrong to "cave in" to pressure from a small, well-organized group.

In the committee's debate, the Conlan amendment and the issue of censorship produced interesting alignments and made for strange bedfellows. Olin Teague of Texas, its Democratic chair, supported Conlan, its most conservative Republican. Both were opposed by Charles Mosher of Ohio, its ranking Republican, who was in agreement with most of the committee's Democrats, which included James Symington of Missouri, who strongly supported MACOS. Moreover, a number of Republicans on the committee, who agreed with Conlan's position on the morality of MACOS, were reluctant to engage in any form of censorship. After a good deal of debate, the Conlan amendment failed by a vote of 17–14, and the committee endorsed Symington's more moderate call for an end to NSF support for MACOS until a full and impartial review of the program and its publishing arrangements could be carried out.

A few days later, Dow testified before the committee, presented the MACOS materials, and answered questions. George Archibald was in the room during Dow's presentation, taking notes and frequently interrupting to take issue with what Dow had said. Archibald was well informed about the program and seemed fervently dedicated to removing it from schools. If Archibald's attitude was indicative of Conlan's commitment, or so it seemed at the time, NSF would be in for a prolonged fight. Moreover, NSF had a lot more at stake than just MACOS. Conlan's campaign against federal support threatened to derail the entire NSF science curriculum reform program.[75]

The committee discussion and the danger it posed prompted NSF Director H. Guyford Stever to write a five-page letter to Committee Chairman Olin Teague, indicating his intention to terminate all funding for MACOS and placing a moratorium on the NSF curriculum implementation program pending an NSF internal review. On March 17, 1975, Stever wrote,

> Because of the concerns expressed on all sides of several issues, I have decided that, regardless of what action is taken by Congress, no further 1975 funds will be obligated for MACOS, and no 1976 funds, if authorized and appropriated, will be obligated either for MACOS or any other precollege science course development and implementation until we have conducted a thorough review of the NSF effort in these areas and reported to the National Science Board and Congress with recommendations.[76]

Fearing for the future of the entire NSF budget, Stever caved in to the possibility of congressional oversight raised by the Conlan amendment. Interestingly, not everyone within the NSF supported this decision. When asked about Stever's decision to cut off funds "at the outset" Lowell Paige, assistant director for education, stated to an interviewer a few months later, "When Conlan questioned how we were doing it [awarding grants]...I think there was a rather strong reply to that, namely, that we do it on the basis of merit...and good programs get supported. If we had maintained a strong offensive thrust...[and] taken a less defensive posture...we would have come out better." He then went on to elaborate:

> I mean Conlan—well...they say you never get in a pissin' match with a skunk, and there is no question who occupies the latter position [laughter]...I like a good fight. And I think that we should have just fought stronger...I would have just stuck right to my guns, saying these were our program plans, and we're going to keep on funding them, and if they're going to cut Education off entirely in Congress...that's just too damn bad, and it will be a ridiculous reaction...And I think the proof of the pudding is finally coming to rest. The state of California adopted the program. It's on their approved list of programs...And it's just obvious that there was a well-coordinated, vitriolic minority that was doing this, and we should have just taken them on.[77]

Regardless of what NSF's Education Directorate and educators outside Washington may have thought of it, Stever's decision meant the end of funding for MACOS, as well as the virtual end of funding for new social studies programs.

Despite Stever's letter, Conlan pressed his attack by reintroducing his amendment at a committee hearing on March 19, 1975. Dow was invited to Washington again on the chance that an opportunity might arise for him to give informal testimony. A chance meeting with Margaret Mead in the hallway led Dow to enlist her support for MACOS and the teaching of anthropology to young students. In the course of explaining MACOS to Mead, who agreed to testify on its behalf, and after relating the "Old Kigtak" lesson in which an Eskimo, a poor hunter who feared for his family's survival, places his aging mother-in-law on an ice flow, Mead's exasperation grew. "What do you tell the children that for? . . . Don't you know that Eskimos are famous in the anthropological literature for their kind treatment of old people?" Dow replied that the story was presented as a moral dilemma to illustrate their humanity. Sensing that Mead was beginning to warm to the cause, he made the case for MACOS by stating that the schools typically have a very ethnocentric curriculum, and that the aim of the course was to "expose students to the way others live," enable them "to observe and think about human behavior" and contribute to their "appreciation of cultural diversity."

Mead responded:

> No, no, you can't tell the senators that! Don't preach to them! You and I may believe that sort of thing, but that's not what you say to these men. The trouble with you Cambridge intellectuals is that you have no political sense!
>
> Tell them what they want to hear. You point out that the reason we teach about Eskimos is to help children understand the differences between our culture and theirs, that we have choices they don't have . . . that we are a culture of abundance, not scarcity, and we don't have to leave our old people behind to die on the ice like the Eskimos— if we choose not to.[78]

Notwithstanding what appeared to be a noticeable shift among members of the committee toward increased support for the course, it appeared that much of the support centered on academic freedom and the question of whether a congressional committee should get involved in detailed supervision of an NSF program. The committee took no vote on the Conlan amendment, but it seemed likely that Conlan would reintroduce his proposal when the appropriation bill came to the floor of the House.

By late March, the MACOS debate in Congress was garnering increasing media attention. Nationally syndicated columnist James J. Kilpatrick devoted a column to MACOS, which appeared under provocative titles such as "Teaching Fifth-Graders about Eskimo-Style

Sex" and "Is Eskimo Sex Life a School Subject." Quoting Conlan extensively, Kilpatrick charged that the "barely concealed purpose" of MACOS was "to teach children how to think—to think, that is, as Bruner would like them to think." And, following Conlan's strategy, he wrote that the "most serious question" was, "Is it wise for the federal government...to commission the writing and promotion of any textbooks at all." He charged that the government's involvement echoed "the Soviet Union's promulgation of official scientific theory" and was a "significant step down the road to 1984."[79]

In an effort to respond to what appeared to be a growing campaign against the course, Dow prepared a four-page open letter that he sent to "Friends of Man: A Course of Study" on April 4, 1975. The letter described the growing controversy, made the case for academic freedom, and offered support materials to help school systems defend the course in the local controversies that would inevitably arise. The letter read, in part:

> Recently you may have heard or read news reports about a controversy that had arisen in Congress regarding Education Development Center's Social Studies Program [MACOS]...that would deny further funding for support [of MACOS]...During the past two weeks I have spent several days in Washington at NSF's request showing materials and talking with Congressmen about the *Man: A Course of Study* program. Behind the criticism appears to be a small but well organized group of people who see anti-American motives behind federally supported curriculum innovation. Mistaking our aims, our critics have tried to show that we are undermining the moral values of children by exposing them to cultural patterns of the Netsilik Eskimos.[80]

In closing the letter, Dow asked the "Friends" of MACOS to "contact your Congressman" to voice support for the materials. Unfortunately, the letter eventually fell into the hands of Conlan who saw it as "further ammunition" to use in his campaign against MACOS. Conlan sent a copy to Stever at NSF, with a cover letter accusing EDC of using the NSF "curriculum promotion network" as a "political weapon" and a "call to arms to malign and intimidate parents and citizens at the local level" who oppose MACOS. He described MACOS as an attempt at "imposing a uniform national social studies curriculum with NSF funding" that was aimed at "changing children's social values and behavior and questioning their religious upbringing."[81] Though well intended, Dow's letter was another reflection of the political naivete of EDC in its efforts at curriculum reform.

Conlan's tactics shifted somewhat when he brought the issue to the House floor on April 9, 1975. This time, the Conlan amendment was broadened to require a thorough congressional review of all NSF curriculum projects before implementation. Apparently set on avoiding the issue of censorship, Conlan focused on the questions raised by the federal role in curriculum development and implementation, on the accountability and openness of federal agencies, and on the controversial nature of the social sciences. Conlan cited EDC's dissemination activities as "a dangerous plan for a federally-backed takeover of American education," and he declared, "We must reassert effective congressional authority over all NSF activities in the area of developing and promoting school materials."[82]

The Conlan amendment provoked a vigorous debate in the House for more than two hours. Some, including Frank Annunzio of Illinois agreed with Conlan, while others including Symington and Mosher offered a strong defense of the course and against "thought control" by the federal government. As debate continued, the question of the appropriateness of congressional oversight of curricular materials became the key issue, and discourse returned repeatedly to the emotional issue of censorship. Before a vote on the Conlan amendment, Symington rose again to review the issues and make a final pitch on behalf of MACOS. He said, in part:

> My impression is that a misinformed national consciousness concerning other races and other peoples has been in part responsible for our participation in wars and other mistakes simply through want of understanding of how other races and cultures live and how other peoples gather themselves together to meet the problems of life. To broaden the perspective of the young citizen in this regard improves the judgments he will make both for his own and the country's benefit.[83]

When the vote on Conlan's proposal was finally cast, the amendment was defeated by the relatively slim margin of 215 to 196. The legislators passed an amendment that called for all instructional materials, including teachers' manuals, to be available to the parents of children engaged in NSF supported programs. But the debate was not over. Later that day, the House passed the Bauman amendment—a much broader measure that would have given Congress much greater power over the grant proposal application and review process and given it veto power over all proposed awards—by a vote of 212 to 199, despite its impracticality. Though the Bauman amendment was later killed by the Conference Committee before reaching a vote in the Senate, both sides recognized its significance as a sign of political attitudes toward the NSF and the threat it represented to the autonomy of science.[84]

Bruner, Behind the Scenes? Dow had tried to keep Bruner, who was teaching at Oxford, abreast of developments during the growing controversy, and wrote to him on April 7, 1975, with news of the congressional debate. Their exchange of letters provides an insider perspective and raises an interesting question. Dow wrote, in part:

Dear Jerry:

> If you haven't already heard...you have been getting a bit of publicity. In fact, *Man: A Course of Study* may become the best known and least used curriculum effort of the entire sixties...My life, alas, has turned into a perpetual vigil at the barricades. Had I ever known it would come to this, I would have poisoned your soup on that famous evening in Philadelphia. We may have made it smoothly from Widener to Witchita, but we sure are having a devil of a time in Phoenix.

In its closing note, Dow's letter posed a question, for at least the second time during the controversy, about Bruner's previous experience in psychological warfare. He wrote,

> One of the mysteries in all of this is your World War II experience in psychological warfare (we could use a little of it now!). Would you care to set the record straight?[85]

Bruner's April 12 response to Dow's letter and package of materials updating him on recent developments began:

Dear Peter:

> Thank you for passing on all that material on MACOS. It was as depressing a bit of reading as I've done in some time...Plainly the anti-intellectuals are loose again and, as always, one is appalled at the damage they can do...The links to perversion and "bad" sex education, the innuendoes about "manipulation of the minds of children by a wicked psychologist," all of these things are almost too tendentious to answer without giving undue publicity to what are libelous accusations.

> I am not sure what I could say to "set the record straight." I have always had the conviction that the academic student of human development should take an active part in trying to improve the state of public education...I have tried to resolve the lack of clarity about what constitutes a well educated man by favoring diversity and

openness, *not* trying to shape minds to one pattern, but to make it possible for a growing mind to develop according to its own interests and values and make it possible for people to find their own ways of contributing to the society. That, it seems to me, is the essence of democratic education...but...helping young people develop a broad sense of the alternatives open to man does not always meet with favor among those who think they know the truth as it *really* is. And because these are anxious times, there are probably more frightened and angry reactions to innovations in school curricula than before.[86]

What else can I say? Am I a manipulator of the mind of the young as the Congressman from Arizona implies? I wish he would read some of my books. Or perhaps he might talk to Senator Proxmire who was a student of mine the year he spent at Harvard after the war.

I remember Charles Eames, the designer, saying to us that if we failed in getting the acceptance we hoped for, we should fail well, having done something good and something honest. Well, Peter, perhaps that is what is happening now, a worthy failure. But I am not ready to admit defeat. There are too many teachers, too many kids, too many curriculum people who have expressed their confidence and delight in studying MACOS. A small minority of frightened, often misled people are surely not going to bring it all down.[87]

Bruner's letter addressed many aspects of the controversy quite directly. However, Bruner did not fully address the "mystery" of his experience in psychological warfare during World War II, as Dow had seemingly asked.

As discussed in a previous chapter, Bruner did serve in the psychological warfare division of the Office of War Intelligence during World War II and was a veteran of Project Troy and several other wartime research projects. At Woods Hole, the work group on the apparatus of teaching lamented the lack of modern technology in education and believed that application of "systems development principles" held great promise for educational improvement because it would "further the application of modern technology to improve education." As described earlier, the group put forth a template for curriculum design drawn on the systems development approach: (1) define course goals; (2) determine the functions to be performed; and (3) assign functions to men and machines to optimize the effectiveness of the entire system.[88] The model was borrowed directly from wartime research projects such as Hartwell and Troy, and as such it had direct links to Bruner's involvement in "psychological warfare." In the minds of the reformers, it was a powerful model to be emulated. Moreover, as John

Rudolph has pointed out, several techniques were borrowed from a defense systems engineering perspective, including the use of the summer study; a fast paced and loosely structured working environment; and, an emphasis on engineering the whole system.

Bruner, Zacharias, and at least a few other participants were well aware that they were applying this model.[89] While on the surface, it appears logical and imminently useful to apply such a powerful and successful model to education, in the application of any model one must proceed with caution. Based on an analogy to a weapons system, the application may break down in use. As suggested in an earlier chapter, weapons are used for military purposes, to defend, to destroy, to kill, and to conquer. Institutionalized education, on the other hand, has, as its central aim, the goal of helping the student learn about and understand a complex world, a world in which values and cultural traditions often run deeply beneath the surface, embedded in myriad ways.

How much did all of this influence the MACOS materials? Did a link to a "weapons system" and "psychological warfare" make for a subliminally powerful curriculum that could not only challenge student's preconceived values and world-view, but trouble their parents? It seems at least plausible that it could. MACOS appeared to embody the principles of wartime research quite powerfully, applying the model over several years of development. Despite Bruner's disclaimer, the link between MACOS and psychological warfare, though it now appears a ludicrous assertion, probably seemed a plausible inference to many critics, one that Bruner chose to brush aside. Bruner and the MACOS team had created an innovative curriculum that evidently had the power to deeply influence children. Whether that influence was wanted was the central question. Bruner's letter stating that he favored "diversity and openness, *not* trying to shape minds to one pattern," must be taken at face value. Nonetheless, the course aimed to develop in students a broader conception of humanity and a deeper sense of cultural understanding that could help counter the ethnocentrism of human societies. Perhaps it is the ultimate irony that such a worthy goal was anathema to many of the critics.

Senate Hearing. The debate in the House was followed by a Senate hearing on April 21, 1975, when the issue came before a Special Subcommittee on the NSF, chaired by Senator Edward Kennedy. Though the matter never came up for a floor vote in the Senate, the committee hearing drew quite a bit of attention when it heard the testimony of McGraw, who appeared as a witness against the program.

McGraw presented a chart that purportedly illustrated the collaboration of EDC, CDA, and NSF to impose MACOS on the Nation's schoolchildren at taxpayer expense. McGraw questioned the publishing arrangement that MACOS had worked out with CDA after EDC had failed to find a commercial publisher. Like Conlan, McGraw asked, "Why should we taxpayers have to support and subsidize promotion and sale of any school materials when the best test for their need is the private marketplace?" She charged that the combination of professional educators and government bureaucrats put local school authorities and parents at a disadvantage. She invoked "academic freedom" as an argument against the use of pubic funds for development and dissemination of curriculum materials. Despite her condemnation of MACOS as an embodiment of "secular humanism," the questions she raised about public funding for the creation and dissemination of innovative curricular materials were legitimate policy issues, described by Dow as the "Achilles heel" of the MACOS project.[90]

The congressional debate over MACOS and the ongoing investigations that resulted were partly a reflection of the times. The controversy reached the halls of Congress after the Watergate affair had ended and reflected subsequent concerns over government secrecy and accountability. Moreover, it occurred at a time of national failure; the same year as the fall of Saigon.

Media attention to the MACOS controversy, which had been minimal before 1975, suddenly mushroomed as an increasing number of newspapers and magazines carried stories on the controversy. WCR TV, Washington DC's NBC affiliate, carried a sensational story on the controversy that was advertised in the *Washington Post* under the title "Horror flicks. Is your ten-year-old watching 'X-rated' films at school?" The *Chronicle of Higher Education* ran a series of stories covering the congressional debates. In addition, a story written by the United Press International education editor appeared in late June of 1975. The story cited a report from the CBE that had appeared in its most recent *Bulletin*, and echoed Conlan and McGraw's criticisms of the course. Stories also appeared over the next several months in a number of other nationally circulated venues, including the *National Enquirer, Newsweek,* the *Wall Street Journal, Readers Digest*, and the *New York Times*. Articles about the controversy also appeared in a growing list of national magazines and professional journals, including *Scientific American, Social Education,* and *Phi Delta Kappan*.

The Fed Investigates. While the congressional debate was going on, three review committees initiated by Congress began their investigations of MACOS, conducted during the spring and summer of 1975. The NSF launched its own internal investigation on April 7, ordered by Director Stever as a direct response to congressional concerns. A second investigation, an Ad Hoc Review Committee appointed by Chairman Teague, began its investigation at about the same time. Finally, a third probe, a General Accounting Office (GAO) investigation focused on accusations of financial irregularities, also launched its inquiry at Teague's request.[91]

Each of the three committees filed separate reports in the ensuing months. The NSF internal review panel, which published its findings in May, found very little fault with the various aspects of the development and implementation of MACOS, but was critical of the way NSF had managed fiscal and contractual arrangements. Reviewers found that NSF had been somewhat lax in its review procedures, had failed to monitor the development of the project closely, and that fiscal and contractual arrangements between EDC and CDA, though somewhat unusual, appeared "fiscally sound." In summary, the internal review recommended that NSF exercise more rigorous oversight of projects, among other recommendations.[92]

The Ad Hoc Science Curriculum Review Group appointed by Olin Teague, and chaired by Chancellor James Moudy of Texas Christian University, a personal friend and constituent of Teague, began its work in May 1975 in the highly charged atmosphere created by media attention and by a flurry of protests launched by critics of the course, including Conlan, McGraw, the Heritage Foundation, the CBE, and Leadership Action, Inc. Though there were a few supportive letters and articles, the weight of public outcry seemed overwhelmingly against the course. On May 13, Dow and Edwin Campbell, president of EDC, appeared before the Moudy Committee to explain EDC's role in the development and implementation of the course. In his testimony, Dow discussed many of the issues brought up during the congressional debate and read a letter from a seventh-grade student describing his experience with MACOS during the previous school year. The student, Ben Kahn, rejected critics claim that the course taught negative values and suggested that the course helped him better understand his other social science courses, because MACOS "helped me to understand another culture."[93]

As the committee was conducting its investigation, the Heritage Foundation weighed in with a lengthy and scholarly looking analysis of MACOS written by Susan Marshner, Education Director for the Foundation. The analysis suggested that the NSF was using federal funds in an attempt "to place the controversial course in every district in the country" and thus "competing unfairly" with private publishers. After a thorough analysis and description of the course's development and contents, an examination of the role played by the theories of Bruner and psychologist Richard Jones in course development, and an analysis of several specific activities, Marshner wrote,

> If the discovery method must depend on the constant probing of children's social-emotional growth to succeed, clearly "discovery" is the wrong word, and "psychoanalysis" or perhaps "manipulation" is the more accurate one. Whether or not Bruner intended discovery education to turn out as it has in MACOS, clearly this method has opened itself to incredible abuses.[94]

She then cited the MACOS seminar for teachers that quoted theorist Lawrence Kubie at some length on the goal of education to "make it possible for human beings themselves to change...[aiming for] a progressive freeing of man." Marshner implied that violent scenes in the Netsilik films and the role playing and discussion activities embedded in the course would provide a kind of shock to students. Many of the discussions probed students' personal values, which she described as "psychotherapy in the schools by unlicensed teachers."[95]

Marshner also quoted extensively from several letters describing unpleasant experiences with the course, letters received by Congressman Conlan. One from Dr. Armand DiFrancesco, a family doctor from Buffalo, told of a twelve-year-old girl who had been referred to him because of "severe anxiety, and insomnia, school phobia, and who began to have sexually obsessive thoughts...brought about by...MACOS." Other children developed "anxiety and conflicts" as a result of MACOS materials that were in conflict with their "religious beliefs and teachings at home." Another letter, from Dr. Rhoda Lorand, a former psychotherapist with a doctorate from Columbia in educational psychology, argued that the program forced children to be "preoccupied with infanticide and senilicide," the "gory details of animal slaughter," and aimed at "making children accepting of these practices." Calling it an "exercise in sadism" she questioned whether the materials should be "foisted upon a captive audience of children who are undergoing the crucial process of adaptation to our culture and civilization...[with] government support."[96]

Marshner's analysis concluded by questioning "federal support for development and promotion" that gave MACOS an "undeniable edge" over privately developed courses. She charged that the course involved "experimentation" on "human subjects" and offered a kind of "intellectual pablum" through its role playing and play acting. Finally, she noted that the course was replacing traditional courses in history and geography. She closed with the following sentences:

> The best that could be said for the so-called open-ended discussions is that they lead to values obfuscation. The worst is that they push children toward very particular and divergent political, moral and philosophical ideas which have been subtly imbedded in the course...It is clear that a course, which has so few positive benefits to students and teachers, and which is so hard to sell that it requires special promotional and financial arrangements, should either be completely rewritten or allowed to sink into graceful oblivion.[97]

Given the charged atmosphere surrounding the congressional committee investigating MACOS, it is virtually certain that the committee members received the Heritage "analysis" though it is more difficult to assess its probable impact. Moreover, Heritage continued its assault on the course and other "objectionable" school materials the following year with its publication of McGraw's "Secular Humanism and the Schools," a thirty-page pamphlet that provided "a case study of the growth of humanistic teaching in the public schools and the efforts of local parent groups to stymie the humanistic trend," and which proved to be one of Heritage's most popular early publications.[98]

The Moudy Committee, split 5–3 against the course during its initial meetings, postponed a final report at the urging of one of its members, Gerard Piel, the publisher of *Scientific American*, who offered a persuasive defense of NSF curriculum work and MACOS. Contrary to the charges of Conlan and other critics, the curriculum reform movement that had produced MACOS was not a federal government attempt to control the curriculum, but was instead, in Piel's words, the product of "a self-governing democracy of science" that utilized a rigorous peer review system and employed a diverse variety of reform approaches based upon initiatives received from scholars and teachers. After two particularly intense sessions in June and July, Piel succeeded in convincing a majority of the committee to support continuation of the NSF curriculum reform program, with two members dissenting, arguing that NSF should confine its efforts to natural science and mathematics. The committee's report agreed with the NSF internal review and offered a similar call for tighter structuring of management and review procedures. Joanne McCauley of Dallas, a parent representative on the committee, was not persuaded by the testimony and discussion and submitted a minority report in which she called for Congress to "terminate" NSF's curriculum activities. Her position reflected the thinking of a growing body of conservatives who wanted the federal government to get out of education completely.[99]

The GAO audit of EDC, conducted at the request of Chairman Teague, was by far the most thorough review of MACOS and EDC's programs and procedures. Its report cleared the foundation of any wrongdoing, but recommended that NSF should have monitored the publishing arrangement between EDC and CDA much more closely and reviewed all contractual arrangements in detail.[100]

The consequences of the congressional foray into a variation on textbook criticism were, in the end, quite serious. As a result of the extended controversy, NSF terminated several science and social science curriculum projects and support for others was curtailed. Except for completion of a pending evaluation study, federal funding for MACOS ended completely. Though the Conlan Amendment, which would have placed a congressional veto on the content of curricula, was defeated, MACOS took a public relations beating because of the adverse national publicity. Sales of the program took a "precipitous fall" and never recovered.[101] Implementation funding was suspended on all NSF curriculum development projects for the fiscal year, and the appropriation request for the following year was modest compared to past outlays. Moreover, the NSF promulgated onerous review procedures intended to avert future controversy.

Dow and the staff of EDC and CDA were the chief advocates in defense of MACOS, but others joined in to offer help. The National Council for the Social Studies (NCSS) issued a statement in support of MACOS and the continued funding of curriculum development and implementation. Later, support for MACOS and concern over the incident came from other sources. Gerard Piel, publisher of *Scientific American*, wrote a paper in 1976, titled "Congress Shall Make No Law..." in which he lamented the success of "the vigilante textbook watchers" behind the MACOS incident and called for political action to defend first amendment rights.[102]

Earlier, controversies regarding academic freedom had contributed to the decline of progressive education. In this case, the impact of conservative critics was especially ironic, because the new social studies was a discipline-based response to progressive education's excesses and seemed to match conservative preferences. The controversy over MACOS and other new social studies materials proved that even the disciplines and the new inquiry models, with students as junior social scientists, could be controversial because they asked students to develop their own conclusions. Educational conservatives and many members of the public, it seems, wanted a more traditionally "American" and authoritative perspective fed to students.

The Controversy Continues. Given increased media attention that came with the congressional debate, and the continuing efforts of conservative activists, the controversy over MACOS continued to spread for some time, across the nation into more cities and towns. In May 1975, the California State Board of Education held an open hearing on adoption of MACOS. Among the testimony it heard was that of Floyd Fenocchio, Principal of Birch Lane Elementary in Davis, who called MACOS, "The most significant, all-around educational program I've ever been involved with!" Subsequently, California made MACOS a state adoption, which must have been a major boost to the program's sagging fortunes.[103]

Controversies occurred over the remainder of 1975 and well into 1976 in a variety of states and cities. During the 1975–1976 school year, the number of local controversies reached an unprecedented level. A controversy occurred in Guilford, New Hampshire, in September as concerned parents organized the Guilford School Forum, and the state Department of Education reportedly received scores of calls from irate parents.[104] A controversy over MACOS and other school materials developed in Quincy, Massachusetts, in October and November 1975. South Shore Citizens against Forced Busing held a meeting to discuss the MACOS program on October 7, at which a Mrs. Libby took the stand to explain her objections to MACOS. She played a tape from Mrs. Gabler citing films of Eskimos "gouging eyeballs" and alienating children from their parents through exposure to Netsilik life and the course's subsequent "role playing and playacting." When asked, "Why can't you get the churches and clergy behind you?" she replied, "I am from Boston. We're trying. It takes a courageous man to stand. This is in the billions of dollars. They are not going to give up easily. Teddy Kennedy thinks this is super." Carl de Esso, social studies coordinator for the Quincy schools rose and said, "Your concerns warrant study. You should see the films." School officials then held a series of seven meetings to help familiarize parents with the program and allay concerns.[105]

Later that fall, a controversy developed in Collier County, Florida (Naples) schools. Tom Morris, Principal of Pine Ridge Middle School, which was at the heart of the controversy, was convinced that "the opponents of the course, who were small in number but very well organized, were being fed from a national effort...[and were] constantly taking quotes out of context and routinely twisting their meaning." He said he suspected "members of the John Birch Society and of the American Party" were behind the attacks. At a board meeting on December 4, some forty speakers made presentations and were approximately evenly divided in terms of their position on the course. The principal speaker against the course was Rev. Donald Glenn of Jacksonville, who had instigated the Lake City controversy. A citizen's committee appointed to study the issue recommended that parents be offered an alternative course, and the board agreed with their position. The original complaint in Collier County was brought by Mr. William Morse in June 1975. Morse stated in his filing that MACOS had been brought to his attention by Mrs. Shirley Correll when she spoke at an American Party Executive Committee meeting on May 12. Correll was a member of the Florida Action Committee for Education (FACE) that was working throughout the state against MACOS and other state-adopted texts they found objectionable. Morse's complaint against the course focused on such issues as "federal control versus local control of education; communism versus democracy; liberalism versus conservatism; 'religious humanism' versus Christianity; and gun control," all of which were common John Birch Society complaints.[106]

According to an EDC internal memo, the growing nationwide controversy led to an increasing number of calls for help to EDC during May 1975, "especially heavy in June and the first half of July" and tapering off a bit after that. The calls came from all parts of the nation: in Massachusetts, from Quincy, West Boylston, Paton, Holyoke, Brookline, Westborough, Leverett, Lynn, Boston, Northampton, and Salem; in New York, from East Greenbush, Hempstead, Jamaica, Newfield, Terrytown-on-Hudson, Norwich, New York City, Port Chester and Castleton; from Laconia and Dover, New Hampshire; from Summit and Westfield, New Jersey; from Bryn Mawr, Westchester, and Havertown, Pennsylvania; from De Kalb, Rockford, and Evanston, Illinois; and from Kenosha, Milwaukee, Thorp and Eau Claire, Wisconsin. Calls came from western states: in California, from Orange, Modesto, Tarzana, Berkeley, and San Francisco; from Vermillion, South Dakota, Lincoln, Nebraska, Pocatello, Idaho, Decorah, and Iowa City, Iowa; in Minnesota, from Minneapolis, Duluth, and St. Paul; from Greeley, Colorado, Naples and Pensacola, Florida, and Atlanta, Georgia; from Kirksville, Missouri, and Hampton, Virginia. Calls also came from abroad, from Queensland and Canberra City, Australia and from Joensuu, Finland.[107]

According to the EDC staffer who seemed most familiar with the process, upon receiving a call, EDC sent the caller a "controversy package" that included materials about the course and suggested strategies for handling local disputes or parental concerns. "Of several hundred requests, we have had only a handful of responses letting us know how things turned out. I interpret this as being a good sign by and large—that is, had the controversy not died down in relatively short order, they would have asked for more help."[108] Perhaps, but given the outcome in so many places where conflict had led to compromise followed by eventual elimination of the course, it is very likely that many districts where controversies occurred did not continue the course for very long. The growing number of state and local confrontations reflected an increasingly powerful network of resistance and the new level of prominence bestowed by congressional debate and investigation, along with the subsequent increase in national media attention.

The Wingspread Conference. During the 1960s and 1970s, NCSS took steps to actively involve itself in the social issues of the day. Resolutions were passed in 1969 regarding the war in Vietnam, academic freedom and censorship, enforcement of desegregation, and financial support for the Martin Luther King, Jr. Memorial. In addition, definitive statements were adopted regarding urban education and racism.[109] Also, the organization created the NCSS Legal Defense fund to offer initial assistance to teachers in academic freedom cases. On the whole, the organization, for a time at least, seemed to adopt a social activist stance on a host of fronts.

In response to the MACOS controversy, NCSS held a conference in May 1976, on "Freedom and Responsibility in the Selection and Use of Educational Materials and Learning Strategies in the Social Studies," at the Wingspread Conference Center in Racine, Wisconsin. The conference received financial support from the Johnson Foundation. Congressman Conlan, who was invited to speak, instead sent his legislative assistant, George H. Archibald, whose remarks were revealing and offered a cultural conservative's critique of the new social studies.

Archibald stated that since the efforts to stop federal funding to promote and market MACOS had begun:

> We have found that hundreds of thousands of parents throughout the coun-
> try view the academic-bureaucracy complex—comprised of the nation's
> colleges of education, the NEA and its state affiliates, in league with the
> Federal government with its vast power and resources—as the principal
> national threat to their values, families, spiritual, social, economic, and
> political freedoms, and our national heritage itself...MACOS is an obvi-
> ous example of global education—now called "world order education."[110]

This was, in essence, an updated version of the "interlocking directorate" allegation frequently leveled against progressive education.
Archibald went on to present a partly factual history of an episode where
the new social studies "got its start" at the Wingspread Conference in
June 1968, when "40 educationists met for a week's discussion about
the need to radically revamp social studies." According to Archibald,
the conference theme of "survival" recommended a curricular focus
on the "arms buildup," the gulf between rich and poor, "alleged social
and economic injustice," pollution and natural resources "threatened"
by "corporations and government," and the population explosion.
"The Wingspread Report declared," Archibald noted, "that traditional practices and approaches were no longer adequate" and called
for a new, interdisciplinary social studies emphasizing "Socratic dialogue, role playing, [and] debate" with more time devoted "to inquiry,
analysis, and decision, less to the acquisition of facts."

Archibald described the 1968 Wingspread Conference as "a
classic example of an unrepresentative minority of educationists...[seeking]...to radically alter American education for the purpose of socio-economic and political change, without the approval of
the people. This call for a new nationwide social studies curriculum
centered around global studies and de-emphasizing American history
and our American heritage, completely disregards the wishes of local
citizens and taxpayers." Archibald then offered a strong argument for
traditional history and a return to the basics, a return "to perpetuat-
ing in their schools each community's social, religious, political, and
economic way of life."[111]

He closed his speech with the following warning:

> If you educators and the National Council for the Social Studies choose
> to press this ideological approach to public education, there will be a

collision of major proportions between yourselves and the general public in every community throughout America...Make no mistake about
it: taxpayers and parents are ready to marshal every resource at their
disposal to ensure that they win. And win they will.[112]

Archibald's speech on behalf of Congressman Conlan reprised the
ominous tone of the war on social studies that had been going on for
decades. Defenders and eloquent statements in support of academic
freedom notwithstanding, the bottom line in the aftermath of the
MACOS controversy was that there would be profound limitations
on teacher freedom and government support for curriculum materials development. Archibald voiced many of social studies reformers'
deepest fears.

Conclusion

The overall cycle seemed largely a repeat of what had occurred during
the progressive era, experimentation and growth followed by attacks
on teacher freedom and defensive statements from NCSS and assorted
social studies leaders. Boom and bust, innovation and reaction had
undoubtedly become a familiar pattern to many in the social studies
profession. To teachers, the impact was likely somewhat bewildering,
at least to those who were paying attention.

Like many of the other academic freedom controversies of the
period, the MACOS controversy had its origins in the reaction of a
few religious fundamentalists whose concerns were magnified by a
national network of textbook protesters. The breadth and depth of
the controversy grew until it was national in scope. The Phoenix controversy was a turning point at which it appears, protesting MACOS
became a rallying cause for critics. After the Kanawha County textbook controversy, the seeming explosion of controversy over MACOS
appears, in hindsight, a logical next step. The controversy had a
direct impact on sales and distribution of the MACOS materials, and
it ended up marking the end of the period of funding for MACOS
and for the new social studies.[113] A watershed in the history of social
studies, the MACOS controversy meant the movement for reform, for
inquiry and innovation in social studies as a national and government
backed initiative, was largely over.

MACOS was a brilliant, pedagogically innovative curriculum that
asked deep and important questions about life on earth. That it was
ultimately rejected by American schools is a sad commentary on the

nature of American schooling, even though the rejection may have been orchestrated by a relatively small group. As Dow commented:

> It doesn't take very many people to bring something down. I realized, in a sense, how naïve we were not to be more sensitive to some of the issues that were upsetting some people. And I guess it never had dawned on me how political education really is, and how much choices about what we teach our children are motivated by issues of value.[114]

Despite its ultimate rejection, MACOS remains a shining example of what is possible given brilliant ideas, hard work, and pedagogic innovation. Recently, when asked about the controversy and lasting contribution of MACOS, Bruner said, "I do think it [the controversy] was inevitable," but the project made an important contribution, it was "a step along the way...a beacon a little bit."[115] Unfortunately, what happened to MACOS in the controversy and its aftermath illustrates what can happen, what has happened, when innovation confronts the reality of the American political and cultural landscape.

6

The Conservative Restoration

After the nationwide MACOS controversy had more or less subsided, another heated textbook controversy occurred in Warsaw, Indiana, a northern Indiana town of about 9,600 people, a conservative community with "a strong religious feeling" and the home of 36 churches. Like the controversy in Kanawha County, this one involved questions over who would determine the curriculum, and whether the right to know and the right to read would be prized over the concerns of conservative and fundamentalist groups who felt their values and way of life were being threatened. As one observer noted, the controversy in Warsaw turned the back-to-basics movement into a crusade to purify the curriculum, ban books, and obstruct change.

Books Burning in Indiana

The story begins with a school board decision in the spring of 1977 to review, then drop the Individually Guided Instruction (IGE) program at Washington Elementary School after receiving complaints from parents who said their children were not learning basic skills in reading, writing, and arithmetic. The board also voted to establish "strict parameters" that would standardize the curriculum and teaching practices at all nine district elementary schools, appointed a new principal at Washington, and transferred four of its teachers. Despite protest from an attorney representing 230 disgruntled parents and the resignation of Superintendent Dr. Max E. Hobbs, the board sustained its decision.[1]

In June, the board approved a policy foreshadowing what was soon to come, stating, "Any multi-page teacher-made material used as a source of instruction must have prior approval by the principal and superintendent...before it can be formally utilized in the classroom."[2] At its meeting on July 19, the board set its sights on another target of various pressure groups and voted to drop the "Values for Everyone" course from the Senior High School, after board member William I. Chapel brought a copy of a book used in the course to the meeting and read passages after a concerned parent brought it to his attention. The board voted that the book *Values Clarification* by Simon, Howe, and Kirschenbaum was to be "thrown out, removed, banned, destroyed and forbidden to be used," despite protests from English teachers that "only ten of...two hundred exercises in the book" were used in class, and despite the districts own policy requiring a review process. The book had been part of the English curriculum for two years following an in-service by the Indiana Department of Public Instruction at the invitation of the former superintendent. According to the local newspaper, the *Times-Union*, the school board "banned the book last moth because it contained passages that asked students to share their views on premarital sex, masturbation and other experiences. Board members said they believed exercises in the book could encourage students to reject their family values and those of churches, government and other institutions."[3]

Then on August 25, the new superintendent, Dr. Charles Bragg, announced major changes in the English program as the board voted unanimously to make the following changes: to discontinue several English courses, including Gothic Literature, Black Literature, Science Fiction, Good Guys, Folklore and Legends, Detective and Mystery Fiction, and Whatever Happened to Mankind; to discontinue the phase-elective APEX program at the end of the coming school year; to add three courses to be offered that year, in composition and college prep developmental reading; and to develop a required English program for grades seven through eleven with electives for grade twelve.[4]

As the fall semester began at Warsaw High School, Principal C. J. Smith asked English teacher Teresa Burnau not to use several books that she had ordered for the phase-elective course titled "Women in Literature." On October 18, Principal Smith sent a memo to faculty stating, "Any classroom materials that you have in your room that might be objectionable, please bring them to the office." By November, at least four more books had been banned, including *Growing up Female in America*, which contained pictures of nude women; *The Stepford Wives*, which depicted suburban housewives replaced by robots and was critical of traditional female roles; *Go Ask Alice*, a diary by a teen girl who died of a drug overdose and contained "dirty words"; and *The Bell Jar*, about a nineteen-year-old girl's struggle with mental illness. According to Ms. Burnau, the principal had dismissed the books because "someone in the community might be offended by their criticism of traditional roles for women."[5]

On December 15, 1977, ten days before Christmas, the Senior Citizens Club of Warsaw carried 27 copies of *Values Clarification* to a parking lot, doused the books with gasoline, and set them ablaze. The president of the 200-member group claimed that he was only carrying out his obligation to the club. In defense of a ban on "objectionable materials" dramatically expressed by the book burning, one board member quipped that at least teachers will "have no problem knowing the will of this community."[6]

On January 9, 1978, board member Chapel read the following resolution at the meeting, which was passed unanimously:

> Be it resolved that the teachers, administrators and staff of this school district shall be directed to teach students to avoid the use of profanity and obscenities, also books and materials that could be construed as objectionable in this community shall not be used.[7]

Five days earlier, the president of the Warsaw Community Education Association (WCEA) filed a complaint with the Indiana Education Employment Relations Board citing eleven unfair labor practices by the district centering on working conditions, curriculum revision, and book banning.

In the spring of 1978, the board went after teachers. In all, eleven teachers were asked to resign. Three teachers who refused, including Burnau and Joann Dupont, were then notified that their contracts would not be renewed. Dupont was an outspoken teacher and secretary of the WCEA who was, it appears, ousted largely because of antiunion sentiment.[8]

After controlling the teachers, the administration went after the students. In late May, Anne Summe, editor of the student newspaper, wrote an editorial expressing dismay at the dismissals and forced resignations. Initially, Smith told Ms. Summe that she could not publish the editorial. After she called the Student Press Law Center in Washington, DC, and then threatened to appeal his decision to the board, Smith permitted publication of the editorial. Subsequently, the student newspaper was shut down.[9]

Behind the book banning, the teacher dismissals, and the entire controversy was the conservative owner of the *Times-Union*, Reub Williams, a powerful figure in the town who had strongly influenced appointment of the four new school board members who were most vigorously pursuing censorship. Before and during the four-day unfair labor practice hearing in June, the newspaper ran a series of editorials, cartoons, letters to the editor, and full page ads that left no doubt about its position on the controversies. A few days before the hearing, it ran a front-page announcement by Carl Davis and Sharon Lowry of People Who Care, an organization aimed at removing "filthy, vulgar material from the classroom," an organization that "seeks to rally support for the beleaguered school board." The group had been meeting for some time. One member expressed the group's philosophy as follows: "Children seek the parent to restrain them. A woman inherently seeks for man to be in authority over her and man seeks God to be in authority over him. It is not a questions of equality...it is a required condition for a stable society." Another member stated simply, "School decisions should be based on the absolutes of Christian behavior." Comments from a number of Warsaw residents suggested that authority was "a central issue in these people's lives—authority of men over women, of fundamentalism over secular humanism, of the school board over the teachers, of the family over the school board, and of parents over children."[10] Many citizens of Warsaw believed that their values were being threatened, and they were willing to censor books, obstruct the legal process, and destroy careers if necessary.

The hearing, which was described as "parallel to the Scopes Monkey Trial" of 1925, resulted in a recommendation that the school board be ordered to "reverse all policies" and to restore the school "to status quo positions." During the fall of 1978, a panel composed of two members of the school board and two members of WCEA agreed on a compromise: it would write letters of explanation to transferred teachers, follow textbook review procedures, discuss possible curriculum changes with teachers before they are made, and consult WCEA before making any changes in working conditions.[11]

The period of controversy was followed by four lawsuits on behalf of teachers, parents, and students. The Indiana State Teachers' Association filed suit on behalf of two teachers who had been dismissed, and the Indiana Civil Liberties Union (ICLU) filed suit on behalf of students, alleging that the board's actions had violated students' "right to know" and "right to read." At issue in the cases were questions involving the rights and responsibilities of various parties, centering on the academic rights of teachers and students in public schools, and the rights of parents to protect students by controlling the curriculum. In a class action lawsuit, Zykan v. Warsaw Community School Corporation, a district court judge ruled in favor of the district, stating that school boards have the right to determine the curriculum and to regulate library materials. On appeal in 1980, the appellate court judge agreed with the district court and stated that high school students do not have the same rights of academic freedom as college students, but opened the door to further litigation if the plaintiffs could find evidence of constitutional violations. However, by that time the Zykan family had left town, and the ICLU attorney gave consent to dismissal of the case.[12]

The book burning and larger controversy in Warsaw was symptomatic of a much larger wave of book banning and school controversies. Judith Krug, director of the American Library Association's Office for Intellectual Freedom estimated that there were more book banning incidents in the 1977–1978 school year than at any other time in the past twenty-five years, and that 90 percent of the incidents involved schools. Mrs. Norma Gabler, who was interviewed by a reporter regarding the Warsaw controversy, reframed it in her comments:

> For years we taught the academic skills. The important thing was to teach the child to read and write. We had good wholesome stories. We taught the good, the true and the beautiful. Now, it is a steady stream of violence and disrespectful attacks on the home. The aim is no longer to teach fact, skill and knowledge. The aim is to change the thinking and the values of children.

She argued that writers, editors, and publishers "are censoring the right of the parent to be heard."[13]

Ultimately, the immediate issue was who will control the mind of the student, and the larger issue was whose version of the American way would be prized. The contending sides in the textbook dispute, as always, were struggling over their competing visions of the future American society. The text censorship battles in Warsaw and Kanawha County were not isolated incidents, but were especially dramatic cases symbolic of a broad wave of controversy over books and materials used in schools that occurred in every part of the nation, though there seemed to be more in the East, North Central, and midwestern states. Moreover, most such incidents were not simply the act of individual parents acting alone, but were the acts of parents and community groups prodded by a number of national groups and organizations that wanted to change the schools.

Censorship Pressures. There were many other book banning controversies across the nation during the 1970s and into the 1980s. In Spanish Harlem, parent objections to the author's use of four-letter words led to removal of *Down These Mean Streets* from school libraries; in Strongville, Ohio, three books were banned as "required" texts, including *Catch-22* by Joseph Heller and two books by Kurt Vonnegut; in Chelsea, Massachusetts, an anthology titled *Male and Female under 18* was removed from the school library, then returned following litigation; in Mississippi, a realistic state history textbook titled *Conflict and Change* by James W. Loewen and Charles Sallis, originally struck from an approved list, was placed among state adoptions only after a court decision.[14] In general, the courts served as final arbiter of the law and usually held in favor of academic freedom for libraries, but on the side of school authorities when it came to the question of who controlled the curriculum and the materials students would be required to read.

Censorship pressures came from a number of sources and played a role in most of these cases and certainly contributed to the national climate. In one midwestern state, a questionnaire revealed that 16 percent of high school social studies teachers had been contacted by at least one censorship organization. In the larger high schools, 59 percent perceived at least some censorship pressure. Censorship organizations included patriotic organizations such as the Daughters of the American Revolution and the American Legion; conservative groups such as the John Birch Society or America's Future; religious organizations such as the Jehovah's Witnesses or B'nai B'rith; and miscellaneous groups such as the National Association for the Advancement of Colored People (NAACP) or a Teenage Republican Club. The author of one study also found that the patriotic and conservative groups were most militant, best coordinated, and well financed. They rallied around the theme that true "Americanism" was no longer being taught by textbooks and teachers, and they sought to purge the schools of all materials and teachers who did not conform to their notion of the American ideal. Protests based on religion tended to be largely uncoordinated and poorly financed and centered on materials that were too "scientific" or that were too immoral, that is, in language or sex. The study also found that many teachers were subject to self-censorship, as one teacher reported, "To avoid any unpleasantness...I know my school parents and community and so I know just how far to go."[15]

Another study, national in scope and published in 1975, examined teacher freedom to discuss controversial topics. It found that teachers felt very free with some topics and less free with others. Among the most restricted topics were homosexuality, heterosexual sex, prostitution, pornography, and abortion. The most common source of criticism or pressure to avoid controversial topics was parents, followed by administrators and the community. Moreover, an index purporting to measure the climate for innovation in social studies classrooms had dropped rather noticeably, from 32 to 23, and showed a "probable decrease in educator's optimism about the climate for innovation in the nation."[16]

Taken together, the academic freedom cases and the studies reported suggest a climate of growing restraint on teacher freedom and led one observer to ask, "Is Academic Freedom Dead in the Public Schools?"[17] While a number of the contestants in the cases related earlier received support from the National Education Association's (NEA's) DuShane Fund, the National Council for the Social Studies (NCSS) Defense Fund, the American Civil Liberties Union (ACLU) or other sympathetic groups, the damage done by the charges and the interruption of teachers' lives sent a message across the land that freedom had its limits.

The Conservative Restoration in School and Society

From the mid-1970s to the mid-1980s and beyond, social studies, especially the progressive issues-centered approach experienced a decline, paralleling a conservative restoration in politics, schools, and American culture. The aim of this chapter will be to document and explain the rise of the conservative restoration and the revival of history, the decline of issues-oriented approaches to social studies, and to reflect on the process of curriculum change. What were the origins of the conservative restoration and the revival of history? Why, in recent years, has curricular attention to social issues had limited impact in schools? What lay behind the decline of a broad and interdisciplinary approach and the increasing insistence on history and geography as the core of the social studies curriculum?

The conservative restoration in schools and society, a backlash against the legacy of the 1960s, grew out of 1970s concerns over declining standards during a period of experimentation and turmoil. It followed a generally conservative shift in public mood regarding the perfectibility of humankind, the role of science in helping us understand society and life, and a shift in attitudes regarding the proper role of government in curricular reform. Major episodes of the era included the literacy crisis, back-to-basics, the excellence reports of the early 1980s, and the revival of history.

Although many of the trends of the 1960s had begun to erode by the late 1970s, they were subjected to direct attack following the election of Ronald Reagan. By the early 1980s, the liberal consensus on schooling had begun to unravel, and two related but distinct forms of educational conservatism had already gained favor. The first of these came in the form of the New Right, led by the Heritage Foundation, a Washington-based think tank discussed in the previous chapter consisting of several conservative scholars, including Onalee McGraw, Eileen Gardner, Russell Kirk, E. G. West, David Armor, Thomas Sowell, and George Gilder. Other important voices in the New Right movement included Senators Orrin Hatch and Jesse Helms, fundamentalist ministers Jerry Falwell and Tim LeHay, textbook critics Mel and Norma Gabler, and Arthur Laffer, the supply-side economist. The New Right called for a much smaller federal government role in education, championed an extremist position against "secular humanism," and favored active censorship and teaching of creationism. A larger and less cohesive group of neoconservative educators, politicians, and businesspeople, who could be described as "centrist conservatives" called for a shift in federal policy away from equity to an emphasis on excellence. Though the two groups overlapped on a number of issues, they had basic differences regarding the mission of schooling and the role of government in education.[18]

From the perspective of the New Right, most of the schools' problems could be linked to overcentralized decision making caused by rising federal power. In resistance to the mainstream, the New Right supported educational free choice and diversity. Many New Right advocates believed that vested interests created a unified curriculum based on principles of secular humanism. The New Right sought to promote its agenda, and to counter the spread of secular humanism in schools and society, through multiple interlocking organizations, think-tanks, and political action committees with extensive mailing lists; a network of nationally circulated magazines, tabloids, and newsletters;

and through an "electronic church" composed of nearly 40 television stations and more than 1,000 radio stations. Its agenda included the following:

- developing and propagating "model" legislation for states,
- promoting prayer in public schools,
- promoting creationism,
- censoring textbooks and school library books,
- ending unionism and union tactics in education,
- promoting the interests of Christian schools,
- cutting taxes and school expenditures,
- nurturing conservative ideas,
- fighting "secular humanism" in public schools, and
- channeling corporate gifts and funds into colleges and universities that promote "free enterprise."[19]

Leaders of the New Right used propaganda skillfully, making scapegoats of the NEA, the public school system, "secular humanism," the United States Office of Education (USOE), and textbook writers. Moreover, their attacks came at a timely moment, when public education was at a low point—ravaged by inflation, declining student enrollment, increasing costs, and fading public confidence. Many critics charged schools with nearly total failure, citing a lack of discipline, lack of serious study, teachers unprepared in their subject matter, social promotion, subjective grading systems, and "too much pedagogical faddism."[20]

The New Right sought to achieve their objectives through three main approaches: searching out and destroying those elements in the schools that promote free inquiry through attacks on secular humanism; limiting and controlling learning materials in classrooms and school libraries via censorship; and, injecting into classrooms the essence of the Christian Bible, with creationism as the initial vehicle. The first of these had direct ramifications for social studies instruction. The term "secular humanism" was used by the New Right as a code word with which to brand offenders, in an attempt to eradicate the person or practice from schools. For hardcore Christian fundamentalists, humanism was viewed as an evil so insidious as to be at the heart of most of what was wrong with humankind.

The New Right critique of humanism was expressed clearly in a pamphlet produced by the Fort Worth, Texas, Pro-Family Forum, titled "Is Humanism Molesting Your Child?" The pamphlet charged that humanism "denies the deity of God, the inspiration of the Bible, and the divinity of Jesus Christ...believes in equal distribution of America's wealth to reduce poverty...Humanism is being inculcated in the schools." Humanism was viewed as "destructive to our nation, destructive to the family, destructive to the individual."

In one tract circulated by a Moral Majority-related group, seemingly aimed mainly at social studies classes, students were urged to follow a list of commandments:

- Don't—discuss values.
- Don't—write a family history.
- Don't—play blindfolded games in class.
- Don't—write an autobiography.
- Don't—take intelligence texts. Write tests only on your lessons.
- Don't—discuss boy/girl or parent/child relationships in class.
- Don't—confide in teachers, particularly sociology or social studies or English teachers.
- Don't—join any social action or social work group.
- Don't—take "social studies" or "future studies." Demand course definitions: history, geography, civics, French, English, etc.
- Don't—role play or participate in sociodramas.
- Don't—get involved in school-sponsored or government-sponsored exchange or camping programs that place you in the homes of strangers.
- Don't—submit to psychological testing.
- Don't—get into classroom discussions that begin:

  What would you do if...?
  What if...?
  Should we...?
  Do you suppose...?
  Do you think...?[21]

New Right critics also engaged in a widespread movement to ban, remove, and occasionally burn materials designed for student use. Censorship efforts focused on textbooks, works of literature, poetry, films, school dramas, records, comic books, magazines, reference works, and coloring books. For censors, the targets frequently involved "dirty words," but also included alternative images of family life, evolution, race relations, religion, politics, patriotism, free enterprise, communism, or other topics that may have been improperly treated. The censors proclaimed themselves to be Christian, patriotic Americans.

Perhaps the most well known were Mel and Norma Gabler and Phyllis Schlafly's Eagle Forum, but there were many other censors as well.[22]

The overall plan of the New Right included infusing education with Christian/Protestant religion, injecting large doses of the Bible; transmitting the rightness of Victorian morality, free enterprise, and militarism; minimizing student inquiry or investigation; isolating educational theory and practice from experimentation and innovation; and, finally, weakening and eventually eliminating the public system of education by creating rival Christian schools that would bleed the public schools of financing, students, teachers, and community support.[23]

Centrist neoconservatives, on the other hand, were a more diverse and thoughtful group, though their activities lent credence and support to the conservative cause. Their intellectual core was made up of individuals with ties to the American Enterprise Institute (AEI), a conservative think-tank, and to *The Public Interest* and *Commentary*, conservative journals. This group included Nathan Glazer, James Q. Wilson, Chester E. Finn, Daniel P. Moynihan, James Coleman, Joseph Adelson, Diane Ravitch, and columnist George F. Will. Neoconservatives argued that the basic causes of educational problems in the 1980s were the social experiments of the 1960s and 1970s that made too many demands on the schools in the name of reform and excessive federal intervention to promote educational equity.

Centrist conservatives posited three overarching missions for the schools: promoting economic development for the nation; preserving a common culture; and, promotion of educational equity through color-blind access and improving quality. They generally agreed on the need to strengthen educational standards, establish a more limited and selective role for the federal government, increase the amount of homework, reduce nonacademic electives, abolish social promotion, and strengthen requirements for admission and graduation. They also agreed on the need to impose traditional classroom discipline, to improve the quality of teachers, and to promote business/education cooperation.[24]

The neoconservative, centrist philosophy lay behind much of the educational agenda of the 1980s and 1990s and was the driving force behind many of the reports on educational reform during the time. Much of the conservative activism was a backlash against the legacy of the 1960s, for its political sins, or against a perceived decline in standards.

The neoconservative movement, combined with the New Right, found expression in the back-to-basics movement. Many reforms of the 1960s, including the new and newer social studies, flew in the face of the traditional teachers' demand for order and content orientation. This emerging sentiment, and reactions describing open education as a "fad," was expressed in 1974 in school districts across the nation. In 1975, the College Board revealed that Scholastic Aptitude Test (SAT) scores had declined steadily since 1964. Public concern about declining test scores combined with complaints about lax standards and charges that students were doing less reading and writing led to loud calls for instruction in the basics, reading, writing, and arithmetic. In response to this demand, by 1977, thirty-eight state legislatures had passed laws requiring minimum competency tests in the basic skills.[25] In most instances, the movement focused on a single objective, improvement in the three R's. In other's it expanded to include a wide range of aims, including patriotism and puritan morality. On the whole, the movement lacked clear conceptualization and seemed to thrive without identifiable leadership. The Council for Basic Education (CBE), organized by Arthur Bestor and associates in the 1950s, seemed nominally in the forefront. However, its leaders held a broader definition of "the basics" than did many latter day proponents.[26]

What did back-to-basics advocates want? Because they had no single organization, spokesperson, platform, or declaration of principles, the closest we can come is a composite. According to one educational writer in the late 1970s, with a good deal of regional and temporal variation, advocates of back-to-basics wanted the following policies implemented:

1. Emphasis on reading, writing, and arithmetic in the elementary grades. Most of the school day is to be devoted to these skills. Phonics is the method advocated for reading instruction.
2. In the secondary grades, most of the day is to be devoted to English, science, math, and history taught from "clean" textbooks, free of notions that violate traditional family and national values.
3. At all levels, the teacher is to take a dominant role, with "no nonsense about pupil directed activities."
4. Methodology is to include drill, recitation, daily homework, and frequent testing.
5. Report cards are to carry traditional marks (A, B, C, etc.) or numerical values (100, 80, 75, etc.) issued at frequent intervals.

6. Discipline is to be strict, with corporal punishment an accepted method of control. Dress codes should regulate student apparel and hair styles.
7. Promotion from grades and graduation from high school are to be permitted only after mastery of skills and knowledge has been demonstrated through tests. Social promotion and graduation on the basis of time spent in courses are out.
8. Eliminate the frills. The *National Review*, a conservative journal, put it this way: "Clay modeling, weaving, doll construction, flute practice, volleyball, sex education, laments about racism and other weighty matters should take place on private time."
9. Eliminate electives and increase the number of required courses.
10. Ban innovations (a plague on them!). New math, new science, linguistics, instruction by electronic gadgets, emphasis on concepts instead of facts—all must go [the new social studies would also go].
11. Eliminate the school's "social services"—they take time from the basic curriculum. "Social services" may include sex education, driver education, guidance, drug education, and physical education.
12. Put patriotism back in the schools. And love for one's country. And for God.[27]

The most extreme advocates of the new back-to-basics approach wanted to purge the school of its impurities gained during the previous decade. Most did not support all of these planks, yet a consensus was emerging around several of the main ideas, and others were tacitly supported by centrist conservatives, if not openly advocated.

Educators responded in a variety of ways. Because back-to-basics covered a range of convictions, many educators embraced some of them while rejecting others. Some argued that the schools had never left a focus on the basics. Others argued for an expanded version of the "basics" with inclusion of teaching children to think and analyze problems. Still others viewed the back-to-basics movement as "a simplistic solution for complex educational problems" with the potential to "throw us back 100 years." There was, by many accounts, a good deal of disagreement over what "basics" were to be included.[28]

On the whole, schools responded to the new demand with movement toward a new educational trinity: minimal competency, proficiency testing, and a performance-based curriculum. These were the early stages of a movement to establish a system in which no student would go from grade to grade or graduate from high school unless he or she could prove, via test results, mastery of at least a minimal body of skills and information. School administrators and school boards generally lent support to the general idea of a back-to-basics approach by stressing greater emphasis on reading, writing, and arithmetic, though relatively few districts restructured their policy statements or made wholesale changes in instructional programs. More common were a range of efforts from the cosmetic to the new initiative designed to satisfy the demand for more emphasis on the basics, something that had continued uninterrupted in the vast majority of schools through the earlier periods of reform. State legislatures and state departments of education generally jumped aboard the back-to-basics and minimal competency movement.

Despite a strong level of public support for the movement, many educators feared the growth of state power over the schools that it signaled, along with the spread of testing. "What worries me most," said one curriculum director, "is that we shall actually be asking teachers to teach to the test—a practice already condoned." The overwhelming worry of many educators appeared to be the possibility that schools were moving toward producing a generation of "minimal mediocrity," stressing student progress in rote mechanical skills of communication and computation and neglecting critical thought, social criticism, and creativity.[29]

Behind the back-to-basics movement lay the nation's periodic pendulum swing from liberalism to conservatism and back. This paralleled a strong public appetite for accountability, a high divorce rate, disintegration of the family, demands for discipline, and a curb to the excesses of permissiveness. These were combined, for many critics, with a bundle of causes ranging from Dr. Spock and the passive influence of television to creeping socialism. Of course there were many more immediate causes. Parents were taking a larger role in school affairs and frequently tried to reshape policies and programs. Many African Americans and Latino Americans believed that their children were being shortchanged with respect to basic skills and became strong advocates for the basics. For years, teachers had been urged to focus on creativity and the development of independent thinkers. It was not always clear whether this focus was in addition to or instead of instruction in basic skills. Employers had long complained that high school graduates could not read instructions and lacked computational abilities. To the slogan, "Johnny can't read," industrialists added, "And Johnny can't work, either." Many college professors lodged longstanding complaints about the declining level of student preparation. Moreover, public perception held that schools would benefit from beefed-up standards. In 1975, when the Gallup poll asked a sample of parents the reason for the declining student test scores, a significant number of respondents said, "Courses are too easy; there is not enough emphasis on basics." All of this coincided with a financial crunch during which a bare-bones, low-cost school program had a certain appeal to taxpayers.[30]

To some extent the back-to-basics movement was also a media construction. Articles appeared in countless national publications extolling the move "Back to Basics in the Schools," or asking, "Why Johnny Can't Write." Typical was an article from 1975 that alleged, "Willy-nilly, the U.S. educational system is spawning a generation of semi-literates."[31] *Newsweek* reported, in October 1974, that "all across the nation, parents, school boards, and often the pupils themselves are demanding that the schools stop experimenting and get back to basics—in reading, writing, arithmetic and standards of behavior to boot." Open classrooms, "relevant" topics and course materials, permissive discipline, and lax standards had been introduced at the expense of work in the traditional disciplines like English composition, history, the hard sciences, and foreign languages. Professional educators were clearly held responsible. *Newsweek* concluded that "the growing call for a return to the basics seems a healthy signal that masses of Americans are no longer willing to accept a pharmacopoeia of educational nostrums that has been handed to them by a relative handful of well-meaning, but sometimes misdirected innovators."[32]

Social studies was one of the chief targets of the movement as critics alleged that secondary educators had stressed the "fun and the relevant" in the social sciences with the result that students were "quite conversant with local, national, and international problems, but they can't write three consecutive declarative sentences in the English language." The response from many social studies educators was to argue that instruction in basic skills and content were already a key element of the curriculum, and that infusion of work focused explicitly on reading and writing skills could help to improve student learning. In the late 1970s, *Social Education* ran two theme issues devoted to back-to-basics. In the first of these, "Teaching Basics in Social Studies," Barry K. Beyer reported that many basic skills are not really taught in social studies classrooms, and that too many social studies teachers simply assume their students already possess the requisite reading and writing skills necessary to complete written work. Moreover, he charged, these teachers make few if any attempts to diagnose student skill deficiencies or to provide systematic instruction in skills to help their students succeed. Beyer suggested that social studies teachers develop strategies for teaching reading and writing skills while simultaneously seeking to achieve common social studies objectives.[33] A special section the following year was titled "Improving Reading in the Social Studies." In a later article, a cartoon depicted the new social studies as Moby Dick, with Captain Ahab and a back-to-basics harpoon strapped to his back. Alongside was a social studies teacher clinging to a floating "1980s?" casket. The cartoon was captioned "Is teaching basic skills in the social studies a constructive response to the conflict?" Apparently, many social studies scholars and practitioners thought it was. The first article of the section proposed a "constructive response to the challenge of basic skill development" and argued, as had Beyer, for the integration of basic skill instruction in reading and writing into the content of social studies.[34]

By 1980, NCSS had linked up with a number of other leading groups of professional educators to support the essentials of education, acknowledging that "public concern about basic knowledge and the basic skills in education is valid," but arguing that society should shun the easy tendency to limit the essentials to the three R's and that teachers should fight pressures to concentrate upon "easy-to-teach and easy-to-test bits of knowledge." Despite these disclaimers, an NCSS declaration labeled the "Essentials of Social Studies" exposed the profound influence that the conservative restoration was having on the field. In its account of the subject matter of social studies, the statement gave precedence to the academic disciplines and suggested a more traditional focus on content, along with inculcation of democratic beliefs, the hallmark of social efficiency education. A curious document, it melded a reaction to the back-to-basics movement with social efficiency and critical thinking skills. In a sense, it signaled the co-optation of social studies by a rising conservatism.[35]

There were critics of the movement as well. One noted detractor, a professor of English at Wesleyan, Richard Ohman, charged that the literacy crisis was "a fiction, if not a hoax." Ohman wrote, "The available facts simply do not reveal whether young Americans are less literate than their counterparts in 1930 or 1960." He cited a number of facts and findings that supported his view, including a rise in preliminary SAT scores, an National Assessment of Educational Progress (NAEP) study showing that the percentage of good writers among seventeen-year-olds had gone up and that all three age groups tested adequately handled the basics. Also, a study by the American Institutes for Research that found slight improvement in reading test scores for high-school seniors between 1960 and 1970, and the NAEP found that functional literacy for seventeen-year-olds had actually increased between 1971 and 1974. Moreover, a wide survey of reading test results conducted in 1975 by Educational Testing Service (ETS), USOE, and other organizations found "no solid evidence of a decline in reading ability," and concluded "We are now convinced that anyone who says he knows that literacy is decreasing…is at best unscholarly and at worse dishonest." Ohman charged that the literacy crisis was a "media-created event."

The decline in test scores was, he argued, due to other factors being uncovered by researchers, including a drop in enrollment in English courses and a reduced dropout rate resulting in more students taking standardized tests. Moreover, the decline in American College Testing Program (ACT) scores had taken place almost entirely among women due to a dramatic increase in the percentage of women test-takers, meaning women were less excluded from education and that more were choosing higher education. Thus, the "literacy crisis" was partly a result of increasing social justice.

A cogent explanation for the literacy crisis and the back-to-basics movement might suggests that each time the American educational system has rapidly expanded, admitting previously excluded groups to higher levels, the trend has been greeted by a chorus of voices charging a decline in standards. Moreover, in this instance, much of the fuss came from members of the cultural and educational elite and focused on the "grammatical, stylistic, and conceptual abilities" of an elite group, college students. In addition, a conservative spin was in evidence, including a tendency to indict the movements of the 1960s both within and outside education.[36] In succeeding years, the literacy "crisis" and the charge that our schools were failing, would become an underlying and central premise for conservative reforms.

A Nation at Risk?

By the early 1980s, the conservative restoration was more fully taking form. The movement garnered support from a consensus of Americans both within and outside educational institutions and received a major boost from an unprecedented flurry of reports on the status and future of schooling published in 1983 and after. The watershed for the new direction of reform came with publication of *A Nation at Risk: The Imperative for Educational Reform*, the report of the National Commission on Excellence in Education, a blue-ribbon commission appointed by President Ronald Reagan. Though the report contained no new research and was based on a compilation of findings, its timing and the language in which it was written created a heated atmosphere and attracted a great deal of media attention, as well as spawning a secondary literature of reaction and critique from scholars.[37] This report and a flurry of others with a similar theme set the agenda for schooling, signaling the official, US government supported stance. The central thesis of the report was that our nation was "at risk." The commission blamed US schools for the nation's decline in international economic competition, alleging that the position of the United States in commerce, industry, science, and technology was overtaken by "a rising tide of mediocrity in our schools which threatens our very future as a nation and a people." The report went on:

> If an unfriendly foreign power had attempted to impose on America the mediocre educational performance that exists today, we might well have viewed it as an act of war. As it stands, we have allowed this to happen to ourselves. We have squandered the gains in student achievement made in the wake of the Sputnik challenge...We have, in effect, been committing an act of unthinking, unilateral educational disarmament.[38]

The commission supported this inflammatory thesis with a section captioned "Indicators of Risk," which cited the poor performance of American students on international comparisons made in the 1970s. Yet the report contradicted this evidence later, acknowledging that no other nation approaches the United States in the proportion of youth completing high school and going on to higher education. The report also included reference to test comparisons that indicated that the test scores of the top 9 percent of American students compared favorably with their peers in other nations.

The commission also made several reform proposals. They proposed establishing a "core" of studies as the "Five New Basics" for the high school. The core included four years of English, three years of math, three years of science, three years of social studies, and one-half year of computer science, all required for graduation. Health and physical education went unmentioned, and the arts were clearly relegated to a secondary status. Other proposals included the establishment of national standardized tests that had to be passed before promotion, requiring more homework, lengthening the school day and year, merit pay and eleven month contracts for teachers, and creation of more rigorous textbooks and curricular materials.[39]

There were other similar reports as well, though all shared the central thesis of *A Nation at Risk* that the US decline in international economic competition was to be blamed on a mediocre educational system. Most prominent among the other national reports on education published in 1983 were *Action for Excellence*, the Report of the Education Commission of the States, and *Making the Grade*, the report from the Twentieth Century Fund Task Force. *Action for Excellence*, the work of a panel of business and industrial leaders, echoed the thesis of *A Nation at Risk* and offered similar remedies for regaining our preeminent position in global industrial competition. In clear and unabashed language, the report called for a broadened definition of education to meet the demand for "highly skilled human capital" in the "new era of global competition." It outlined what it called "Basic Skills and Competencies for Productive Employment" that included reading, writing, speaking, listening, math, science, along with "competencies" in reasoning, economics, computer literacy, and basic employment. "Good" citizenship was listed under basic employment. *Making the Grade* offered a similar message, specifying the components of a new "core" to insure the availability of workers to sustain a "complex and competitive economy."[40] As Joel Spring observed, these reports called for businesses to hook up with the public high school system "to ensure an adequate and docile supply of unskilled labor." However, he lamented, "The resulting distortions of education would condemn many to a life of low wages and limited career advancement."[41]

Though the aim of the various commissions may have been to suggest that "inattention to our schools puts the well-being of the nation at risk," and the goal may have been to rouse schools from encroaching "mediocrity" and stir them toward excellence, the reports were not warmly greeted by many educators.[42] If the nation did have a true educational crisis of the magnitude described by the reports, it was a predicament manufactured by business and political leaders. Perhaps the most thoughtful analysis and one of the most scathing critiques written in the immediate aftermath of the reports was an article by Lawrence C. Stedman and Marshall S. Smith, two policy analysts based in Madison, Wisconsin. Stedman and Smith charged that the reports contained "weak arguments, poor data, and simplistic recommendations" and described them as political documents that made polemical arguments rather than offering a reasoned and well-documented case. On the whole, the reports had a pronounced tendency to regard schools rather narrowly as instruments for training human capital and regaining US dominance over world markets. Each of the commission reports supported reckless accusations making a scapegoat of the public education system in the United States. The arguments in the reports were based on inaccurate, incomplete, and misleading data centered on a faulty thesis.[43] Another reviewer, Daniel Tanner, argued that the commissions revealed "an appalling lack of understanding of the function of general education in a free society."[44] Others were critical of the commission reports for different reasons. An article in *Fortune* complained that the National Commission failed to address "the systemic cause of U.S. education's inefficiency: monopoly."[45]

Given the makeup of the Commission on Excellence, perhaps these findings were understandable. The commission was made up primarily of administrators from universities and schools, and school board members. Together they accounted for eleven of the commission's eighteen members appointed by Secretary of Education Terrel H. Bell. The group also included a former governor, a business leader, and one public school teacher. Perhaps the most famous commissioners were David P. Gardner, then president-elect of the University of Utah and A. Bartlett Giamatti, president of Yale University and a well-known neoconservative critic of the schools. Notably missing from the commission were scholarly experts in the field of education. It is also important to keep in mind that these were political appointees of the Reagan administration. Regardless, the makeup of the commission did not include sufficient representation from the various constituencies involved in determining school policy and in a position to influence classroom teachers.

Beyond these institutional reports a number of important scholarly works on education were also published in the early 1980s from mainstream, perennialist, and critical perspectives. In each case, these works reflected either primary research in schools, theoretical or philosophical development, or both. Among the works comprising what could be called a "researcher's agenda" were John Goodlad's *A Place Called School*, Ernest L. Boyer's *High School*, and Theodore R. Sizer's *Horace's Compromise*. In contrast to the commission reports, these were research reports with recommendations for school practice. Their findings were both more accurate and more soberly presented. The Boyer study found that one in ten students received an education as fine as any in the world, and that two in ten were condemned to schools that mock the name. The vast majority of students "glide" through with the understanding that they won't demand too much from school, if the school doesn't demand too much from them. More positive than the "at risk" reports, Boyer found that education was slowly improving. He called for a core curriculum, the elimination of tracking, and creation of an interdisciplinary vision with room for electives, in which content would extend beyond the specialties to touch larger societal issues. In *Horace's Compromise*, Sizer's insightful essay of the same name described English teacher Horace Smith's compromise of quality for efficiency, a compromise that many if not most teachers were forced to make.[46]

In the most extensive research study of schools among the reports, Goodlad and his associates in *A Place Called School* found that only 75 percent of class time was devoted to instruction, that the overwhelming proportion of instruction was in the mode of teacher "telling," and that students were rarely involved in making any decisions about their learning. Tests and quizzes stressed mainly the recall of specifics and narrow mechanical skills. Through the practice of tracking or "ability grouping," the upper groups received a rich curriculum while the lower groups were taught largely through drill and rote. Instruction for mixed groups resembled that of the high groups. Goodlad called for a restructuring of the educational system via attempts to improve pedagogy by gaining active involvement of students, providing more personal attention and using a greater variety of teaching methods.[47]

Concurrently, a body of work was emerging from a critical perspective that would challenge the thinking and interpretive framework of conventional educators, both neoconservatives and mainstream liberals. This new criticism reflected the influence of several forms of critical theory and included such works as *Schooling in Capitalist America* by Samuel Bowles and Herbert Gintis, *Ideology and Curriculum* by Michael Apple, and *Education Under Siege* by Stanley Aronowitz and Henry Giroux as well as the work of a number of others.[48] These works, which were discussed in some depth earlier, shared a perspective critical of schools for their persistence in limiting social mobility and of a curriculum, and hidden curriculum, that reflected the influence of power relationships in the society. By and large, the critical theorists held that schools served the interests of those in power and socialized students not to question.

On the whole, the Report of the National Commission and its sister reports expressed a corporate agenda for schooling. Their publication came on the heels of the back-to-basics movement and demanded improved traditional schooling for the development of human capital.

This was the latest incarnation of education for social efficiency, a turn away from the progressive impulse, and a step back from the potential redemptive power of schooling. However, the calls for change were more than empty rhetoric. They reflected the anxieties and aspirations of the time and offered an image of a preferred future. In conservative times, the 1890s, the 1950s, and the 1980s, the keynotes have been a focus on the talented with hopes of outperforming the Russians or the Japanese, calls for greater emphasis on the basics and the traditional disciplines, and concern about incoherence in the curriculum and a lack of student decorum. In more liberal eras, the 1930s, the 1960s, and early 1970s, the focus has shifted to equity for the disadvantaged, a broadening of the function of schools, and greater flexibility and innovation in teaching. From a long-term perspective, competing values such as equity and excellence are often in tension while schools have continued to go about their business largely in traditional ways, changing only slowly over time.[49]

Social Studies during a Conservative Era. During the initial years of the conservative restoration, the back-to-basics movement, and the business driven thrust for excellence, social studies appeared to be a field adrift. The era of the new social studies had ended, yet no correspondingly influential movement for reform had risen to take its place. Moreover, the disappointing impact of the new and newer social studies on classrooms led to a great deal of hand-wringing. By the late 1970s, it seemed that social studies was a subject in search of itself. The journal *Social Education* reflected this soul searching. From the late 1960s, *Social Education* had become a potpourri, taken over by special issues with a focus on what seemed to at least one observer, "one damn thing after another." First it was an issue on Russia, then Japan, then back-to-basics, and so on, seemingly without end. Even though there were many thoughtful articles and special issues published, the journal of the late 1970s and early 1980s appeared to lack conceptual focus. Social studies, it seemed, could be most anything one wanted it to be.

Definitional dilemmas within the subject appeared to be a major feature of social studies during the late 1970s and early 1980s, making the time appropriate for alternative initiatives. Suggesting the depth of social studies' malaise, a front cover cartoon accompanied a special issue of *Social Education* in 1980, entitled "Discussion and Debate on New Proposals for the Social Studies Curriculum." The cartoon depicted seven social studies professionals sitting at a table considering a jigsaw puzzle with pieces labeled to reflect various parts of the enigma: social sciences, history, decision making, concepts, ethnic studies, international human rights education, generalizations, social action, global education, geography, futurism, career education, consumerism, moral education, law-related education, citizenship, drug education, geography, factual knowledge, skills, socialization, and so on. One of the participants commented, "It might help if we had a picture of what this is supposed to look like."[50]

In addition, by the 1980s there was increasing recognition of the difficulty of changing social studies, an awareness that diffusion did not necessarily lead to significant curricular change, and a feeling that the theory/practice divide was conceivably the key dilemma of the field. One letter to the editor bemoaned the paradox between the "real" and the "ideal" in social studies.[51] Another article shared the valuable insight that "diffusion" does not equal "change."[52] Larry Cuban's *How Teachers Taught* revealed that despite repeated attempts to improve teaching, habitual practices relying on teacher talk, seatwork, use of textbooks, and recitation were remarkably persistent.[53]

In sum, social studies appeared without direction for a time partly because there were no new reform initiatives with the power of either the new social studies or the progressive movement. Moreover, many scholars in social studies had watched the failure of both these movements and had gradually begun to appreciate the enormous difficulty of large-scale transformation. So there emerged, for an instant, a chasm between reform movements, a retreat in the face of the conservative restoration, and a return by many teachers to more time-honored approaches to teaching. Much of the blame for the deterioration in the vitality of social studies reform efforts lay in the context of the times. In the Reagan years and afterward, progressives in social studies were swimming against the flow of a torrential flood.

The Revival of Traditional History

Into this void of near "directionlessness" came a new initiative more in touch with the mood of the times, the revival of history. The sources of the revival of history may be traced to the same kinds of anxieties that motivated the back-to-basics movement. It was, in a sense, the citizenship wing of the conservative restoration. Though support for traditional history had never disappeared, such preferences seemed at low tide during the era of the new and newer social studies with its emphasis on inquiry and issues. However, at least a few detractors of the new social studies had called for a return to traditional history, and by the mid-1970s a growing number of historians were expressing distress over the decline of history teaching in schools and the loss of students to other majors in colleges and universities.

A committee of the Organization of American Historians (OAH) chaired by Richard S. Kirkendall issued the most recognized survey of the time in 1975. After reviewing the status of history in schools and colleges, the survey authors concluded that "history is in crisis." The committee found broad disparities in the credentials required of teachers in secondary schools. In a number of states, requisites for the certification of "social studies" teachers were undergoing revision, with a reduction in the number of compulsory courses in history. In their report, the situation regarding teacher certification requirements was characterized as "quite fluid," with the inference that history's preeminence was endangered.[54]

History's standing in the curriculum was also diminishing, according to the report. The committee perceived a dynamic circumstance with movement away from history, at least as history was "traditionally defined and taught." History was slowly being de-accentuated and integrated into social studies units with trends favoring a "multidisciplinary approach." In many cases, it seemed, a chronological approach had been replaced by the "inquiry method" and efforts "to link courses to the issues facing society."[55]

The report met robust disapproval along several lines. Some alleged that the committee was poorly informed about secondary schools. Others argued that the report reflected a traditional approach to teaching history that should be abandoned. Kirkendall and historians generally seemed to blame social studies for failures in the teaching of history. It was an attack reminiscent of Allan Nevins and the *New York Times* crusade of the 1940s. Moreover, the "survey" published in the *Journal of American History* supplied little substantive evidence to corroborate a "crisis" in history teaching in the schools and appeared to be almost completely anecdotal.

In an article in *Social Education*, Allan O. Kownslar offered something of a counterpoint. Though he largely agreed with the report, Kownslar supported the "newer methods" and reported on an ETS study that found that students who claimed they had been exposed to the newer pedagogies in the history classroom scored slightly higher on standardized tests than those who had not. He also noted that the OAH report did not include student opinions about the reasons for declining interest in history. Kownslar reported several common student complaints: a focus on "accumulation of data strictly for knowledge's sake"; that students were expected to be passive listeners, passive note-takers, or passive memorizers. For the disgruntled student, "memorization of everything" seemed the primary reason for endless hours of traditional history. Kownslar was a strong supporter of history, but confided, "Personally, I suspect that in many cases history courses are unpopular simply because they are taught so badly."[56] A later article confirmed that many students found little value in the study of history, that the methods of teaching were too often dull, the content irrelevant to their personal lifestyles, and that many resented the fact that they were required to take history throughout their educational careers.[57]

In 1980, a special issue of *Social Education* was devoted to "Teaching American History." The introduction made note of the increasing media attention to the teaching of American history. "The rationale, the content, even the methodology" were inspiring a great deal of comment, opinions, and prescriptions. *Time* magazine ran a cover story on the new generation of historians, 60 Minutes devoted most of a program to a story on the teaching of history, the CBE named a special commission to investigate the place of history in schools, Frances Fitzgerald's series of articles in the *New Yorker* on American history textbooks stirred interest and controversy, and many schools and agencies were undertaking studies of ways to improve the teaching of American history. One of the authors of the special issue called for better teaching and recommended: creating a sense of time in students; teaching history as a rigorous discipline with respectable intellectual standards; insisting that history be taught by history teachers; and, shaping alliances with persons and groups that could contribute toward more effective history teaching.[58]

The critique of social studies that lay behind the "crisis" was trumpeted most pointedly by Kieran Egan, a Canadian curriculum theorist. In a provocative article titled "Social Studies and the Erosion of Education," Egan found "a fundamental conceptual confusion inherent in social studies." He cited social studies aims focused on "attitudes and skills" for furthering the "democratic form of life" and "inculcating the ability to think critically" about the major problems of the past, present, and future. Egan charged that such aims were plagued by "vacuous generalities…mindnumbing vagueness…and ideological innocence." Such conceptual confusion, he wrote, results in a social studies curriculum that "has not worked, does not work, and cannot work." Egan went on to argue that the basis for the "expanding horizons" curriculum was psychologically flawed and that social studies was designed primarily to socialize students. He concluded that we would be better off "letting the 20th century American curriculum experiment called social studies quietly die." He argued for a revival of narrative, academic history and concluded that history and the other "foundational disciplines" of social studies should be separated from social studies to "preserve the disciplinary autonomy of these areas and thereby their educational value." Their educational value, he alleged, "is precisely what is eroded when they become handmaidens to the socializing purpose that pervades social studies."[59]

Several neoconservative writers contributed to an escalating upsurge among historians, politicians, and more than a few teachers to back the revival of traditional history. The "crisis" served as preface to the revival, which was spurred by a *New York Times* involvement. An article written by educational historian Diane Ravitch appeared in the November 17, 1985, issue of the *New York Times Magazine* titled "Decline and Fall of History Teaching." Ravitch argued that history was in trouble in the schools and that social studies was culpable. In the succeeding years, publications by Ravitch, Lynne Cheney, Paul Gagnon, Chester Finn, and others, along with support from political figures such as California Superintendent of Public Instruction Bill Honig and US Secretary of Education William J. Bennett, contributed to a growing call for the revival of history in schools and made the case for a return to history and geography as the core of citizenship education. A number of scholars made significant contributions: Cheney in *American Memory: A Report on the Humanities in the Nation's Public Schools* (1987), Gagnon in an article titled "Why Study History?" that appeared in *Atlantic Monthly* (1988), and Finn, as coauthor with Ravitch of *What Do Our 17-Year-Olds Know? A Report on the First National Assessment of History and Literature* (1987).[60] However, by the late 1980s it became obvious that Ravitch was the driving force.

In her writing, Ravitch argued, first, that history was in trouble. Requirements had eroded as history was forced to share time and space with the ill-defined social studies, leaving students ignorant of even the most basic facts of US history. Moreover, social studies was, in her view, a watered-down form of "tot sociology," an unholy concoction brewed by professional educationists. Second, internal disorder within history as a discipline had minimized the idea of history as story and replaced it with process-centered schemes through which students learn how to engage in historical inquiry as if preparing to be historians, resulting in less attention to learning the content or facts of history. Third, she argued, "History is above all the retelling of what happened in the past" and should emphasize content knowledge, appeals to the imagination, and empathy so that students could experience a dissimilar time and place.[61]

Ravitch portrayed a "golden age" of history in schools during the early years of the twentieth century, and held up traditional history centered around a textbook, chronology, and history as "a story well told," as a model curriculum. She argued that this archetype had been displaced by a "social efficiency" oriented social studies program focused on direct social utility, on "relevance and student interest." In contrast, she held out the new California Framework as "a historic-step towards the national revival of the teaching and learning of history." The framework positioned history in almost every grade, chronologically sequenced to build student knowledge. It emphasized democratic values and standards of democratic governance "throughout the curriculum."[62] The underlying intention, the use of history to instill American democratic values and build a common culture and a sense of national identity, was a slightly adapted version of Nevins's aims from the 1940s. If the problem was social studies, the solution, in Ravitch's view, was to return in spirit to the 1890s and reinstitute traditional history.

Ravitch, Gagnon, and a cadre of distinguished historians, including Kenneth T. Jackson, William H. McNeill, C. Vann Woodward, Michael Kammen, and William E. Leuchtenburg formed the Bradley Commission on History in Schools. Generously funded by the Lynde and Harry Bradley Foundation, the Bradley Commission published a pamphlet outlining its program in 1988 entitled *Building a History Curriculum*. The commission adopted a platform of nine resolutions calling for the study of history to be required of all students; for the kindergarten through grade six social studies curriculum to be history-centered; and, requiring no fewer than four years of history in grades seven through twelve.[63] The platform contained many useful recommendations, but took an extreme position regarding the balance of history and other social sciences in the curriculum. Furthermore, it all but ignored one of the key difficulties facing history teachers in the schools, the quandary of making the study of history relevant and meaningful to students.

In 1989, the Bradley Commission published *Historical Literacy: The Case for History in American Education*. Edited by Gagnon, the volume included contributions from numerous members of the Bradley Commission. Most chapters were authored by historians. Markedly, not one educational theorist or curriculum specialist appeared among the authors. The few professors of education included were those who had already clearly established their support for history as core. The book was a polemical argument for more and better history in schools, with little or no consideration of the place of the other social sciences. Disingenuously, historians argued that the social sciences would be incorporated within history.[64]

Critiques. Social studies educators offered a rather tepid response given the challenge to their stewardship of the field. Richard Gross portrayed the critics as "a small but vocal, highly motivated, well-funded, and very visible interest group...promoting the primacy of history and geography in the school curriculum." Gross observed that there was "little evidence from the past, when history and geography held sway, that the study of these subjects produced the results that today's proponents' desire."[65]

Ronald W. Evans appraised the revival of history and its chief advocate, Diane Ravitch. Evans remarked that Ravitch was making a scapegoat of social studies and ignoring the history and intentions of the social studies movement, choosing to make simplistic condemnations instead. The actuality, he wrote, was that "history continues to hold a dominant position among the social studies, and that one goal of the social studies movement has been to make instruction in history and the social sciences more meaningful and relevant to the average citizen." He criticized Ravitch and her colleagues for presuming that a chronological narrative, the "tell a story" approach to history teaching, was some sort of answer, when a traditional method had continued without interruption in most classrooms and had been largely unsuccessful in the effort to interest and educate students.[66]

In his critique of the reform movement, Stephen J. Thornton inquired, "Should we be teaching more history?" Thornton questioned whether the proposed reforms were well founded, and whether a renewed stress on acquiring content would bring a return to a "golden age" as Ravitch suggested. He found "scant support in the research literature for the reformers' views, and that the substitution of history for other social studies courses will be to little avail unless entrenched patterns of instruction and learning are also changed."[67]

Sid Lester, a professor at San Jose State University, wrote a critique of the California Framework in which he decried the short shrift given to the social sciences and the failure of the Framework Committee to be more inclusive. "There were no professors of economics, anthropology, sociology, psychology, or political science," he wrote. "None! Not any! Zip! Nada!...According to most authorities," he countered, "the 'social studies' should be comprised of the disciplines of history, geography, anthropology, economics, political science, sociology, and psychology, with some humanities, philosophy and law thrown in."[68] Another professor from California, Duane Campbell at Sacramento State, objected, in a letter printed in *Social Education*, that the framework had been "railroaded through" the adoption process by undemocratic means, despite strong objections. In sum, critics charged that the nascent revival of history was an attempt to overturn a decades old attempt at a compromise position between historians and social scientists, brokered by educators with the needs and interests of students at heart.[69]

What were the fundamental causes underlying the revival of history? The movement came to fulfillment because of the convergence of people and ideas during a time of rising support for conservatism. It received strong backing from those in positions of power, and munificent funding from the Bradley Foundation, a philanthropic group with a strong conservative bias and the goal of influencing policy.[70] This kind of financial support, from a private foundation leaning in a particular direction, was a growing presence in the history of social studies. Moreover, there were elements of truth in some of the critiques leveled against social studies. The new social studies did emphasize the social sciences and social issues, and it was undeniably the case that classroom practice in social studies was a shadow of what was possible, regardless of orientation.

Clearly, the movement touched a nerve among historians and the general public, who always seem vulnerable to appeals to tradition and a "golden age," and developed at an opportune time. In synopsis, the revival of history was yet another episode in the social studies wars. Yet, this new initiative was different in a few significant ways. Though polemical, its arguments were more powerfully developed than those of many previous critics. Moreover, Ravitch and her supporters garnered substantial support among respected historians, found strong organizational and financial backing, and established a firm beachhead by developing a "model" curriculum in the most populous state in the nation. By all appearances, this was a movement to reform social studies that would have influence for some time.

Explaining the Conservative Restoration

The problem set forth near the beginning of this chapter was to explain the conservative restoration in schools and society, declining attention to reflective, inquiry, and issues-centered social studies and the continuing failure of attempted reforms. Several possible explanations can help contribute to our understanding of the conservative restoration, the decline of progressive social studies, and the revival of history.

First, the educational reforms of the period, back-to-basics, the pursuit of excellence, and the revival of history, were motivated by educational, political, and economic forces in the society outside of education. This was fundamentally a response to a manufactured crisis, based on a faulty thesis and flawed assumptions, driven by persons in positions of power with control of considerable financial resources in government and the private sector. New Right and neoconservative activists were methodical, well organized, inspired, visible, articulate, and well funded. Attacks on the new and newer social studies received support from a broad array of conservative groups, as we have seen. Only a few years later, the Educational Excellence Network and the Bradley Commission were major supporters of the neoconservative revival of history. In part, the political trends culminating in the conservative restoration originated in reactions to the perceived excesses of reforms of the 1960s and 1970s. The swing of the pendulum to the right seemed a perennial trend in American education, which typically followed any period of innovation.

The conservative restoration forestalled reform, truncated possibility, and brought an end to a remarkable era of school reform. Several elements converged during the period to give the conservative movement its power. A conservative intellectual movement had been brewing since at least the 1940s, marked by the publication of Freidrich Hayek's *The Road to Serfdom*, an anticollectivist treatise published in 1944, and growing with the rise of a cadre of thoughtful conservative thinkers in the 1950s and 1960s. Among them were "libertarians" who resisted the threat of expanding government; the "new conservatives" who urged a return to traditional religious and ethical absolutes and rejection of the "relativism" that had corroded American values and produced a vacuum filled by demonic ideologies; and, a militant, evangelistic anticommunism. These groups shared "a deep antipathy to 20th century liberalism" and gradually consolidated through the medium of various journals and organizations, most prominently William F. Buckley's *National Review*, founded in 1955.[71]

The evangelical resurgence was an equally powerful force and represented a form of status politics with no compromise. To evangelicals, the struggles over social studies were an effort to return the certainty of absolutist values to schools and society corrupted by un-American ideologies. They were seeking to restore dominance for their world view, for "a cluster of values derived from Victorian middle-class society." While the social revolutions of the 1960s had empowered many, it also diminished the influence and cultural domination of those whose values had previously held sway. The ultrafundamentalists saw the secular education system threatening their belief that there are absolute truths, and their campaigns against the schools were a "direct attempt...to gain equal status for their view of the world" and to convert nonbelievers to their cause.[72]

The evangelical resurgence was given greater political, organizational, and financial potency by the emergence of a new generation of conservative funders and influence-peddlers. They grew into a wide-ranging conservative "counterintelligentsia" aimed at breaking a "liberal stranglehold" on politics and restoring "limited government, free enterprise, hard-line anti-Communism, 'traditional' family values, and individualism" as prevailing norms. During the 1970s, a handful of conservative foundations and individuals provided what one assessment called the "venture capital" for a proliferating array of "conservative think tanks, advocacy organizations, professional associations, university-based research institutes, publications and policy advocacy organizations" that led to a sweeping move to the right. Major funders on the right, through individual donations and their foundations, played a key role in the campaign against the new and newer social studies and for the revival of traditional history. These included Lynde and Harry Bradley, Joseph Coors, JM, Smith Richardson, the Koch Family, Richard and Sarah Scaife, and now-prominent organizations such as the Heritage Foundation, the Cato Institute, the Manhattan Institute, the Hudson Institute, the John M. Olin Foundation, and the American Enterprise Institute (founded in 1943). Through their publications, lobbying, and financial contributions these groups helped make the 1970s a "seedtime" for conservative reform via an alliance between business and conservative intellectuals. This became a "counterrevolution from above" that tapped into decades of built up frustrations against what conservatives viewed as an "interlocking directorate" among members of the northeast liberal establishment in politics, academia, and education.[73]

Though it is tempting to suggest a broad conspiracy of conservatives behind the conservative restoration, the word conspiracy often suggests the workings of secret societies, operating behind closed doors. The reality is that a coalition of conservative activists, evangelicals, neoconservatives, and wealthy individuals worked together in a coalition built around common causes and beliefs, including the sanctity of private property, free enterprise, low taxes, the traditional family, law and order, and traditional education. The coalition was funded by a multitude of groups and individuals, many of whom were from the wealthiest segment of American society. Though it undoubtedly had its hidden aspects, by and large the conservative directorate operated quite openly. Suggesting a conspiracy would only aggravate a sense of helplessness and diminish our ability to deal with the seriousness of the situation.[74] It might breed apathy at times when we need to take action against the conservative forces, still a vocal and well-funded minority, that have had such a profound influence on the direction of social studies and schools.

Second, the conservative restoration was erected upon widespread myths about American schooling and the notion of a fabled golden age. In the broad realm, this took the shape of the assertion that schools were failing. Not just a few of the schools but schools in their entirety. Thus, advocates suggested, back-to-basics, reassertion of tougher standards, and a return to more conservative traditions were warranted. In support of the revival of history, the myth of a golden age was merged with the scapegoating of social studies as the factor that led to the hypothetical decline of history in schools. A return to the golden age meant revisiting the familiar "grammar of schooling" and the conviction that the only bona fide social studies was traditional history.

Third, many of the doubts regarding the reforms of the 1960s and 1970s were based on the realistic judgment that the reforms were not effective. The limited success of reforms in the era of the new and newer social studies was a large element giving rise to the conservative restoration, creating an easy target for criticism from the New Right, neoconservatives, and concerned historians. In part, the reforms failed due to the reformers' neglect of institutional obstacles to change. Impediments to the encouragement of higher order thinking in social studies classrooms seemed prevalent in schools. Among these were the omnipresent practice of instruction as knowledge transmission, a curriculum concentrated on coverage, teachers' low expectations of students, larger numbers of students per teacher, a dearth of adequate planning time, and a culture of teacher isolation.[75] Additional constraints on teaching such as the number of students per class, the length of the class period, the readily available materials, and the content to be taught were influenced and sometimes mandated by factors outside the classroom. Although teachers did have authority over classroom space, student grouping, classroom discourse, tools, and activities, pedagogy could not escape at least two foremost commands from outside: maintain decorum and cover the mandated curriculum. So, despite potential for teacher beliefs to deeply impact what occurred in classrooms, organizational constraints resulted in a remarkable pattern of persistent instruction, of constancy marked by teacher-centered forms of pedagogy, particularly at the secondary level.[76]

Moreover, these constraints were shaped by a remarkably resilient grammar of schooling that seemed to impose structural constraints on school reform. In the high school, for example, the grammar of schooling included hourly shifts from one subject and teacher to another, teachers and subjects divided into specialized departments and instructing 150 or more students a day in 5 classes, and students rewarded with grades and Carnegie units. Over time we have seen little lasting change in the way schools divide time and space, classify students, and allocate them into classrooms, splinter knowledge, and award grades. This standard "grammar of schooling" has proven remarkably durable, persisting partly because it enabled teachers to perform their duties in a predictable and efficient fashion: controlling student behavior, sorting students into social roles for school and life outside. Such conventional organizational forms take on a life of their own, becoming the universal attributes of a "real school." Fixed by custom, legal mandates, and cultural beliefs until they are so entrenched that they are scarcely noticed. As Tyack and Cuban explain it, "They become just the way schools are."[77] In practical terms, the new reforms of the conservative restoration were easier to sustain because they matched stakeholders' notion of a real school.

Fourth, philosophically, the conservative restoration and the revival of history both conformed to what were perceived as the traditional purposes of education. Traditionalist members of the school culture and the public rose up, through a growing system of conservative influence, and reasserted a movement toward more conventional forms of schooling. During the era of the new social studies, a significant number of teachers and students raised doubts about American social structures. During the conservative restoration, that questioning was turned on its head. Instead of education for social criticism, the emphasis was on socialization, social control, and the creation of human capital. It seemed that many Americans did not want schools to reform American society, but simply to restore its luster. Employers wanted workers who were punctual and followed instructions without asking too many questions. Behind this was a school system that seemed to have more to do with maintaining the class structure rather than equalizing opportunity. As Shirley Engle, a social studies luminary once suggested, "More citizens than we would like to think are really hostile to democracy. They do not want the schools to teach their children to think."[78] It seemed that an emerging consensus of politicians and the American public viewed social studies as a means of inducting youth into the traditional values of the social order—even if it had to be done by rote indoctrination.

Conclusion

Following the conservative restoration, the continuing series of developments seemed to follow a very logical progression that included the imposition of standards and high stakes testing. This was combined with the reinstitution of core academic subjects, especially history and geography, instead of a broader form of social studies. As we have seen, these developments grew out of postwar attacks on progressive education and were an extension of long-term criticisms of the progressive direction of social studies reform from at least the years of the Rugg controversy if not before. Seen in long perspective, the 1960s era of the new and newer social studies was instrumental, both as an era of innovation and reform and for the reaction it provoked. Though social studies advocates and curriculum activists such as Peter Dow and Ted Fenton, and organizations such as NCSS, the NEA, and People for the American Way attempted to defend schools and social studies against conservative attacks, in the end they were no match for the clarity, sense of purpose, and political and economic power held by conservative activists. Driven by money from conservative foundations, backed by several of the wealthiest and most conservative Americans, and supported by business and culturally conservative religious groups, it seems, from a vantage point only slightly removed from the fray, that social studies was for sale, and with it the direction of citizenship education in the United States.

III

Making Sense

7

Can We Transcend the Grammar of Social Studies?

In 1977, on the basis of his survey of social studies, Richard Gross proclaimed, "The traditional pattern of high school social studies offerings, rather stable since 1917, finally has been shattered." Some states required fewer social studies courses, others permitted more local options, and an increasing proportion of social studies time was devoted to electives. In the mid-1980s, Carole Hahn took another look at the findings of the Gross survey using data collected in 1982–1983 and found that several of his conclusions warranted revision due to changes in the intervening years. She found that the dual trends of reducing social studies requirements and increasing electives may be reversing. The most frequently required courses remained US history and US government. Other frequently required courses included state history or government, economics or "free enterprise," and world geography or cultures. Social studies electives were on the decline and Problems of Democracy had become a distant memory. As in the Gross survey, elementary social studies was in a continuing decline. Additional trends included an increase in mandates for economics education, sometimes labeled "free enterprise," and new emphases on law studies, ethnic studies, global studies, and career education. Several other trends reported in the Gross survey from the mid-1970s were likely to be missing. These included peace education, future studies, women's studies, family studies, and human rights education.

In the 1980s, academic freedom was still a concern. Though many respondents to Hahn's survey reported only sporadic and isolated attempts to censor materials, several stated that teachers seemed to be more self-censoring. In the face of budget cuts and staff reductions many were "playing it safe." Pressures most often centered on particular books that included topics such as evolution, values clarification, or global education. Issues mentioned as being controversial in 1983 included evolution/creationism, abortion, right to work laws, nuclear freeze, school prayer, and minority group relations.

In 1977, Gross reported limited use of material from the new social studies projects in schools. Hahn confirmed this finding, reporting that the materials "never reached widespread use" and that the "era of the new social studies" had passed. Yet, many of the materials were still in use in some classrooms. Respondents reported moderate to widespread use of law programs. American Political Behavior received moderate to slight use. Materials from a number of other prominent programs were used slightly or moderately, if at all. These included the Carnegie Mellon Project, Citizenship Decision Making, the Harvard Public Issues Booklets, the HSGP, MACOS, Our Working World, the Taba Social Studies Program, and SRSS. As we shall see, Gross and Hahn were not the only ones to report limited influence.

Status Studies

In the years immediately following the era of the new social studies, the National Science Foundation (NSF) and United States Office of Education (USOE) issued contracts for studies of schooling to assess the impact of the reforms. The "status studies," as they came to be called, revealed a social studies landscape rich in new rhetoric but little changed in practice. So, during the mid-to-late 1970s, reports on the status of social studies proliferated, a result of unprecedented federal funding for such research. Several surveys, based primarily on the NSF funded studies of science, math, and social studies came to somewhat similar and disappointing conclusions on the status of classroom practice in social studies, suggesting that recent reform efforts had made little difference.[1] An interpretation of the NSF data, written by Shaver, Davis, and Helburn, summarized the general findings. With the caveat that many exceptions can be found, their study revealed the following:

1. The teacher is the key to what happens to students in the social studies classroom. For example, it is the teacher who decides how new curricular materials will be used, if at all.

2. A major concern of teachers is with classroom management and the control of students. The perceived need to deal with large groups of uninterested and often disruptive students during the day occupies much of their attention.

3. Instruction is primarily textbook oriented. The textbook is not only viewed as the central tool of instruction but as *the* source of knowledge. Discussion is largely recitation, with students often asked to reproduce the same language as used in the text.

4. Despite the lack of state or federal control of education, there tends to be a national curriculum through the independent adoption of textbooks by individual school districts, all selecting from the same pool of similar books.

5. Social studies is largely the study of US history and government, along with geography, especially at the lower levels.

6. Although most teaching objectives are stated in cognitive terms (e.g., learning knowledge), a major underlying goal in the presentation of social studies content is affective—to instill positive feelings about American society—its history and government.

7. Teachers, university professors, and district supervisors seem to be concerned with different school realities. University professors tend to see knowledge as an end in itself and stress the importance of learning how to inquire like social scientists...Teachers tend to see university professors and curriculum developers as not aware of classroom realities.

8. Innovative "New Social Studies" materials developed during the 1960s and early 1970s...are not used widely in social studies classes. Approximately 10 to 25 percent of social studies teachers' report having used material from at least one of the new social studies projects. The inquiry methods and suggestions for student participation fly in the face of teachers' content orientation and promote techniques that challenge teachers' methods for maintaining order. Teachers also report that they have not been prepared to use inquiry techniques.

9. Teachers generally like their students, and students sense that they are liked, even though they find social studies to be boring. Students generally find social studies content and modes of instruction uninteresting.

10. Despite considerable change in some districts and outstanding teaching by some teachers, there has generally been little change in social studies instruction in the great majority of classrooms.[2]

A similar depiction of the status of social studies classroom practice was expressed by a number of other writers and researchers summarizing the NSF data and other sources.[3] Two additional sources from the period provided historical and anthropological perspectives on the constancy of classroom teaching in social studies and other subjects. The first of these was an article by James Hoetker and William P. Ahlbrand titled "The Persistence of the Recitation." The article concluded, based on a review of historical studies, that recitation, a question and answer pattern of instruction dominated by teacher talk, was a remarkably stable and dominant form of classroom verbal behavior over the past half century or longer. More recently, Larry Cuban argued much the same thing, that during the past sixty years, the social studies classroom has been dominated by teacher-centered instruction that includes lecture, the textbook as the solitary source of information, discussion, texts, and seatwork.[4]

Another important study of the 1970s with serious implications for social studies was Alan Peshkin's *Growing Up American,* an ethnographic account that described education in the typical American town of Mansfield. The book provided strong evidence of a virulent socialization process with little or no countersocialization as did the Lynd's study of Middletown half a century earlier. The richly detailed anthropological study described an educational system clearly in-step with community desires for conformity and social control, and a social studies curriculum that inculcated allegiance to "God and Country" through a fairly traditional pattern of content and instruction.[5]

At least one work on the status of social studies drawing on data collected in the middle of the 1970s drew a more optimistic conclusion on the possibilities for the future. This assessment came from the directors and staff of one of the NSF-sponsored research projects, Project SPAN, a loose acronym for "Social Studies/Social Science Education: Priorities, Practices, and Needs." After reviewing the same studies as Shaver, Davis, and Helburn, they concluded that there is "a large unrealized potential for learning among youth and that it is possible for our school systems to move toward greater realization of that potential." They argued that "we know a great deal about learning and teaching" and about educational change and intervention, but that knowledge has been "insufficiently applied." Moreover, they suggested, the educational reform efforts of the 1960s and 1970s, "while viewed by many as a source of chaos and frustration, supply many building blocks that can be used fruitfully in new efforts to improve the social studies...(including) knowledge of new approaches to content and method, a large array of social problem areas from which to choose, a greatly expanded data base...and an expanded corps of interested and experienced persons concerned with social studies improvement."[6] Despite this note of optimism, conceptual linkages to the curriculum politics of the 1970s were apparently lost in the haze of the research-ers desire to put a positive spin on what can only be described as an overarching and growing sense of futility.[7] James Becker, back in 1965, had predicted that social studies was largely unchangeable. As it turned out, he was more or less correct. Institutional obstacles and external reactions exemplified by the MACOS controversy suggested, once again, that reformers face a difficult task in any effort to change social studies.

In 1980, Project SPAN reported that the dominant curriculum pattern of yearlong courses had regained strength, recovering from the temporary changes of the minicourse explosion of the mid-1970s. They described it as a seven-year "expanding environments" sequence (K-6), followed by "contracting environments" (7–9, 10–12). The persistent modal pattern was long familiar and was presented in an earlier chapter of this book. As to the ways in which social stud-ies was being taught, SPAN reported that ever-present commercially published textbooks were the central tool for teaching, and that teachers relied most heavily on lecture and discussion. Nearly two-thirds of secondary social studies teachers reported lecturing at least weekly, or daily, while 60 percent reported using discussion daily, and another 30 percent "at least once a week." Discussion likely involved informal talking, question and answer recitation, and give and take. Many other teaching techniques were used on a less-frequent basis, including student reports, library work, role-plays, simulations, and use of "hands-on" materials.[8]

Irving Morrissett, who had participated in the SPAN survey, con-ducted an updated assessment of the status of the field in the mid-1980s, with data from 1985 to 1986. Despite certain commonalities, he found, "a great diversity of practices and requirements in social studies exists" among the states and school districts. He also found a great deal of variation in the degree of state power and influence, ranging from rather complete mandates to little or nothing. The prin-cipal "flavor," however, was a strong trend toward state-prescribed standards, about what teachers, students, and to a lesser extent, courses must do. Moreover, the trend in many states was a move back to the old "tried and true" courses, approaches, and materials. In fact, while many states reported the creation of new standards or guidelines for social studies, many other states were instituting some kind of competency testing and a shift toward a historical focus. The most frequently mentioned new course requirement was economics, with many states indicating a "free enterprise" emphasis. The second most frequent course change was institution of global education courses. A frequent complaint concerned the low status of or deemphasis on social studies, or competition with other subjects, mainly science and math. On the whole, the trend was toward institution of more state requirements, a tightening of graduation requirements, more prescripts for teacher certification and training, and increased course requirements in the schools.[9]

One interesting outside perspective on social studies theory and practice in US secondary schools was provided by two Australians, Michael Elliott and Kerry Kennedy, who spent over a year studying and observing social studies in the United States. Before their visit, the two had garnered distinct impressions of social studies in the United States based on reading a range of methods textbooks, the journal *Social Education*, and by talking with a number of educators from the United States who had visited Australia. Following their visit and firsthand observations, they found what they described as "a considerable 'lack of fit' between our expectations and the classroom practices we observed." Though they did see some excellent teaching, their more realistic views following their year in the United States were revealing and, undoubtedly, quite disappointing. Among their observations:

1. We have not seen much teaching organized around concepts. Most courses of study (especially history courses) emphasize a chronological approach...In almost all of the history classes we observed, the textbook has played a dominant role.
2. The social studies is primarily seen as a collection of single disciplines, taught separately, with history and government predominating. In many states, mandated requirements help to ensure the perpetuation of this single subject emphasis.
3. Much, if not most, social studies teaching is expository in nature. The lecture appears to permeate practice at the secondary level.
4. In nearly all the schools we have visited, the curriculum has been determined long before it is presented to students in the classroom. Such practices seem to work against the chance that the needs and interests of students will be incorporated into what is taught.
5. No matter how content is organized and presented in a social studies classroom, there is always an element related to values issues: but such issues are rarely explored.[10]

These observations reflected the general lack of success of attempts to reform social studies. As another writer put it, diffusion of new materials does not equal change, and reformers often overlook what teachers and students are already doing, to their peril.[11]

Beyond status reports, there were also a number of studies that gave attention to teachers, as improving teachers had become part of the conventional wisdom for improving schools. A special issue of *Social Education* presented a profile of social studies teachers and led to the following general conclusions: 75 percent were moderately or very religious; 80 percent had traveled outside the United States at least once; an overwhelming majority were white and male; more men than women enter teaching, and men were more likely to leave; 75 percent had in-service training in the previous two years; they participate in political activities at a higher rate than the general public; they both enjoy teaching and take pride in their work, yet one-third would consider leaving the profession; they enjoy interacting with students; and, their political and educational views are similar to those of the general public.[12]

More revealing of the realities of teachers' working lives was a book by a professor who returned to the classroom as a teacher and wrote about his experiences. In *900 Shows a Year*, Stuart B. Palonsky described teaching as a difficult, demanding job. He found that there never seemed to be enough time to prepare for classes, and that it was not possible for teachers to assign as much work as necessary because there was not enough time to grade the papers. The school lacked an academic focus, a cohesive curricula, or an agreed-upon plan, leaving teachers to conclude that they were on their own. Teachers spent most of their working lives away from colleagues, supervisors, administrators, or other adults, delivering 900 classes each year. Moreover, teachers rarely discussed teaching. "Their conversations were typical of those who were without power in large organizations: irreverent, sometimes crude, and filled with gossip and rumors."

The faculty, it seemed, was often united by little more than a common bell schedule. Bells defined the teacher's working day, telling the teacher when to begin a class, when it ended, when to eat lunch, "when you could have coffee; and when you could go to the lavatory." According to administrators and supervisors, "good teaching was bell-to-bell teaching." Administrators seemed as concerned with order as with instruction. Emphasis on discipline seemed to be based on an implicit assumption that if school masters were not vigilant, "the barely controlled energy of adolescents would explode." Teachers sensed that the school treated them poorly with a pattern of rudeness and minor insults: classes were routinely interrupted, conferences scheduled without consultation, teaching recognized only when unsatisfactory, and teachers could not leave the campus on their own during school. Other teachers advised Palonsky to "avoid controversy and to cover myself at all times." Moreover, through the school's approaches to learning, its course offerings and tracking system, some students learned that they were "dumb" or "stupid," and teachers generally reinforced the pattern of ability grouping offering the lower track students "watered-down" courses with less-provocative reading and lower expectations.[13]

Still other work focused on students. One important article, especially for the question it posed, reported on why kids do not like social studies. Based on interviews with students, the authors found that students appeared not to consider social studies very important, and that it seemed to have little meaning for their future lives. Their attitude was generally one of indifference. As a correspondent later pointed out, it was essentially a finding that the content they were taught was not perceived as meaningful.[14]

Others were beginning to address what seemed perennial dilemmas of the social studies field. Howard Mehlinger described several "gulfs" in social studies, including the gulf between a liberal leaning profession and a more conservative public seemingly bent on censorship; a gulf between social studies leaders, mainly professors, and classroom teachers who saw little relevance in theories to daily practice in schools; and the gulf between social studies specialists and academic scholars who too often moved into distant and hostile camps. In an attempt to deal with these dilemmas, Fred M. Newmann called for creating a common agenda focused on depth in the curriculum, student engagement in the classroom, and collegiality among teachers.[15]

Constancy and Change

Given the findings of numerous research studies suggesting that the unprecedented attention to reform brought little lasting change, it may be helpful to reexamine and reframe the research findings in a search for deeper understanding. Continuity in the mode of instruction, as seen in the persistence of certain low-level instructional practices and the infrequency of meaningful approaches to learning, results in a general lack of student interest in social studies classes and is the greatest single problem facing the social studies field. I am calling this persistence of instructional practice the grammar of social studies.

Globally, the grammar includes a wide range of factors that stand in the way of meaningful teaching and learning occurring in more social studies classrooms. These factors, the prevailing conditions in schools and classrooms, tend to inhibit the possibility of meaningful learning. Meaningful learning in social studies refers to teaching and learning practices that include critical thinking, inquiry, and consideration of persistent social issues and diverse perspectives. It refers to a variety of approaches that emphasize raising and pursuing questions about the ideas and concepts encountered in the curriculum, examining diverse perspectives, considering values, evaluating and generating interpretations, developing hypotheses, and drawing tentative conclusions based on evidence. In short, meaningful learning embodies what Fred Newmann and others have labeled "thoughtful" or "authentic" approaches to teaching.[16]

Despite the best efforts of social studies reformers over many years, the grammar of social studies has largely inhibited the growth and spread of meaningful learning in social studies classrooms. In what follows, we will examine several of the main factors, in school and out, that make up the grammar of social studies and that contribute to curriculum constancy. Following that, I will discuss the failure of the new and newer social studies, and explore possibilities for the future of the field.

Of course, the grammar of social studies is not a new problem. A number of scholars over the years have written about the issue of classroom constancy under a variety of names. In the 1950s, J. D. McAulay reported from a study of classrooms and teachers that while teachers knew the buzzwords of education, they could not put the words into practice.[17] In the 1960s, Bellack and colleagues examined the language of the classroom, finding that teacher talk, focused on recitation of factual meanings, takes up 70 to 80 percent of classroom time. Seymour B. Sarason examined the school culture and the problem of change and concluded that the culture of the school provided major impediments to reform.[18] In the late 1960s, two historians discussed earlier, Hoetker and Ahlbrand, investigated the persistence of recitation and argued that educational procedure was marked, historically, by continuity and routine and most often focused on a question and answer format in which students were asked to recite factual information from texts.[19]

During the 1980s and 1990s, a number of scholars devoted attention to the problem of change and the resiliency of classroom constancy, the persistence of relatively low levels of instruction centered on textbooks, worksheets, and teacher talk. Larry Cuban's work, mentioned earlier, examined the persistent patterns in how teachers taught and found a remarkably stable pattern of classroom constancy. Linda McNeil studied contemporary patterns of instruction during the 1980s and found evidence that many teachers engage in what she called "defensive teaching" in which teachers simplify content and reduce demands on students in return for classroom order and minimal student compliance on assignments, thus controlling students by limiting and fragmenting classroom knowledge.[20] And, in a slim volume examining a century of school reform, David Tyack and Larry Cuban explored the tendency of schools as an institution to deflect a variety of reforms and theorized that many attempts at reform made little headway because of what they called "the grammar of schooling," as discussed in a previous chapter. The "grammar" as they described it includes many standard features of schooling such as a bell schedule, division of students into subject-centered or graded classes, and emphasis on efficiency—features that have become ingrained as the common formula for schooling.[21]

In more recent years, several scholars in social studies have addressed issues related to classroom constancy and the persistence of low-level teaching in social studies classrooms from different researcher perspectives. Keith C. Barton and Linda S. Levstik asked, "Why don't more teachers engage students in interpretation?" and found that many teachers do not because it conflicts with their "two primary tasks: controlling students' behavior and covering content." They argued that those teachers who do choose inquiry and interpretation have different purposes that are not well served by a focus on content and control, and that emphasis on the citizenship goal of preparing students for participation in a pluralist democracy required going beyond coverage and control.[22]

Catherine Cornbleth examined the issue of constraints on teaching, concluding that teachers would be well advised to cope with climates of constraint by exercising their professional options as far as possible in their own classrooms and by pursuing more limited goals that support them in that quest, such as forming support groups with like-minded colleagues. Diana Hess investigated questions surrounding the lack of controversial issues discussion in social studies classrooms and argued that with directed effort, teachers can learn to facilitate good discussions as an essential means to democratic empowerment. Indeed, she has strongly suggested that thoughtful discussion of controversial public issues can lead to democratic empowerment.[23]

Unfortunately, recent research suggests that classroom discussion of controversial issues has decreased in the current era of high-stakes testing and that the accountability movement has intensified the tendency toward superficial coverage of content making teachers less likely to experiment with alternative pedagogies.[24] Moreover, in a recent field study John Saye and a collaborative team of researchers found that high levels of meaningful pedagogy were quite rare in the nation's social studies classrooms, and that very few teachers exhibited a substantial level of authentic pedagogy.[25]

In short, the grammar of social studies, the persistence of low-level forms of instruction that leave the vast majority of students uninterested, is the most serious problem in the field. It undermines every effort at improvement. While other questions are important, that is, questions of definition and rationale, content selection and focus, methods, and so on, it is clear from the history of the field that the grammar is more than a "puzzle," and that it could more appropriately be called a tragic failure. Innovative and engaging approaches to teaching social studies are well established with thorough grounding and development from several theoretical perspectives. Yet, the constancy of low-level classroom practice appears unyielding.

In this regard, the era of the new social studies and its aftermath serves as an instructive case study. The founders and advocates of the curriculum reform movement envisioned a "revolution" in the teaching of social studies that never really materialized. They raised expectations, only to have their hopes and dreams dashed by hard experience with the realities of schooling. During the 1990s, several scholars who were leading participants in the new social studies projects examined its failure to live up to expectations. Several wished they had done some things differently, but most agreed that expectations were raised far beyond what could realistically be expected.[26]

Moreover, a point we must not forget, the nature of the attempted reform matters. Its congruence with established patterns and its relative ease of adoption can make a huge difference in the rate and acceptance of change. The new social studies emerged as a response to a perceived external threat and to the perception of anti-intellectualism and quackery in public schools. University scholars served as the model for reform. However, the patterns of inquiry and concepts drawn from university scholarship, which might be seen as logical components of the "church of reason," were not congruent with the traditions and culture of the schools.[27] The reform, linked to empire, and the military-industrial-academic-complex that served its interests, was artificially induced and imposed from above, an innovative "fix" or solution for schools that were assumed to be dysfunctional. In a loosely coupled system, with a long tradition of local control, relatively few in the schools bought into the reform.

The Grammar of Social Studies

The weight of historical evidence reviewed for this chapter and presented in the two volumes of this history of the new social studies strongly suggests that curriculum reforms aimed at improving social studies instruction in schools are unlikely to lead to significant or major changes toward meaningful learning. In part this is due to the fact that social studies teaching occurs in a context that tends to severely limit the possibility of change. Despite the best efforts of reformers over many years, the grammar of schooling has largely inhibited the growth and spread of meaningful learning in social studies classrooms. In the remainder of this chapter, we examine several of the main factors, in school and out, that make up the grammar of social studies and that contribute to curriculum constancy. Key elements of the grammar consist of facets related to the curriculum, teachers, textbooks, instructional practices, students, administrators, teacher education, and the culture of school and society.

The Curriculum. In the curriculum, traditional subject matter linked to the disciplines has staying power.[28] Despite rhetorical struggles among interest groups in social studies, traditional approaches to history, geography, and government are especially dominant. In schools, there is historically minimal attention to issues. Problems of Democracy, which had been a major component of the social studies in many schools, was in decline, hampered by its old fogey image, and eclipsed the social science emphasis brought with the new social studies. Reform movements can bring temporary changes in subject matter, which are easier to implement than changes in classroom practice. The new and newer social studies did result in a temporary shift toward more emphasis on the other social sciences, the minicourse explosion, and an emphasis on relevance, but the scope and sequence had returned to the modal pattern in most areas by 1980. In the lower grades, the expanding horizons model remained dominant, along with the persistence of the "holiday curriculum." Despite local control, we had what amounted to a national curriculum via independent adoption of textbooks from a pool of similar books.

Thus, despite temporary shifts, the subject matter of the curriculum remained relatively constant.

Teachers. Teachers are controlled, for the most part, by school system administrators and by parent, student, and teacher expectations. Though teachers are the "key" to what happens in classrooms, there is great variability in teacher experience, style, and quality. Most teachers tend to focus on coverage of the content of the curriculum and control of the students under their charge. Teachers are expected to cover the curricular content thoroughly and to manage large groups of uninterested students. Many administrators evaluate teachers on the basis of their classroom control.[29] Few teachers use inquiry or reflective approaches in their classrooms. The system offers few incentives for innovation, and the reward system in schools and absence of a meaningful career ladder are not conducive to change. While teachers and professional organizations devote some attention to the academic freedom needed for sustained innovation, and there is some support in many districts, the process of teacher socialization imposes constraints.[30] According to one perceptive teacher, "You have to survive in the community in which you teach. They are paying your salary...so they have the right...to keep certain things out of the school."[31] Finally, teachers tend to value stability and what works over innovation or enacting a purposeful program. Teachers are also constrained by common images of teaching and school that fit a traditional model, with the teacher in charge and doing most of the talking, and the textbook as the backbone of the course, if not the sole source of information. In recent years, with the introduction of standards and testing, teachers are also evaluated by student scores on standardized achievement tests, further reinforcing the mandate for coverage.

Textbooks. The predominant tools or technology of instruction include textbooks, films, worksheets, and other media. The heavy, one volume history or social studies textbook is the most common resource in social studies classrooms and is frequently treated as the main source of content, and often the final arbiter of truth. Teachers find that textbooks are relatively easy to use and that they provide a base of information and material that can be easily covered in class and tested. Textbooks are a commodity strongly influenced and shaped by market forces and by the influence of critics and interest groups via the textbook adoption process.[32] They present a rather lifeless depiction of the social world of past and present and devote very little attention to issues or problems. Moreover, most textbooks are not conducive to inquiry or divergent interpretations. In American history, for example, they present "an image of America sculpted and sanded down," devoid of controversy and great issues, "whitewashing" and sanitizing war and other dilemmas, and frequently embodying "lies," omissions, and distortions.[33] Innovative, nontext materials of the type produced during the era of the new social studies are harder to manage and use. While computers have potential as an instructional tool, their typical use has failed to live up to the much-hyped potential for instructional change. Finally, the persistence of a codified textbook adoption process that regulates their production, appropriately labeled "the great textbook machine,"[34] provides a strong barrier to reform.

Instructional Practices. Instruction in social studies is marked by the persistence of traditional patterns in which teacher talk is dominant.[35] Studies of classroom interaction show that teacher talk takes up 70 to 80 percent of classroom time, mostly in large group instruction, and that the major activity of teachers is recitation, asking and reacting to questions that call for factual answers from students. Much of teacher and student time is also spent on noninstructional activities such as bureaucratic routines and maintaining order. Classroom interaction patterns tend to be governed by a set of rules in which teacher talk is dominant, students respond to teacher solicitations, and the largest proportion of discourse involves factual meanings.[36] Recitation appears to be functional for most teachers as a means of covering content, maintaining control, and meeting the demands of the system and its administrators. Student expectations also play a strong role in reinforcing instructional patterns and make up a major part of the teacher's social system. Student expectations are shaped largely by prior instruction that has been traditional and textbook centered. For students, recitation and textbook-oriented teaching is simply "the way it spozed to be." It has persisted as the dominant instructional pattern for more than a century, and it is part of what Tyack and Cuban have called the grammar of schooling.[37] The grammar of schooling includes basic institutional patters such as the ways that "schools divide time and space, classify students and allocate them to classrooms, splinter knowledge into 'subjects' and award grades and credits," which are largely taken for granted as "the way schools are."[38] For many teachers, it appears that recitation is also a form of "defensive teaching," a coping strategy in which teachers "simplify content and reduce demands on students in return for classroom order and minimal student compliance," though its use may vary depending on school climate.[39] Moreover, recent observational studies have documented the virtual absence of meaningful discussion in social studies classes.[40] The persistence of recitation means that in most classrooms, there is very little use of inquiry, interpretation, or open-ended discourse.

Students. Students, like their teachers, bring a range of aptitudes, attitudes, and abilities with them to school. Unfortunately, many students fail to see the relevance and importance of the material studied in school, and this is especially true in social studies. That lack of relevance was captured in the statement of one student who responded to a teacher query, "I heard the question, I just don't care."[41] Problems with student attitudes and the perceived lack of relevance of social studies is made worse by the fact that students are tracked into ability groups by the school system, sorted by their supposed abilities and performance. However, this sorting, which usually leads to differentiated curriculum, with low-track classes receiving the most perfunctory type of instruction, is weakly justified and sloppily carried out. Teachers, students, administrators, and parents generally seem to accept ability grouping as one of the commonplace features of schooling, even though there is a good deal of literature critiquing the practice and the limitations it often places on student growth.[42] A preponderance of evidence suggests that students do not like social studies very much, that most find it boring.[43] While this would seem to make curricular innovation in social studies a priority, in most cases it has not worked out that way.

Administrators. Administrators tend to want stability. While many administrators lend rhetorical support to reform and innovation in the classroom, most try to avoid conflict and controversy, integral to meaningful approaches to social studies, whenever possible partly because it is difficult and time consuming. Despite claims to being a democratic institution and the hope of serving society as an "embryonic democracy," the schools tend to be top-down, hierarchical, and undemocratic. Moreover, administrators and curriculum supervisors are viewed by teachers as out-of-touch with the realities of classrooms. Most administrative supervision is rather perfunctory, focused on coverage of content and control, and offering little authentic help to teachers. Some administrators evaluate teaching on the basis of adherence to an oversimplified "Hunterized" protocol of seven steps thought to be associated with effective teaching, even though the Hunter model has been severely criticized and its use may stand in the way of more meaningful approaches such as inquiry and other reflective teaching strategies.[44] Administrative directives such as writing behavioral objectives, common during the 1970s and 1980s, and writing the standard being covered on the board in recent years are viewed by teachers as "a waste of time" and do little to promote more effective teaching.[45] Moreover, the business efficiency models that are often applied to school administration contribute to a lack of focus on improving classroom practices and instead tend to substitute compliance, control, and rising test scores for meaningful learning. Finally, there is considerable inertia in the loosely coupled educational system and the traditional of local control. Though state and federal influence has grown considerably in the era of standards and accountability, its main impact has been to reify traditional teaching practices.

Teacher Education. Teacher education, certification, and in-service education has also largely failed to lead to meaningful change in social studies classrooms. While some of what goes on in teacher education programs is helpful to beginning teachers, such programs are marked either by a heavy focus on theory, or an emphasis on providing beginning teachers with practical strategies for survival via a "bag of tricks" approach. While many beginning teachers find some of their teacher preparation coursework and field experiences very helpful, others report that much of what they learned is "ivory tower" theory that does not work in the "real world" of the schools. Teacher education programs have long been criticized for their anti-intellectualism or their technocratic rationality, a focus on what to do, methodologies, rather than development of a full-bodied rationale connected to practice. In-service programs, often selected by administrators, frequently have a generalist focus and are viewed by many teachers as another "waste of time."[46] During the era of the new social studies, teacher education programs were slow to infuse the inquiry methods championed by reformers. Reformers purposefully chose to target teachers directly and to bypass the teacher education and certification establishment, giving only minor roles to education professors and virtually none to credentialing agencies. In hindsight, this was a mistake.[47] Finally, professional development in the form of continuing education is not seen as important in the school social system that sanctions and rewards teachers. The school as a social system largely controls teacher choices and behaviors.[48]

Culture of the School. Part of the resistance to change in social studies is related to the culture of the school.[49] Schools are machine-like institutions that sort students by their supposed ability levels and acculturate them for life and work in capitalist America, in a society stratified by race, class, and gender. Though schools simultaneously transmit messages of socialization and countersocialization, the socializing function is dominant. Socialization occurs on at least two levels: the inculcation of American values and ideology, and behavior socialization whereby students learn to follow instructions and school rules, and learn from authorities, teachers, and texts. Active citizenship, inquiry learning, and other intellectually engaging approaches to social studies instruction are fundamentally inconsistent with the enculturation of students into the American ideology of the modern state, which is bureaucratically organized for social stability and control. Stability is assured via a passive citizenry, which schools have, ironically, helped to create. Thus, apathy, indifference, boredom, and following instructions are all part of the larger web of enculturation. As Jules Henry reminds us, "School is an institution for drilling children in cultural orientations."[50] In the political economy of schooling, schools function for purposes of social efficiency. They embody principles of Taylorism with the aim of producing human capital. The physical structure of the school and its curriculum, built on industrial era assumptions, employs an egg-crate design and variations of the platoon system along with a system of buzzers and bells—a clockwork that acculturates students for work in a similar economic system.[51]

The administrative and organizational structure of the school replicates the hierarchical pattern of business and other similar institutions. School leadership is increasingly patterned after a business model, with specific aspects of the current reform focused on standards and testing borrowed directly from principles of business efficiency.[52] Social studies reform during the era of the new social studies exhibited the clash of two cultures, the culture of the school and the culture of the university, which were fundamentally incompatible because of their differing realities. Reformers, steeped in the culture of the university, made mistaken assumptions about students, teachers, and the culture of schooling based upon their experiences in the culture of the university. They assumed that students were naturally curious about the questions investigated by social scientists and that similar forms of inquiry would work in schools. They assumed that teachers lived lives of intellectual curiosity similar to their own, and that intellectualized approaches to the subject matter would have great appeal to teachers. Finally, they adopted a technological concept of innovation that defined school reform as a process of merely replacing the teacher's methodologies and instructional materials with their own version, an approach that conceived of the school as something similar to a weapons system to be modified for a more effective attack on ignorance and anti-intellectualism.

Social Context. In the larger context, schools are driven by the hegemony of dominant interests in society. Schooling is the machine of the state, reproducing social patterns and the larger culture. The social context that gave rise to the new social studies reforms was focused on excellence and national security. Over time, the focus shifted to social problems and social change by the late 1960s, then to a new and virulent conservatism by the mid-1970s. With each change in cultural emphasis, the rhetoric of school reform shifted. Despite these shifts, the underlying grammar of social studies remained largely unchanged, leading several analysts to conclude that significant change would only come about with substantial change in the structure of society.[53] Cultural constraints also take very real political form in controversies over textbooks, materials, and approaches to teaching. During the early 1970s, as controversies over the new social studies were gathering steam, Ted Fenton described a social studies field held hostage by a "nationwide conspiracy" of conservative critics and organizations. Much later, Jerome Bruner suggested that behind the limited success of the reform was his perception that many Americans do not want to question.[54] Moreover, a significant number of parents do not support the aims of inquiry or of fostering meaningful discussion.[55]

The culture of American school and society is dominated by its capitalist/industrial structure. Anthropologist Jules Henry once wrote that the essential characteristic of American culture is its "drivenness." We are driven by "achievement, competitive, profit, and mobility drives, and the drives for security and a higher standard of living." The school, in American culture, becomes a place "where children are drilled in cultural orientations" and in which subject matter becomes "the instrument for instilling them," fettering and freeing at the same time, but insistently drilling children with messages that drive us away from the "essential nightmare" of failure and toward success in social and economic terms.[56] The market economy promotes aims directly related to obtaining credentials and preparing for the workplace and thus tends to undervalue civic education. A recent survey of adults in the United States lends support to the pervasive influence of this orientation. Moreover, concerns over student performance in math and science have contributed to the devaluation of civic education.[57]

Given the wide range of factors serving as barriers to reform, what is remarkable is not that the new social studies did not live up to the unrealistic expectations of some of its major advocates, but that it enjoyed the level of success that it did achieve.

Failure of the New and Newer Social Studies

In reflecting on the legacy of the new social studies, it seems that curriculum change in social studies is possible but difficult to sustain and spread beyond a small group of adherents. The ultimate failure of new social studies reform efforts to have greater influence on classroom practice is related to a multifaceted context that makes any reform difficult. As to the extent of adoption of new social studies materials, terminology, and practices, there is little evidence that the adoption of materials got very far. Analysts of the NSF case studies reported that fewer than 20 percent of teachers heard of or used the materials. John Haas, who authored the most complete previous history of the new social studies, suggested that it had an influence on, at most, 5 percent of teachers. Nonetheless, a number of studies found that teachers reported using the approaches associated with the new social studies movement, particularly inquiry, concepts, and simulation games. Moreover, respondents to one survey agreed that teaching styles were materially influenced by the new social studies projects, though the projects themselves had only minimal influence on textbook selection and materials adoption. Furthermore, they reported very limited use of the new projects in schools. Yet, a number of projects did wield influence, among them the High School Geography Project, the Carnegie Mellon Social Studies Project, Sociological Resources for the Social Studies, American Political Behavior, and the Public Issues Series of the Harvard Project. At the elementary level, among the most influential were MACOS, the Taba Social Studies Program, and Senesh's *Our Working World*.[58] Evidence from other sources indicates that the movement's terminology had a wider though cursory effect. So, it is clear that the new social studies reform was not a total disaster. Nonetheless, it fell short of the unrealistically ambitious expectations of its strongest proponents and staunchest advocates. Reasons for its failure to reach expectations relate to the sociopolitical context of the 1960s and early 1970s, the nature of the reforms proposed, and key attributes of the school as an institution as well as elements of the culture in which teaching and learning take place.

The social, political, and cultural context of schooling powerfully influenced the origins of the new social studies and hastened its decline. As we have seen, the new social studies was a stepchild of Sputnik. It had origins in the curriculum politics of the cold war, and its general orientation was, in part, a legacy of manpower studies conducted by the CIA, and of the general climate of the times favoring the academic disciplines and taking a critical stance toward progressivism and its meliorist focus aimed at social progress. From 1968 onward, the social studies was confronted by a new context created by protests against the Vietnam war, the civil rights movement, a youth rebellion, a new focus on the problems of the disadvantaged both in school and out, the widespread alienation of youth, and the paradox created by the distance between purported national values and social realities. As a consequence, the society, and curriculum reform projects, were subject to a more critical assessment. Instead of being seen as a smoothly functioning institution operating for the benefit of all, schools were increasingly viewed as problematic.

Another major factor in the failure of the new social studies was related to the nature of the reforms proposed. The reforms were largely aimed at replacing the existing social studies curriculum, a revolutionary rather than evolutionary intent. Yet, taken as a program, the new social studies projects and materials did not offer a coherent alternative to what had become the standard scope and sequence and the traditional approach to teaching relying on textbooks, lecture, seatwork, discussion, and tests. There was no overall plan or scope and sequence alternative proposed as part of the reform. In addition, many of the reform projects and the materials generated lacked a strong rationale or a clear purpose, an element that is crucial for any reform's success.[59] Though almost all of the materials that resulted from the projects were of high quality, their interest generating power was "misperceived" by many teachers who adopted the materials. As it turned out, their use frequently required thoughtful and committed teacher preparation and did not result in a magical and automatic increase in student interest.[60] Many of the projects created materials especially for the same slot in the school program, senior year social science electives, thus limiting their influence in the total school program.[61] Moreover, many of the materials created were not highly readable for the majority of students. Average and below-average students were generally not well served by the materials.

The reformers and project directors also made unarticulated and mistaken assumptions about the culture of schooling. They assumed that the project materials and their conceptualization would be compatible with the prevailing culture of the schools. Unfortunately, this turned out not to be the case. The philosophy and materials produced were largely incompatible with the prevailing culture of schools. In fact, one analyst suggested that the new social studies movement proceeded in the absence of a well-developed and explicit theory or conception of the social foundations of schools and schooling. The architects of the new social studies assumed that old content could be extracted and replaced with new content; that if social studies teachers could be taught to think seriously about their work, they would adopt the new reforms; and, that schooling as an institution served functions of social equality, individual development, and social integration.

Unfortunately, on the whole, these assumptions were faulty. The integrative function was predominant, with schools serving to socialize students to a society characterized by extensive social stratification. Schools serve as selection and certification agencies, measuring, sorting, and labeling students. Thus, instructional materials, teaching practices, and the content itself became mechanisms for the process of socialization and were functional in the school environment as they contributed to the process of sorting and labeling. Reforms in social studies were valued, at least in part, for the degree to which they were compatible with this function. As Jerome Bruner recently observed, "American education is about what you know and can achieve, and can be tested on." Many key elements of the new social studies were inherently at odds with this basic purpose and sociocultural function of schooling.[62] In Bruner's words, "It didn't fit."[63]

From a critical perspective, the discipline-centered curricula created by the majority of new social studies projects served to draw a veil between students and more immediate concerns in the community. The projects generally focused upon forms of knowledge that moved students away from the particular and the local. The scientific and structural nature of the knowledge encapsulated in the reform served the latent function of socializing students into a way of thinking that too frequently discouraged students from making connections with everyday realities. Detachment from social relationships can make those relationships less amenable to individual control and gives greater power and legitimacy to experts who interpret reality. Thus, the new social studies could be seen as a curriculum driven by secondary abstractions that move students away from face-to-face confrontation with value dilemmas and conflict situations.[64] Moreover, creation of teacher-proof materials treated teachers as mere technicians. By and large, the new social studies projects did not ask teachers to arrive at their own philosophical rationale for social studies and to develop their own congruent approaches to teaching. Instead, teachers were often offered the opportunity to implement materials created by university researchers, an opportunity proffered from above. Hence, this was an approach to reform that was in many instances, undemocratic.

The reform plan under which these new social studies programs were implemented was equally flawed. According to many postmortem evaluations, the new social studies movement and other curriculum reform efforts of the time made serious strategic errors. It was a top-down, hierarchical approach to reform designed by university researchers who had little experience in schools. Teachers and professors of education were seldom involved in the design of the materials. A Rand study of the process of educational change suggested that district-level support and commitment were crucial, and that projects designed by "outside experts," or which utilized commercially prepared materials, generally failed to gather the necessary support.[65] Another evaluation study implied that reformers sought to influence too many schools, that objectives and techniques were not sharply defined, that many projects failed to reach clear agreement on their specific purpose, nature, and limitations. Those projects that were most successful had a clear operating design and a charismatic, hard-working, and omnipresent director.[66]

Critical aspects of the school as an institution also created obstacles to the success of the reform movement and made it probable that teachers would stick with the more conventional teaching techniques, or return to them after a period of experimentation. The reformers generally seemed to hold naïve conceptions on the perspectives of teachers and students and the inertia and persistence of traditional teaching practices. As Bruner later recalled, "Excessive optimism...[we were] idealistically optimistic about what could be done."[67] Yet, most teachers were severely constrained by the conditions under which they worked: five classes a day, thirty or forty students per class, two or three preparations per night, and additional nonteaching duties. Difficult to change institutional factors, which Tyack and Cuban have called the grammar of schooling, made it hard for teachers to embrace new ways, even when they desired to.[68] Moreover, students, other teachers, parents, and most administrators expected conventional forms of instruction. By the 1970s, many of the teachers who used new social studies materials had come to regard the programs as "a parade of fads."[69]

The newer social studies, which materialized in the late 1960s, was in many respects a revitalized, reconstructionist-oriented progressive education. With the new social studies it shared a pedagogical preference for discovery or inquiry, but there the similarities ended. The newer social studies were motivated by the very social transformations and turmoil that made the new social studies seem less relevant. Where the previous program concentrated on the structure-of-the-disciplines, the newer tendency promoted valuing, relevance, and social activism. During a time of civil rights marches, antiwar protests, student sit-ins, and the sexual revolution, the new social studies appeared outmoded. However, the newer movement did share a comparable fate with its predecessor. Its impact on classrooms was equally limited.

Beyond the nature of the reform and schools as an institution, the politics of the curriculum and the conservative restoration combined in the 1970s to produce a strong reaction to the new and newer social studies that seemed to stop the movement in its tracks, and eventually brought an end to funding. Academic freedom controversies centered on individual teachers and national projects, textbooks, and course materials combined with the back-to-basics movement and business-driven reforms to create a climate that was much less conducive to innovation, eventually resulting in the end of the period of reform.

Several aspects of the era have continuing implications for us today. First, money and power, from the government, foundations, and other sources, seem to readily influence the direction of rhetoric on social studies and may have some influence on curricular content, though they have less influence on pedagogy and entrenched patterns of classroom and school practice. The "grammar of schooling" seems largely resistant to reform.[70]

Second, manpower concerns have played a critical role in the rhetoric and influence of educational reform since the mid-twentieth century and earlier. The perceived need to develop technical manpower to win the cold war in the form of developing more scientists and engineers, and then social scientists and students who could emulate the social scientist mode of thought and research, was a mainstay of the curriculum reform movement. In more recent years, reformers have continued to push for schooling to develop other forms of human capital, with a continued focus on improving performance in math and science. In each case, the direction of reform created a skewed and limited vision of education that largely ignored important value questions and social issues.

A third implication may be found by considering the top-down, scientific model for reform embodied in the new social studies projects, and the science and math reforms that preceded them, which had origins in wartime weapons research. The current reform movement, built around accountability via the imposition of standards and high stakes testing, also employs a top-down, scientific model for reform, though with more significant influence from a business orientation and mentality. In both cases, a link to national security and economic progress is a central component.

Fourth, the inquiry and structure-of-the-disciplines approach common to the era of the new social studies, and the social reconstructionist, issues-oriented approach of the newer social studies have their counterparts today in the current literature of school reform. Moreover, many of the projects of the new social studies "made a worldwide impact" that, in a few cases, is still being felt.[71] The relatively recent interest in authentic pedagogy and constructivism has many similarities to the Brunerian reforms of the new social studies era. The banner of the issues-oriented newer social studies maintains a strong presence in the literature of the field. All of these similarities suggest the cyclical nature of efforts at school reform and reflect the general resistance of educational institutions and practices to change, regardless of its origins or direction.

Conclusion: Reflections on Education for Democracy

The central question haunting social studies is whether classroom instruction can be improved in the direction of meaningful learning. This book has examined two persistent dilemmas that have troubled social studies reform throughout its modern existence: curriculum politics and the entrenched dilemma of classroom constancy. Both dilemmas are represented in the history of the new social studies, a hopeful period of curriculum reform during the 1960s. The first dilemma, curriculum politics, is epitomized by the aftermath of the era of the new social studies in schools and the series of academic freedom controversies that resulted in the end of funding for reform and led to the conservative restoration in schools. As we have seen, the era of the new social studies emphasized inquiry oriented reform supported by unprecedented levels of funding from the National Science Foundation (NSF), the US Office of Education (USOE), private foundations, and other sources. It led to the development of new and innovative curricular materials that promised to significantly improve the intellectual quality of life in social studies classrooms. As materials were published and began to reach more and more classrooms in the late 1960s and early 1970s, conservative critics attacked the reform and the trend toward inquiry and issues, aided by a rising tide of religious fundamentalism.[1] Though the materials and the reform movement from which they arose suffered from many other difficulties, the constraint on academic freedom imposed by controversies was a major factor in their decline and served as a significant turning point in the direction of curricular reform.

The second dilemma centers on classroom constancy, the persistence of low-level practices focusing on textbooks and recitation. The era of the new social studies had significant though limited influence on the improvement of classroom practice, for a relatively short span of time. Status studies from the mid-1970s and beyond found that innovative materials from the new social studies projects were not widely used, and that many teachers had not even heard of the reform. Moreover, researchers documented a virulent pattern of constancy in traditional classroom practices, the persistence of recitation style teaching dominated by teacher talk and textbooks. Inquiry methods and suggestions for student participation ran counter to most teachers' content orientation and the need to maintain order. The best estimates suggest that no more than 5 to 10 percent of teachers used the materials. Interpretations of the failure to reach expectations vary, but coalesce around the inescapable conclusion that significant innovation in social studies is unlikely due to a combination of institutional constraints and politicized attacks on the academic freedom needed for sustained innovation.

Dissonance

A brief review of innovations from the era of the new social studies may shed light on differences between that time and our own. In terms of pedagogy, the period stands out as an exciting time of innovation during which social studies was influenced by a fantastic outpouring of new theory, theory into practice, and innovative materials, most of them still useful. At its best, the era brought diverse perspectives, a new openness, and a dramatic shift toward more active roles for students and teachers. In terms of content, the new social studies unleashed a cornucopia of exciting new topics and subject matter into the school, including rich new social science subject matter, an exciting wave of avant-garde topics, and multicultural social issues. The emphasis from the late 1960s on relevance, activism, and values clarification led to an exciting burst of interest in recent and relevant history, a minicourse explosion emphasizing student choice, and a new freedom heralded by the open school movement and new wave critique. For a time, at least, anything seemed possible.

When contrasted with the emphasis on coverage and control in traditional classrooms, portraits of uninspired teaching from research surveys, and the pervasive impact of standards and high stakes testing, what is most noticeable is the comparative freedom that teachers enjoyed during the era of the new and newer social studies. I believe freedom for teachers is healthy and necessary in a democracy. In today's social studies classrooms, pedagogy is increasingly focused on coverage of textbook content, driven by standards and high stakes testing, and imposed by the business-driven mentality of the current reform and its emphasis on education for social efficiency and development of human capital. In many social studies classrooms today a banking approach is dominant, shaped by a technology of control, marked by democratic unfreedom, neglect of issues and values discussion, narrowing of content, and a deadening climate of increasing irrelevance.[2]

The stark contrast between pedagogic innovations from the era of the new social studies and the dominant trends of the current reform raise deep and disturbing questions related to the purposes of education. Whom shall the schools serve? Who benefits? To what extent are schools serving democratic purposes? The answers to such questions have never been simple or straightforward. However, given recent trends in schooling and in social studies, at this moment the answers are less than hopeful. Increasingly, it seems, schools function as an arm of the military-industrial-complex, they discipline and punish, classify, sort, and segment students, while drilling them in a cultural orientation that stresses competition and success. They reify a market society marked by inequality and oppression, making it seem that the current social order is the natural way of things, socializing but doing little to countersocialize. In contrast, education for democracy would focus on active participation, social criticism, decision making, and emphasize freedom and openness in ways similar to the ethos of the new social studies.[3]

Can We Make a Difference?

The weight of historical evidence reviewed for this book strongly suggests that reforms aimed at improving social studies instruction in schools are unlikely to lead to large-scale transformation. In part this is due to the fact that social studies teaching and learning occurs in a context that tends to severely limit the possibility of change. It is a context that is periodically beset with the searing conflict of curriculum politics, and that is constantly faced with the entrenched dilemmas of schooling. Despite the best efforts of social studies reformers over many years, the grammar of social studies, the persistence of low-level textbook-centered recitation, has largely curtailed the growth and spread of meaningful learning in social studies classrooms. In chapter seven, we examined several of the main factors, in schools and out, that make up the grammar of social studies and that contribute to classroom constancy. Key elements of the grammar consist of factors related to the curriculum, teachers, textbooks, instructional practices, students, administrators, teacher education, and the culture of school and society.

The most serious dilemma of the social studies field is the failure of reform to lead to substantial improvements in classroom practice. Because of a variety of institutional constraints that I have labeled the grammar of social studies, the field seems almost impervious to change.[4] Theories to explain the difficulty of changing social studies are rooted in various explanations: the nature of the reform model, characteristics of the school as an institution, the politics of the curriculum, and the social and cultural context of capitalist, postindustrial America.

As for the first factor, the vagaries of curriculum politics have significantly influenced the direction of social studies reform and practice. Controversies in the aftermath of the new social studies resulted in the end of an unprecedented era of reform. They also marked the beginning of the conservative restoration in schools and society that has led to the gradual replacement of progressive social studies with more traditional versions of the field emphasizing history and geography, and giving less attention to inquiry or issues. When asked to explain the failure of the new social studies Jerome Bruner observed, "We don't really want to know about ourselves…One thing that strikes me about the resistance [to MACOS and the new social studies] is the irony of it…We are the most technologically oriented people but we avoid close inspection of what we're doing."[5] A significant number of Americans do not want to think about difficult matters because it can be gut wrenching. Moreover, curriculum is inherently political. Curricular trends in social studies will continue to be influenced by various interest groups and shifting problems and concerns. Though it may prove difficult, it is possible that seeking common ground could reduce the negative impact of curriculum politics and help contribute to sustained innovation.[6]

The second dilemma of social studies, the entrenched dilemma of classroom constancy, is perhaps even more intractable, considering the massive, diverse, and largely uncoupled nature of schooling in modern society. Though political struggles over the social studies curriculum and the institutionalized grammar of social studies are both a persistent presence providing seemingly insurmountable obstacles to reform, it is important to emphasize possibility.

Developments during the era of the new social studies suggest that innovative materials can make a difference, especially for many teachers and their students. The success of MACOS remains a shining example, "a beacon," demonstrating what is possible, given time, money, creativity, and sustained effort.[7] Moreover, many educational initiatives over the years have had influence and offer hope for the future.[8]

Lasting Impressions

One important message to take away from this book is that teachers have choices. Among the choices are traditional approaches emphasizing history, geography, and civics, taught in a traditional manner; a social science approach, emphasizing inquiry and the structures-of-the-disciplines; a progressive, issues-centered approach, emphasizing reflective teaching and learning; social reconstructionist and critical approaches emphasizing education for social justice; and social efficiency, consensus, or eclectic models. For these choices to matter, teachers have an ethical responsibility to examine the choices and to develop their rationales and classroom practices as thoroughly and deeply as possible. The curricular struggles of the past and present are essentially a morality play, and the curriculum is at all times a "loose, largely unarticulated, and not very tidy compromise."[9] For individual teachers to find their own path within the multiple, sometimes confusing, and often contradictory strands of curricular theory and practice can be a daunting prospect. Thus, deep reflection on theory into practice and rationale is at the heart of thoughtful teaching, and one key to counteracting the "mindlessness" endemic to schools.[10] This is perhaps the single most important lesson for teachers to receive. Clear, thoughtful, and fully developed rationales are important, a key element of professional growth and improvement.

The ideas of past reformers continue to live on in the history and foundations of social studies and in the rhetoric of education. They enlarge the present. To make fully informed curricular and pedagogical decisions, teachers must confront and either dismiss, adapt or learn from the alternatives. The ideas of the great progressives, the ghosts of Dewey, Kilpatrick, Rugg, Counts and their colleagues, though largely shelved, can be fruitfully mined for teaching ideas and rationales.[11] So too can the materials and projects developed during the era of the new and newer social studies.[12] The ideas of Bruner, Fenton, and other theorists of the new social studies, also shelved, remain helpful for today's educators, as do materials from their projects.

A second important message is that freedom is powerful, but fleeting. Academic freedom is an essential ingredient for democracy to flourish. We must passionately defend the integrity of the social studies field and the rights of teachers and curriculum workers to make thoughtful choices from among the alternatives. The freedom of the child to learn and for the teacher to make well-informed curricular decisions within broad parameters is the essence of caring in education and a prerequisite for authentic improvement in instructional practice. Teacher freedom is under attack by the current generation of policymakers and has been under siege throughout the modern era. Organizations of educators should strive to defend teachers as intellectuals, supporting their rights and hard-won privileges. On the other hand, teachers have a responsibility to exercise their freedom wisely and in a well-informed manner.[13]

At this juncture in curriculum history, the forces supporting conserving approaches to education are riding tall in the saddle. They have created a narrowed curriculum emphasizing standards and testing, limiting both the time and climate necessary for inquiry and deep social thinking to flourish. Academic freedom for teachers must necessarily emphasize free speech but should also include curricular time and institutional support for meaningful approaches to learning. As we have seen, academic freedom controversies roiled the educational landscape in the 1970s and contributed to the conservative restoration. Behind the controversies lay a politics of rage and intolerance, a climate in which free thought and inquiry were constrained.[14]

A third message is that over the history of the field, discipline-based approaches seem to have staying power. In part, this may be related to the fact that the disciplines have a large number of eager advocates in colleges and universities across the nation, fans among the populace, and allies in the teaching field. It is also a reflection of the fact that social studies educators and scholars often get little respect outside schools of education. The trouble with advocating any one discipline as the core for social studies is it ignores the balance required for the broad education of citizens. Each of the social sciences contributes to our knowledge base, to our cache of concepts, and to our ways of knowing. Together they form an interdisciplinary web from which all students can learn.

Moreover, as they are currently configured for schooling, discipline-based approaches with emphasis on coverage and content acquisition often tend to diminish attention to issues and too frequently limit critical questions about our social and economic systems. As Harold Rugg, the legendary advocate for an issues-centered curriculum once wrote, "To keep issues out of the school, therefore, is to keep thought out of it; it is to keep life out of it."[15] A thoughtful melding of inquiry and issues within a mandate for depth may prove very powerful, that is, disciplined inquiry within an issues-centered frame in which studies are linked to persistent issues of democratic life.

Classroom constancy, the grammar of social studies, and institutional resistance to reform does not mean that schools cannot be changed. As Bruner recently observed, "Schooling has changed" over the years, but there is a "built-in resistance to looking at the process." Most often, "the focus is on the product...[and] nobody stops to look at the long range."[16] Hence, it may be possible for professional organizations such as the National Council for the Social Studies (NCSS) to play, simultaneously, the role of activist for a broad and modern approach to the field, and the role of peacemaker, seeking common ground among interest groups with a stake in the future of social studies. Though compromise may seem unlikely given the field's history, it is possible that an ecumenical reform initiative could center on concerns over textbooks; in-depth student engagement with rich content; authentic and interactive pedagogy; and, the rights of teachers, curriculum makers, and local communities to lead the way in making informed curricular decisions.

In the end, we return to questions of value, questions on the purposes of education in a democratic society. As it stands today, social studies education is in the iron grip of a power game, roiled by curriculum politics, stifled by a mean spirited antidemocratic top-down reform. Ironically, social studies instruction in many schools is held hostage by the pressure for too much coverage and has devolved into a mad rush through the textbook to prepare students for standardized tests.[17] In recent decades, powerful conservative groups with deep pockets have wielded increasing influence supporting a movement away from progressive social studies and toward a more traditional, academic, and conserving approach. In cooperation with a national consensus endorsing application of business principles to schooling, they have created a mechanism of standards and testing fortified with pacing guides that is squeezing the life-blood out of social studies, with too much pressure for coverage of content, and far too little encouragement in the form of space, materials, or curricular time for inquiry, issues, or other meaningful approaches to flourish.

The standards and testing machine functions as a major constraint on freedom to question and often serves to stifle development of engaging pedagogic styles.

If we are committed to education for democracy, it means that we need to develop policies that will support teachers in their pursuit of inquiry-oriented and issues-centered approaches to teaching and learning. The two make a compelling combination when blended in ways that emphasize motivation, interest, and relevance to students' lives. The era of the new and newer social studies offers substantive food for thought regarding the possibility of an approach that seamlessly blends inquiry and issues, Bruner and Dewey, in a powerful form of education for democracy.

Making headway on the central dilemmas of social studies reform, the vagaries of curriculum politics and the grammar of social studies, will require a renewed commitment, and a reorientation focused on what is best for student learning. It is important if we care about our future, the future of our schools, and the prospects for our experiment in democracy.

Abbreviations Used in the Text

ACLU	American Civil Liberties Union
ACT	American College Testing Program, Inc.
AEI	American Enterprise Institute
AHA	American Historical Association
CBE	Council for Basic Education
CDA	Curriculum Development Associates
CIA	Central Intelligence Agency
CME	Citizens for Moral Education
CST	Committee on Science and Technology
EDC	Education Development Center, Inc.
ESI	Educational Services Incorporated
FACE	Florida Action Committee for Education
GAO	General Accounting Office
HSGP	High School Geography Project
ICLU	Indiana Civil Liberties Union
IGE	Individually Guided Instruction
MACOS	Man: A Course of Study
MIT	Massachusetts Institute of Technology
NAACP	National Association for the Advancement of Colored People
NAM	National Association of Manufacturers
NAS	National Academy of Sciences
NCHE	National Council for History Education
NCSS	National Council for the Social Studies
NDEA	National Defense Education Act
NEA	National Education Association
NSF	National Science Foundation
OAH	Organization of American Historians
ODM	Office of Defense Mobilization
PSAC	President's Science Advisory Committee
PSSC	Physical Science Study Committee
PTA	Parent Teacher Association
SAT	Scholastic Aptitude Test

SIECUS	Sexuality Information and Education Council of the United States
SPAN	Social Studies/Social Science Education: Priorities, Practices, and Needs
SRSS	Sociological Resources for the Social Studies
UICSM	University of Illinois Committee on School Mathematics
USOE	United States Office of Education
WCEA	Warsaw County Education Association
WTU	(Warsaw) *Times-Union*
WAN	*Weekly American News*
YWCA	Young Women's Christian Association

Periodical Titles Abbreviated In Notes

AC	*Atlanta Constitution*
AE	*American Educator*
AEQ	*Anthropology and Education Quarterly*
AERJ	*American Educational Research Journal*
AJ	*Atlanta Journal*
AM	*Atlantic Monthly*
ASBJ	*American School Board Journal*
BFP	*Burlington Free Press*
CH	*Clearing House*
CI	*Curriculum Inquiry*
DP	*Discourse Processes*
EE	*English Education*
EF	*Educational Forum*
EJ	*English Journal*
EL	*Educational Leadership*
ER	*Educational Researcher*
FTU	*Florida Times-Union*
HE	*Human Events*
HER	*Harvard Education Review*
HP	*Houston Post*
HT	*The History Teacher*
IJSE	*International Journal of Social Education*
JAH	*Journal of American History*
JRDE	*Journal of Research and Development in Education*
LAT	*Los Angeles Times*
NAT	*The Nation*
NR	*New Republic*
NW	*Newsweek*
NYR	*New York Review*
NYT	*New York Times*
PDK	*Phi Delta Kappan*
PE	*Progressive Education*

PR	*The Progressive*
SA	*School Administrator*
SE	*Social Education*
SP	*Social Policy*
SR	*Saturday Review*
SSRC	*Social Science Record*
SSRV	*Social Studies Review*
TCR	*Teachers College Record*
TRSE	*Theory and Research in Social Education*
TSS	*The Social Studies*
WTU	(Warsaw) *Times-Union*
WAN	*Weekly American News*

Manuscript Collections
Abbreviated in Notes

Carnegie Mellon University Archives
 Edwin P. Fenton Papers   [Fenton Papers]
Dolph Briscoe Center for American History, University
of Texas at Austin
 National Council for the Social Studies
 Records, Manuscript Collection # 17 *   [NCSS]
Harvard University Archives
 Jerome S. Bruner Papers   [Bruner Papers]
 Records of Educational Services Incorporated and
 Education Development Center, Inc.**   [ESI/EDC]
Massachusetts Institute of Technology
Institute Archives
 James R. Killian Papers   [Killian Papers]
National Academy of Sciences Archives
 Central Policy Files
  Advisory Board on Education   [NAS/ABE]
  Woods Hole Papers   [WH]
National Archives II, College Park, Maryland
 Records of the Office of Education, RG 12
  Office Files of the Commissioner of Education   [USOE/OFCE]
 National Intelligence Survey, RG 263   [NIS]
 Records of the National Science Foundation, RG 307
  Office of the Director, Subject Files   [NSF/ODSF]
  Historian File   [NSF/HF]

* At Milbank Memorial Library and Archives, Teachers College, Columbia
  University at the time research was conducted.
** In the personal library of Peter Dow at the time research was conducted.

Notes

Introduction: Challenges of Curriculum Development

1. Robert M. Pirsig, *Zen and the Art of Motorcycle Maintenance: An Inquiry into Values* (New York: Morrow, 1974).
2. Ronald W. Evans, *The Social Studies Wars: What Should We Teach the Children?* (New York: Teachers College Press, 2004).
3. Walter Parker, ed., "Introduction," *Social Studies Today: Research and Practice* (New York: Routledge, 2009), 1.

1   The New Social Studies

1. Ronald W. Evans, *The Social Studies Wars: What Should We Teach the Children?* (New York: Teachers College Press, 2004).
2. Arthur Bestor, *Educational Wastelands: The Retreat from Learning in our Public Schools* (Urbana: University of Illinois Press, 1953); Albert Lynd, *Quackery in the Public Schools* (New York: Grosset and Dunlap, 1953); Kitty Jones and Robert Olivier, *Progressive Education is REDucation* (Boston: Meador Publishing Company, 1956); John T. Flynn, "Who Owns Your Child's Mind?," *Reader's Digest*, October 1951, 23–28.
3. Bestor, *Educational Wastelands*.
4. National Intelligence Survey, "National Intelligence Survey, U.S.S.R., Section 44, Manpower," February 1, 1953, National Intelligence Surveys, 1948–1965, box 125, NIS; National Intelligence Survey, "National Intelligence Survey, U.S.S.R., Section 44, Manpower," January 1, 1958, pp. 13–15, National Intelligence Surveys, 1948–1965, box 125, NIS.
5. National Intelligence Survey, "National Intelligence Survey, U.S.S.R., Section 44, Manpower," March 1, 1963, pp. 1–4, National Intelligence Surveys, 1948–1965, box 125, NIS.
6. Dwight D. Eisenhower to Arthur S. Fleming, August 1, 1953, "Subject files, M," box 11, NSF/ODSF.
7. Arthur S. Fleming, Director, Office of Defense Mobilization, to Dwight D. Eisenhower, January 6, 1954, "Subject files, M," box 11, NSF/ODSF.

8. "Manpower Resources for National Security: A Report to the Director of the Office of Defense Mobilization," 1953, p. 1, "Committee on Manpower Resources for National Security" folder, subject file "M," box 11, 1951–1956, NSF/ODSF.

9. "Russian Science Threatens the West," *Nation's Business*, September, 1954, 42–54, in "Scientists and Engineers" folder, box 71, USOE/OFCE; Benjamin Fine, "Russia Is Overtaking U. S. in Training of Technicians," *NYT*, November 7, 1954, "Scientists and Engineers File," box 71, USOE/OFCE.

10. Zacharias to Killian, memo, March 15, 1956, "13–18 ESI Correspondence A–Z" folder, box 31, Killian Papers.

11. John D. Haas, *The Era of the New Social Studies* (Boulder, CO: Social Science Education Consortium, 1977), 14–15.

12. John L. Rudolph, "From World War to Woods Hole: The Use of Wartime Research Models for Curriculum Reform," *TCR* 104, no. 2 (March 2002): 212–241.

13. Jerome S. Bruner, *In Search of Mind: Essays in Autobiography* (New York: Harper and Row, 1983); William A. Williams, *The Tragedy of American Diplomacy* (Cleveland, OH: World, 1959).

14. Gerald Gutek, *Education in the United States: An Historical Perspective* (Englewood Cliffs, NJ: Prentice-Hall, 1986), 280.

15. Hyman G. Rickover, *Education and Freedom* (New York: E.P. Dutton and Co., 1959).

16. E. Merrill Root, *Brainwashing in the High Schools* (New York: Devin-Adair, 1958).

17. Kermit Lansner, ed. *Second Rate Brains* (New York: Doubleday News Books, 1958).

18. "Proposed Conference on Psychological Research in Education," 1958, Memo from ABE, NAS, to Lanier, et al, March 5, 1958, enclosure, "Proposed conf." folder, NAS/ABE.

19. Randall M. Whaley notes, National Academy of Sciences—National Research Council Governing Board, Advisory Board on Education, Meeting re: PSSC, April 22, 1958, "Coordination with MIT PSSC/Formation of ESI" folder, Governing Board, 1958, NAS/ABE.

20. Bruner, *In Search of Mind*, 180.

21. Jerome S. Bruner, *The Process of Education* (Cambridge, MA: Harvard University Press, 1960), 2–3, 11–12.

22. Ibid., 33.

23. Ibid., 13–14.

24. Bruner, *In Search of Mind*, 181.

25. Ibid., 183.

26. Bruner, *Process of Education*, 10.

27. Jerome S. Bruner, "Memorandum to the Work Group on the Apparatus of Teaching," September 1959, "General" folder, WH.

28. Alan A. Needell, "Project Troy and the Cold War Annexation of the Social Sciences," in Christopher Simpson, ed. *Universities and Empire: Money and Politics in the Social Sciences during the Cold War* (New York: New Press, 1998), 3–38.

29. Jack S. Goldstein, *A Different Sort of Time: The Life of Jerrold R. Zacharias, Scientist, Engineer, Educator* (Cambridge: MIT Press, 1992).

30. Bruner, *In Search of Mind*, 210.

31. Goldstein, *Different Sort of Time*, 164–165; MIT/Oral History Collection. Zacharias always capitalized them because they were of fundamental importance.

32. Charles R. Keller, "Needed: Revolution in the Social Studies," *Saturday Review*, September 16, 1961, 60.

33. Ibid., 61–62.

34. Lawrence Senesh, *Our Working World* (Chicago: Science Research Associates, 1964). Edwin P. Fenton, *32 Problems in World History* (Glenview, IL: Scott, Foresman, 1964).

35. "Report: Conference of Social Studies and Humanities Curriculum Program," 1962, "Endicott House" folder, "Early Development" drawer, EDC. Also, Appendix II, "Advance Reading Material Sent to Conference Participants, 23 April, 1962," "Report," box 1, Correspondence, Miscellaneous, Bruner Papers. See Peter B. Dow, *Schoolhouse Politics: Lessons from the Sputnik Era* (Cambridge, MA: Harvard University Press, 1991), 42.

36. Ibid.

37. Announcement, "Announcement for Project Social Studies," *SE* 26, no. 6 (October 1962): 300.

38. Van R. Halsey, Jr., "American History: A New High School Course," *SE* 27, no. 5 (May 1963): 249–252.

39. Gerald R. Smith, "Project Social Studies—a Report," *SE* 27, no. 7 (November 1963): 357–359, 409.

40. Edwin P. Fenton and John M. Good, "Project Social Studies: A Progress Report," *SE* 29, no. 4 (April 1965): 206.

41. Donald W. Robinson, "Ferment in the Social Studies," *SE* 27, no. 7 (November 1963): 360, 362.

42. James M. Becker, "Prospect for Change in the Social Studies," *SE* 29, no. 1 (January 1965): 20.

43. Editor, "Reactions to the Reports on Project Social Studies," *SE* 29 (1965): 356–360.

44. Mark M. Krug, "Bruner's New Social Studies: A Critique," *SE* 30, no. 6 (October 1966): 401–402.

45. James P. Shaver, "Social Studies: The Need for Redefinition," *SE* 31, no. 7 (November 1967): 592, 596.

46. Jerome S. Bruner, "The Process of Education Revisited," *PDK* 53, no. 1 (September 1971): 19.

2   The Newer Social Studies

1. Todd Gitlin, *The Sixties: Years of Hope, Days of Rage* (New York: Bantam, 1987).

2. Jules Whitcover, *The Year the Dream Died: Revisiting 1968 in America* (New York: Warner, 1997).

3. Melvin Arnoff to Shirley Engle, January 24, 1969, "Impromptu Speakout: NCSS 1968," 1–2, box 6, Series IV B, NCSS.

4. "Minutes, 13th Delegate Assembly, National Council for the Social Studies," *SE* 34, no. 4 (April 1970): 471.

5. "Agenda for Board of Directors Meeting," November 21–22, 1971, 2, NCSS.

6. Stokely Carmichael and Charles V. Hamilton, *Black Power: The Politics of Liberation in America* (New York: Random House, 1967), 5, 37, 159, 167; Martin Luther King, Jr., 1967, as cited in David L. Angus and Jeffrey Mirel, *The Failed Promise of the American High School, 1890–1995* (New York: Teachers College, 1999), 48, 50.

7. James A. Banks, "Relevant Social Studies for Black Pupils," *SE* 33, no. 1 (January 1969): 66–69.

8. Hazel W. Hertzberg, "Editorial Reflections: The Challenge of Ethnic Studies," *SE* 36, no. 5 (May 1972): 470.

9. Hazel W. Hertzberg, "Issues in Teaching about American Indians," *SE* 36, no. 5 (May 1972): 481–485.

10. John R. Browne to Participant, undated 1971, "Clinic I. Changing Racism and Injustice," "Teaching of Values" folder 2, "Teaching of Values" folder 1, box 1, Series X Special Projects, NCSS.

11. Set of Index Cards from a Racism Clinic, handwritten teacher responses assessing current local situation, "Teaching of Values" folder 1, box 1, 1933–1973, Series X Special Projects, NCSS.

12. John R. Browne to Vivian Johnson, Sam Turner, Doreen Wilkeinson, and Wm. O'Connor, "RE: Techniques to employ," February 29, 1972, folder 1, box 1, 1933–1973, Series X Special Projects, NCSS; Evaluations at Denver Clinic, folder 14, box 1, 1933–1973, Series X Special Projects, NCSS.

13. Gerald Leinwand, "The Year of the Non-Curriculum: A Proposal," *SE* 32, no. 6 (October 1968): 542–545, 549.

14. Ibid., 549.

15. Gerald Leinwand, ed., *Problems of American Society* (New York: Washington Square Press, 1968–1972).

16. Frank Simon, *A Reconstructive Approach to Problem-Solving in the Social Studies: A Handbook for Inquiry and Post-Inquiry Activity in Social Process* (Calgary, Alberta: Frank Simon, 1970), v–viii.

17. Nat Hentoff, *Our Children Are Dying* (New York: Viking Press, 1966); James Herndon, *The Way It Spozed to Be* (New York: Simon and Schuster, 1968); John Holt, *How Children Fail* (New York: Pittman, 1964); John Holt, *How Children Learn* (New York: Pittman, 1964); Jonathan Kozol, *Death at an Early Age: The Destruction of the Hearts and Minds of Negro Children in the Boston Public Schools* (Boston: Houghton Mifflin, 1967).

18. Paul Goodman, *Compulsory Miseducation* and *The Community of Scholars* (New York: Vintage Books, 1966); Everett Reimer, *School Is Dead: Alternatives in Education* (Garden City, NY: Doubleday, 1971); Neil Postman and Charles Weingartner, *Teaching as a Subversive Activity* (New York: Delacorte, 1969); Paul Goodman, *Growing Up Absurd: Problems of Youth in the Organized System* (New York: Random House, 1960); A. S.

Neill, *Summerhill: A Radical Approach to Child Rearing* (New York: Hart, 1960); Charles E. Silberman, *Crisis in the Classroom: The Remaking of American Education* (New York: Random House, 1970); Ivan Illich, *Deschooling Society* (New York: Harper and Row, 1970).

19. Harold W. Sobel, "The New Wave of Educational Literature," *PDK* 50, no. 2 (October 1968): 109–111; Robin Barrow, *Radical Education: A Critique of Freeschooling and Deschooling* (New York: John Wiley and Sons, 1978); Ronald Gross, "From Innovations to Alternatives: A Decade of Change in Education," *PDK* 53, no. 1 (September, 1971): 22–24; Diane Ravitch, *The Troubled Crusade: American Education, 1945–1980* (New York: Basic Books, 1983), 235–256.

20. Neill, *Summerhill*, 4, 25, 29.

21. Goodman, *Growing Up Absurd*, 95.

22. Goodman, *Compulsory Mis-Education*, 7, 22, 32–33, 55–57, 67, 126, 141, 145.

23. Kozol, *Death at an Early Age*; Herbert Kohl, *36 Children* (New York: New American Library, 1967).

24. Hentoff, *Our Children Are Dying*; Herndon, *The Way It Spozed To Be*; Herndon, *How to Survive in Your Native Land*; Holt, *How Children Fail*; Illich, *Deschooling Society*.

25. Postman and Weingartner, *Teaching as a Subversive Activity*, 2–3.

26. Ibid., 52–54, 62–66.

27. Ibid., 2–3, 25, 39, 59.

28. Gross, "From Innovations to Alternatives," 23.

29. Theodore Roszak, *The Making of a Counter Culture: Reflections on the Technocratic Society and Its Youthful Opposition* (Garden City, NJ: Doubleday, 1969), 16.

30. NCSS Task Force on Curriculum Guidelines, "Social Studies Curriculum Guidelines," *SE* 35, no. 8 (December 1971): 853–867.

31. Ibid., 860–861.

32. Ibid., 861–862, 865.

33. Richard L. Hart and Victor W. Shapiro, "The NCSS Curriculum Guidelines: Dissemination and Utilization," *SE* 39, no. 2 (February, 1975): 92–95.

34. John Guenther and Patricia Hansen, "Organizational Change in the Social Studies: Mini-Course Subject Options," *EL* 35, no. 1 (October, 1977): 64–68; For an alternative perspective see David Jenness who describes the minicourse explosion as a "1970s trend toward a cafeteria like display of not very well-structured special courses and units" that, he laments, "might have been avoided." See David Jenness, *Making Sense of Social Studies* (New York: Macmillan, 1990), 142.

35. John I. Goodlad and Robert H. Anderson, *The Nongraded Elementary School* (New York: Harcourt, Brace and World, 1963); Charles E. Silberman, *Crisis in the Classroom: The Remaking of American Education* (New York: Random House, 1970), 167.

36. Silberman, *Crisis in the Classroom*, 337, 341.

37. G. Robert Carlsen and John W. Conner, "New Patterns from Old Molds," *English Journal* 51, no. 4 (April 1962): 245–246.

38. John Guenther and Robert Ridgway, "Mini-Courses: Promising Alternative in the Social Studies," *CH* 47, no. 8 (April 1973): 486–489.

39. Leila Christenbury, "The Elective Curriculum: Origin, Development, and Decline," *EE* 15, no. 2 (May 1983): 73–91.

40. Guenther and Ridgway, "Mini-Courses," 488.

41. Anchorage Borough School District, Alaska, "Survey-Elective Social Studies Program for Senior High Schools," ERIC Document # ED 066408.

42. Albert A. Seretny, "Yale-New Haven History Education Project (H. E. P.) Summary Report 1970–1973," New Haven, CT: Yale University, 1972.

43. Ibid., 2, 5–6.

44. Ibid., 6–7.

45. Margaret S. Branson, "The Status of Social Studies: Marin County," *SE* 41, no. 7 (November/December 1977): 593.

46. Arthur D. Roberts and Robert K. Gable, "Mini-Versus Traditional: An Experimental Study of High School Social Studies Curricula," Paper presented at the National Council for the Social Studies Annual Meeting, Boston, November, 1972. ERIC # ED076471; John Guenther and Robert Ridgway, "Mini-Courses: One Way to Provide More Humanistic School Programs," *NASSP Bulletin* 60, no. 399 (April 1976): 12–15; See also Guenther and Ridgway, "Mini-Courses: Promising Alternative"; Guenther and Hansen, "Organizational Change in the Social Studies," 64–68; See also, Arsene Boykin, "Mini-Course, Anybody? *CH* 54, no. 7 (March 1981): 300–301; and, John Guenther and Robert Ridgway, "Mini-Courses Provide More Subject Options for High School History Students, *HT* 6, no. 3 (May 1973): 389–392.

47. Guenther and Ridgway, "Mini-Courses: One Way."

48. Harold O. Rugg, "Do the Social Studies Prepare Pupils Adequately for Life Activities?" In H. O. Rugg, ed., *The Social Studies in the Elementary and Secondary School.* National Society for the Study of Education. Twenty-Second Yearbook, National Society for the Study of Education, Part II (Bloomington, IL: Public School, 1923), 1–27; Harold O. Rugg, *That Men May Understand: An American in the Long Armistice* (New York: Doubleday, Doran, 1941); Harold O. Rugg, "Social Reconstruction through Education," *Progressive Education* 9, no. 8 (1932): 11–18.

49. Allan O. Kownslar, Ed., *Teaching American History: The Quest for Relevancy* (Washington, DC: National Council for the Social Studies, 1974), 3.

50. Ibid., 4–7.

51. Ibid., 7–9.

52. Ibid., 10–12.

53. Louis E. Raths, Merrill Harmin, and Sidney B. Simon, *Values and Teaching* (Columbus, OH: Charles E. Merrill, 1966); Sidney B. Simon, Leland W. Howe, and Howard Kirschenbaum, *Values Clarification: A Handbook of Practical Strategies for Teachers and Students* (New York: Hart, 1972).

54. Lawrence Kohlberg, "Moral Development and the New Social Studies," *SE* 37 no. 5 (May 1973): 369–375; Edwin Fenton, "Moral Education: The Research Findings," *SE* 40, no. 4 (April 1976): 188–193; Jack R. Fraenkel, "The Kohlberg Bandwagon: Some Reservations," *SE* 40, no. 4 (April

1976): 216–222; Ronald A. Gerlach, "Kohlberg's Theory of Cognitive Moral Development: A New Panacea," *SSRC* 14, no. 3 (Spring 1977): 6–10.

55. David L. Angus and Jeffrey E. Mirel, *The Failed Promise of the American High School, 1890–1985* (New York: Teachers College Press, 1999), 135.

3   Larger Trends in Schools

1. Joseph Featherstone, "Schools for Children," *NR*, August 19, 1967, 17–21; Featherstone, "How Children Learn," *NR*, September 2, 1967, 12–25; Featherstone, "Teaching Children to Think," *NR*, September 9, 1967, 15–25.

2. Charles Silberman, *Crisis in the Classroom: The Remaking of American Education* (New York: Random House, 1970), 1, 10, 11.

3. Roland S. Barth, *Open Education and the American School* (New York: Agathon Press, 1972), 50.

4. Anne Swidler, *Organization without Authority: Dilemmas of Social Control in Free Schools* (Cambridge, MA: Harvard University Press, 1979), 2–3.

5. Roland S. Barth, "Should We Forget about Open Education?" *SRW*, November 6, 1973, 58–59; Donald A. Myers, "Why Open Education Died," *JRDE* 8, no. 1 (1974): 60–67; Amitai Etzioni, "Review of Crisis in the Classroom," *HER* 41, no. 1 (February 1971): 87–98; See also, Donald A. Myers and Daniel L. Duke, "Open Education as an Ideology," *ER* 19, no. 3 (June 1977): 227–235.

6. Vito Perrone and Lowell Thompson, "Social Studies in the Open Classroom," *SE* 36, no. 4 (April 1972): 460–464.

7. Robert D. Barr, "Diversifying the Social Studies: The Trend toward Optional Public Schools," *SE* 38, no. 3 (March 1974): 236–242; Mario D. Fantini, "Alternative Schools and Humanistic Education," *SE* 38, no. 3 (March 1974): 243–247.

8. Shirley H. Engle and Wilma S. Longstreet, *A Design for Social Education in the Open Curriculum* (New York: Harper and Row, 1972); Evelyn Berger and Bonnie A. Winters, *Social Studies in the Open Classroom: A Practical Guide* (New York: Teachers College, 1973).

9. James A. Banks, "Multicultural Education in the New Century," *School Administrator* 56, no. 6 (May 1999): 8–10.

10. Thomas J. Famularo, "The Intellectual Bankruptcy of Multiculturalism," *USA Today Magazine*, May 1996.

11. Diane Ravitch, "Diversity and Democracy: Multicultural Education in America," *AE*, Spring 1990, 17–20.

12. Arthur M. Schlesinger, Jr., *The Disuniting of America: Reflections on a Multicultural Society* (New York: W. W. Norton, 1991).

13. Gloria Ladson-Billings, "Through the Looking Glass: Politics and the Social Studies Curriculum," Review of Schlesinger's *The Disuniting of America, TRSE* 21, no. 1 (Winter 1993): 84–92.

14. *Time, Newsweek*, and other popular magazines devoted cover stories to this topic. See also, Dinesh D'Souza, *Illiberal Education: The Politics of Race and*

Sex on Campus (New York: Free Press, 1991); Roger Kimball, *How Politics Has Corrupted Our Higher Education* (New York: Harper and Row, 1990); Mark Edmundson, ed. *Wild Orchids and Trotsky: Messages from American Universities* (New York: Penguin, 1993); Catherine Cornbleth and Dexter Waugh, *The Great Speckled Bird: Multicultural Politics and Educational Policy* Making (New York: St. Martin's Press, 1995).

15. Paulo Freire, *Pedagogy of the Oppressed* (New York: Continuum, 1970), 57–59.

16. Samuel Bowles and Herbert M. Gintis, *Schooling in Capitalist America: Educational Reform and the Contradictions of Economic Life* (New York: Basic Books, 1976), 48.

17. William B. Stanley, *Curriculum for Utopia: Social Reconstructionism and Critical Pedagogy in the Postmodern Era* (Albany: State University of New York Press, 1992), 100.

18. Michael W. Apple, *Ideology and Curriculum* (London: Routledge and Kegan Paul, 1979), 14.

19. Fred M. Newmann, "The Radical Perspective on Social Studies: A Synthesis and Critique," *TRSE* 13, no. 1 (1985): 1–8.

20. Jack L. Nelson, ed., "New Criticism and Social Education," *SE* 49, no. 5 (May 1985): 368–405.

21. Amy Gutman, *Democratic Education* (Princeton, NJ: Princeton University Press, 1987); Ronald W. Evans, "Utopian Visions and Mainstream Practice: Essay Review of William B. Stanley's *Curriculum for Utopia*," *TRSE* 21, no. 2 (1993): 161–173.

22. Diane Ravitch. *The Troubled Crusade: American Education, 1945–1980* (New York: Basic Books, 1983), 237–238.

23. Logan C. Osterndof and Paul J. Horn, *Course Offerings, Enrollments, and Curriculum Practices in Public Secondary Schools, 1972–73* (Washington, DC: National Center for Education Statistics, 1976), 22.

24. Ibid., 12–13, 22, 74, 326; John Guenther and Robert Ridgway, "Mini-Courses: One Way to Provide More Humanistic School Programs," *NASSP Bulletin* 60, no. 399 (April 1976), 12–15; David L. Angus and Jeffrey E. Mirel, *The Failed Promise of the American High School, 1890–1985* (New York: Teachers College Press, 1999).

25. Michael W. Sedlak, Christopher W. Wheeler, Diana C. Pullin, and Philip A. Cusick, *Selling Students Short: Classroom Bargains and Academic Reform in the American High School* (New York: Teachers College, 1986), 37–45.

26. Ibid., 44.

27. Ibid.; Diane Ravitch, "The Schools We Deserve," *NR*, April 18, 1981, 329–340.

28. James M. Benjamin, "What Have We Done to Social Studies?" *SE* 39, no. 2 (February 1975): 88, 90.

29. Allan O. Kownslar, "What Should Be Done to the Social Studies?" *SE* 39, no. 2 (February 1975): 89–91.

30. Arthur G. Powell, Eleanor Farrar, and David K. Cohen, *The Shopping Mall High School: Winners and Losers in the Educational Marketplace* (Boston: Houghton Mifflin, 1985); Phillip A. Cusick, *The Egalitarian Ideal and the*

American High School: Studies of Three Schools (New York: Longman, 1983); Maureen Stout, *The Feel Good Curriculum: The Dumbing-Down of America's Kids in the Name of Self-Esteem* (Cambridge, MA: Perseus, 2000).

31. Maurice P. Hunt and Lawrence E. Metcalf, *Teaching High School Social Studies: Reflective Thinking and Social Understanding* (New York: Harper and Row, 1968).

32. Jules Henry, *Culture Against Man* (New York: Random House, 1963); Herbert Marcuse, *One-Dimensional Man: Studies in the Ideology of Advanced Industrial Society* (Boston: Beacon Press, 1964); Michel Foucault, *Discipline and Punish: The Birth of the Prison* (New York: Pantheon, 1978).

4   Aftermath: "We Face a National Conspiracy"

1. NEA DuShane Emergency Fund Division, "Guarding Your Freedom to Teach," *Today's Education*, November, 1970, 21–22; "Georgia Teacher's Firing Ruled Illegal; Federal Jury Awards $5,000 in Damages," *NEA News*, Press Release, February 16, 1971, "Academic Freedom" folder, box 1, Special Projects, Series X, NCSS.

2. NEA, "Guarding Your Freedom to Teach," 22.

3. Ibid; Merrill Hartshorn to NCSS Legal Defense Fund, May 1, 1972; John Matthews, "Fired Teacher Settles for $40,000," *Washington Star*, June 10, 1975; Confidential Legal Documents: Henry Keith Sterzing, Plaintiff, vs. Fort Bend Independent School District, Defendants, Civil Action No. 69-H-319; Affidavit of Henry Keith Sterzing in Support of Plaintiff's Motion for Summary Judgment, In the U.S. District Court for the Southern District of Texas, Houston Division; Affidavit of O.L. Davis in Support of Plaintiff's Motion for Summary Judgment, Civil Action No. 69-H-319; in "Sterzing Case" folder, box 44, Series 4D, NCSS.

4. NEA DuShane Fund, "Guarding Your Freedom to Teach," 22–23; Frances Ahern to Merrill Hartshorn, November 11, 1969, and attached, "Report of Preliminary Investigation to the Commission on Professional Rights and Responsibilities Concerning the Alleged Violation of Academic Freedom and Unfair Dismissal Procedures at the Grand Island Public Schools," Nebraska State Education Association, August 16, 1969; Frances Ahern, Plaintiff vs. Board of Education of the School District of Grand Island, Filed in the United States District Court for the District of Nebraska, December 2, 1969; Associated Press, "Judge Denies Dismissal Plea," *Grand Island Independent*, February 11, 1970; Brief in support of motion to dismiss; Brief of Defendants; Statement from Frances Ahern; all in "Ahern Case, Correspondence and Briefs" folder, box 3, Series 4D, Executive Reference Files, NCSS.

5. Charles Kochheiser, "What Happened When a Speaker for Gay Liberation Addressed High School Students," *SE* 39, no. 4 (April 1975): 219–221.

6. Edward B. Jenkinson to John Fogarty, NCTE Committee Against Censorship; John Fogarty vs. Board of Education, Fremont County Joint School District, filed in U.S. District Court for the District of Idaho; Barry Siegel, " 'Cuckoo' Drops a Bomb on Private World," *LAT*, March 12, 1978; Fogarty to Ms. Leanne Katz, National Coalition Against Censorship, June 26, 1978; Memo and attached information regarding Fogarty case, May 22, 1978; articles and editorials from Idaho media; "Fogarty Case" folder, file 21, box 6, Accession # 820612 Ochoa (811106), NCSS.

7. The slow learner series sold ½ million copies. Interview with Edwin Fenton, May 18, 2008, South Wellfleet, MA, conducted by the author.

8. Al Linthicum, "Protests Delay Okay of Social Studies Texts," *AC*, November 25, 1971, p. 14-C; Jim Summers to Bob Fitzgerald, December 9, 1971, Holt memorandum re: Georgia-Fenton Materials, both in "Georgia Textbook Controversy" folder 13, box 17, Fenton Papers.

9. Jim Summers to Bob Fitzgerald, December 9, 1971, Holt memorandum re: Georgia-Fenton Materials, "Georgia Textbook Controversy" folder 13, box 17, Fenton Papers.

10. Al Leake to State Board of Education, November 24, 1971, referenced in Mary A. Hepburn, "A Case of Creeping Censorship, Georgia Style," *PDK* 55, no. 9 (May 1974): 611.

11. See Philip Lee Secrist, "The Public Pays the Piper: The People and the Social Studies in Georgia Schools," Doctoral dissertation, University of Georgia, Athens, 1971, Chapter 4, cited in Fenton, "Choosing Curricular Materials," and in Mary A. Hepburn, "The Georgia Situation: Walking the Thin Line between Professional Determination and Censorship," unpublished paper, Fenton Papers.

12. Hepburn, "A Case of Creeping Censorship, Georgia Style," 611–613; Tom Linthicum, "School Board Bars 10 Texts by Fenton," *AC*, December 17, 1971; Edwin Fenton, "Choosing Curriculum Materials: Who and How," Speech to Georgia Council for the Social Studies, March 1, 1974, Savannah, Georgia, " 'Georgia Council for the Social Sciences: Choosing Curriculum Materials: Who and How' Speech, 1974" folder, box 1, Fenton Papers; Tom Linthicum, "Fenton Says Teaching Issue Is Board's Main Criticism," *AC*, December 20, 1971, 16-A.

13. Elizabeth O. Daniel, Carver High School, Columbus, Georgia to Edwin Fenton, December 19, 1971, folder 13, box 17, Fenton Papers.

14. Unsigned letter to Edwin Fenton, undated, "Georgia Textbook Controversy" folder 13, box 17, Fenton Papers.

15. Edwin Fenton to Editor, December 20, 1971, "Georgia Textbook Controversy" folder 13, box 17, Fenton Papers; the letter appeared as, "Textbooks and Americanism," *AC*, January 4, 1972, 5-A.

16. Vernon L Anderson, Director of Marketing, Holt Rinehart and Winston, to Edwin Fenton, January 24, 1972, "Georgia Textbook Controversy" folder 13, box 17, Fenton Papers.

17. J. H. Summers to Andy Anderson, Holt Rinehart and Winston Memorandum, February 17, 1972, "Georgia Textbook Controversy" folder 13, box 17, Fenton Papers.

18. Junie Brown, "Education Board Tosses Out Books," *AJ*, May 19, 1972, "Georgia Textbook Controversy" folder 13, box 17, Fenton Papers; Textbook Controversies, Series IV D, box 12A, Executive Reference Files, "Georgia Textbook Controversy, 1971–1972" folder, NCSS; Beau Cutts, "Educators Won't Finance Textbook: But 'Americans' Is Not Banned," *AC*, May 19, 1972.

19. J. H. Summers to Bobby McGuire, Holt Rinehart and Winston Memorandum, May 19, 1972, "Georgia Textbook Controversy" folder 13, box 17, Fenton Papers.

20. Hepburn, "A Case of Creeping Censorship, Georgia Style," 612.

21. Fenton interview.

22. Edwin Fenton, "Choosing Curriculum Materials: Who and How," Speech to Georgia Council for the Social Studies, March 1, 1974, Savannah, Georgia, 12, "Georgia Council for the Social Sciences: 'Choosing Curriculum Materials: Who and How' Speech, 1974" folder, box 1, Fenton Papers.

23. James Moffett, *Storm in the Mountains: A Case Study of Censorship, Conflict, and Consciousness* (Carbondale: Southern Illinois University Press, 1988), 12–13; see also, Edward B. Jenkinson, *Censors in the Classroom: The Mind Benders* (Carbondale: Southern Illinois University Press, 1979); John Egerton, "The Battle of the Books," *The Progressive*, June, 1975, 13–17; and William Martin, *With God on Our Side: The Rise of the Religious Right in America* (New York: Broadway Books, 1996).

24. Donald J. Rogers, *Banned! Book Censorship in the Schools* (New York: Julian Messner, 1988), 18–19; James C. Hefley, *Textbooks on Trial* (Wheaton, IL: Victor Books, 1976). This is written by an author with a favorable view of the Gabler's work and must be used with care. However, the account of the controversy contained in the chapter "The Truth about West Virginia" provides some details from the perspective of Mrs. Moore.

25. Todd Clark, "The West Virginia Textbook Controversy: A Personal Account," *SE* 39, no. 4 (April 1975): 216–219.

26. Philip G. Jones, "A Clash over 'Dirty Books' Is Dividing a School Board, Threatening a Superintendent, and Shattering a Community," *ASBJ 161, no. 5* (May 1975): 32.

27. Ibid., 41.

28. Moffett, *Storm in the Mountains*, 17, quoting a Charleston Gazette article from June 27, 1974.

29. Catherine A. Candor-Chandler, "A History of the Kanawha County Textbook Controversy, April 1974–April 1975," Doctoral dissertation, Virginia Polytechnic Institute, 1976.

30. Moffett, *Storm in the Mountains*, 17–19.

31. Ibid., 19.

32. Ibid., 20–21.

33. Ibid., 21–22.

34. Ibid., 22; National Education Association, *Kanawha County, West Virginia: A Textbook Study in Cultural Conflict* (Washington, DC: National Education Association, 1975).

35. Moffett, *Storm in the Mountains*, 24; NEA, *Kanawha County, West Virginia*.

36. Staff, "Access Rights to Children's Minds: Texts of Our Times—Problems in Kanawha County, W. Va.," *NR*, January 4, 1975, 19–21.

37. Clark, "The West Virginia Textbook Controversy," 216–219.

38. Carol Mason, *Reading Appalachia from Left to Right: Conservatives and the 1974 Kanawha County Textbook Controversy* (Ithaca, NY: Cornell University Press, 2009), 124, n. 109.

39. Ibid., 215.

40. Trey Kay, "Information about Trey Kay's Kanawha County Textbook Controversy Audio Documentary Project," in Steve Fesenmaier, "Trey Kay Wins Peabody for Radio Documentary on Kanawha Textbook Controversy," *The Gazette: Community Blogs*, April 2, 2010; Mason, *Reading Appalachia from Left to Right*. See also, Karl C. Priest, *Protester Voices: The 1974 Textbook Teaparty* (Poca, WV: Praying Mantis, 2010).

41. Kay, "Information."

5　The MACOS Controversy and Beyond

1. William W. Goetz, "The Rise and Fall of MACOS: A Blip on the Historical Screen?," *TRSE* 22, no. 4 (Fall 1994): 515–522; See also, Buckley Barnes, William Stallings, and Roberta Rivner, "Are the Critics Right about MACOS?," *TRSE* 9, no. 1 (Spring 1981): 35–44; Peter B. Dow, "Innovation's Perils: An Account of the Origins, Development, Implementation, and Public Reaction to Man: A Course of Study," Doctoral dissertation, Harvard University, 1979; Karen B. Wiley. *The NSF Science Education Controversy: Issues, Events, Decisions* (Boulder, CO: Social Science Education Consortium, 1976); Larry L. Kraus, "Curriculum, Public Policy, and Criticism: An Analysis of the Controversies Surrounding Man: A Course of Study," Doctoral dissertation, University of Texas at Austin, 1977.

2. Goetz, "The Rise and Fall of MACOS," 519.

3. Dick Hagood, "Course in Social Studies Creates Furor in Columbia," *FTU*, November 5, 1970; "Summary of Lake City Controversy," Unsigned and undated, "Lake City, FL Controversy" folder, MACOS controversy drawer, EDC; Peter Dow, *Schoolhouse Politics: Lessons from the Sputnik Era* (Cambridge, MA: Harvard University Press, 1991).

4. Hagood, "Course in Social Studies Creates Furor"; "Summary of Lake City Controversy," 6.

5. Hagood, "Summary of Lake City Controversy," 4–5.

6. Ibid., 8–9.

7. Ibid., 9.

8. Dow, *Schoolhouse Politics*, 180–181.

9. Dick Hagood, "Unit's Motives Questioned in Columbia School Issue," *FTU*, November 20, 1970; Dick Hagood, "Minister Cites Objections to Social Studies Course," *FTU*, November 21, 1970.

10. Minority Report of Don Glenn attached to Report of the Review Committee, Enclosure, Frank King to Bob Harrison, November 25, 1970, "Columbia Co.—Lake City, Fla." folder, controversy drawer, EDC.

11. Minority Report of Robert E. Marks attached to Report of the Review Committee, Enclosure, Frank King to Bob Harrison, November 25, 1970, "Columbia Co.—Lake City, Fla." folder, controversy drawer, EDC.

12. Dick Hagood, "Teachers Hit Board Ruling in Columbia," *FTU*, December 4, 1970; "Columbia Co.—Lake City, Fla." folder, controversy drawer, EDC.

13. Robert S. Harrison to John Gentry, November 30, 1970, "Columbia Co.—Lake City, Fla." folder, controversy drawer, EDC.

14. Peter Dow to Don Koeller, December 10, 1970, "Columbia Co.—Lake City, Fla." folder, controversy drawer, EDC.

15. Onalee S. McGraw, "What Educators Are Doing With Your Federal Taxes," *HE*, August 14, 1971, 16.

16. Ibid.

17. Ibid., 17.

18. Dow, *Schoolhouse Politics*, 185; Dow cites a memorandum from James M. Reusswig to Montgomery County Board of Education, September 10, 1971.

19. "MACOS Social? Study?" *WAN*, September 1, 1971, attached to Peter B. Dow to Principal Staff and Project Directors, October 19, 1971, "10/28 Meeting" folder, controversy drawer, EDC.

20. Phyllis Musselman, "We're All Animals—Kids Are Taught Here'," *WAN*, September 22, 1971.

21. Phyllis Musselman, "Part IV—MACOS: It's Your Tax $$ Isn't It," *WAN*, October 6, 1971.

22. M. E. Hatter to Dow Rhoton and Marvin Cornell, September 10, 1971, as cited in Dow, *Schoolhouse Politics*, 186.

23. Dow, *Schoolhouse Politics*, 186–187.

24. Flyer titled, "WHO DO WE EAT?," attached to Peter B. Dow to Principal Staff and Project Directors, October 19, 1971, "Phoenix Controversy" folder, EDC.

25. Phyllis Musselman to School Board, Madison School District No. 38, October 5, 1971; Dr. James Severance to Madison School District, October 5, 1971, attachment, Dow to Principal Staff, October 19, 1971, "Phoenix Controversy" folder, controversy drawer, EDC; Dow, *Schoolhouse Politics*, 187.

26. P. J. MacDonald to School Board, Madison School District No. 38, October 5, 1971, attached, Dow to Principal Staff, October 19, 1971, "Phoenix Controversy" folder, controversy drawer, EDC.

27. Dow, *Schoolhouse Politics*, 187–188.

28. Ibid., 188–189; Minutes of the Board of Trustees, Madison School District No. 38, Phoenix, Arizona, October 28, 1971, 127, "10/28 Meeting" folder, controversy drawer, EDC.

29. Minutes of the Board of Trustees, Madison School District No. 38, Phoenix, Arizona, October 28, 1971, 131, 132, "10/28 Meeting" folder, controversy drawer, EDC.

30. Dow, *Schoolhouse Politics*, 190.

31. Minutes of the Board of Trustees, October 28, 1971, 133–134.

32. Dow, *Schoolhouse Politics*, 191–192.

33. Ibid.

34. Edward C. Martin, Interview with Dow Rhoton, June 1973, cited in Dow, *Schoolhouse Politics*, 195.
35. "MARCOS [*sic*] STIRS MAYHEM," *Arizona Living*, November 12, 1971, "Phoenix—Clippings" folder, controversy drawer, EDC; Peter Dow wrote, "This time it appears to be members of the John Birch Society rather than the Fundamentalists who are causing the trouble." See Dow to Principal Staff and Project Directors, October 19, 1971, "Phoenix Controversy" folder, controversy drawer, EDC.
36. "M:ACOS [*sic*] MAN A COURSE OF STUDY, Official Complaint," "Bellevue, Washington" folder, controversy drawer, EDC; Dow, *Schoolhouse Politics*.
37. "School Book Series Opposed by Group," *HP*, February 7, 1973; Nadine Winterhalter to T. S. Hancock, February 7, 1973; Edward C. Martin to Peggy Chausse, March 1, 1973; Peggy Chausse to Ed Martin, February 16, 1973, all in "Houston" folder, controversy drawer, EDC.
38. Lorna Lecker, "Textbook Controversy Leads to Organization of Schoolbook 'Watchdogs,'" *BFP*, Monday, November 26, 1973.
39. James C. Hefley, *Textbooks on Trial: The Informative Report of Mel and Norma Gabler's Ongoing Battle to Oust Objectionable Textbooks from Public Schools—and to Urge Publishers to Produce Better Ones* (Wheaton, IL: Victor Books, 1976), 114.
40. Peter Wolfson, "The Fight over MACOS—an Ideological Conflict in Vermont," unpublished paper, 1–4, "Vermont" folder, controversy drawer, EDC; John Steinbacher, *The Conspirators: Men Against God* (Whittier, CA: Orange Tree Press, 1972), 51, 53.
41. Maggie Maurice, "Educator Lambastes Innovative School Programs," *BFP*, November 2, 1973; Wolfson, "The Fight over MACOS," 3.
42. Steinbacher, *The Conspirators*, 37.
43. Lorna Lecker, "South Burlington Views MACOS as Atheistic," *BFP*, November 30, 1973.
44. Lecker, "Textbook Controversy."
45. Dow, *Schoolhouse Politics*, 198.
46. Dorothy Nelkin, *Science Textbook Controversies and the Politics of Equal Time* (Cambridge, MA: MIT Press, 1977).
47. Unidentified to Mr. Peter Dow, in "Misc. Other Local Controversies" folder, controversy drawer, EDC.
48. Daniel D. Burns to Education Development Center, Cambridge, MA, February 27, 1975; Peter B. Dow to Daniel D. Burns, Principal, Owyhee School, Boise, Idaho, March 13, 1975, both in "Misc. Other Local Controversies" folder, controversy drawer, EDC.
49. Goetz, "The Rise and Fall of MACOS," 519.
50. Hefley, *Textbooks on Trial*, 15–16; Mel and Norma Gabler with James C. Hefley, *What Are They Teaching Our Children?* (Wheaton, IL: Victor Books, 1985), 10. See also, Nelkin, *Science Textbook Controversies*, and Eugene F. Provenzo, *Religious Fundamentalism and American Education: The Battle for the Public Schools* (Albany, NY: State University of New York Press).
51. Gabler, *What Are They Teaching Our Children*, 127.

52. One source detailing a funding link to the Castle Rock Foundation is MediaTransparency.org; Heritage published and helped distribute Mel and Norma Gabler, *A Parent's Guide to Textbook Review and Reform* (Washington, DC: Heritage Foundation, 1978).

53. Nelkin, *Science Textbook Controversies*, 48.

54. John Steinbacher, *The Child Seducers* (Fullerton, CA: Educator Publications, 1971); William F. Schulz, *Making the Manifesto: The Birth of Religious Humanism* (Boston: Skinner House Books, 2002); Paul Kurtz, *In Defense of Secular Humanism* (Buffalo, NY: Prometheus Books, 1983).

55. Onalee S. McGraw, *Secular Humanism and the Schools: An Issue Whose Time Has Come* (Washington, DC: Heritage Foundation, 1976); Lee Edwards, *The Power of Ideas: The Heritage Foundation at 25 Years* (Ottawa, IL: Jameson Books, 1997), 19.

56. Onalee S. McGraw web page, Women for Faith and Family website, retrieved March 26, 2009, <http://www.wf-f.org/bd-mcgraw.html>

57. John Micklethwait and Adrian Wooldridge, *The Right Nation: Conservative Power in America* (New York: Penguin Press, 2004), 61; John Birch Society website, http://www.jbs.org/ retrieved March 26, 2009; George Johnson, *Architects of Fear: Conspiracy Theories and Paranoia in American Politics* (Los Angeles: Jeremy P. Tarcher, 1983); Jean Hardisty, *Mobilizing Resentment: Conservative Resurgence from the John Birch Society to the Promise Keepers* (Boston: Beacon Press, 1999).

58. Micklethwait and Wooldridge, *The Right Nation*, 82; Edwards, *The Power of Ideas*, 5.

59. Nelkin, *Science Textbook Controversies*, 49; "The Heritage Foundation," Media Transparency, http:/www.mediatransparency.org/recipientgrants/ retrieved March 26, 2009; Dan Baum, *Citizen Coors: An American Dynasty* (New York: William Morrow, 2000), xii.

60. Russ Bellant, *The Coors Connection: How Coors Family Philanthropy Undermines Democratic Pluralism* (Boston, MA: South End Press, 1991), 1.

61. Ibid., 3.

62. Nelkin, *Science Textbook Controversies*, 49; Source, Dorothy Nelkin personal interview with George Weber.

63. Ibid., 49–50.

64. Dan T. Carter, *The Politics of Rage: George Wallace, the Origins of the New Conservatism, and the Transformation of American Politics* (New York: Simon and Schuster, 1995), 14–15, 466–468.

65. Nelkin, *Science Textbook Controversies*, 112.

66. Richard A. Viguerie and David Franke, *America's Right Turn: How Conservatives Used New and Alternative Media to Take Power* (Chicago, IL: Bonus Books, 2004).

67. Ibid., 110.

68. Ibid., 43.

69. Ibid., 111–112.

70. Ibid., 111.

71. George Archibald, "MACOS, A National Controversy," Keynote address at seminar and luncheon, "GOOD EDUCATION OR MIND CONTROL?"

sponsored by the New Jersey Leadership Foundation, January 31, 1975, "Misc. Other Controversies" folder, Controversy Drawer, EDC; Conlan was also a conservative Christian and directed a Christian Freedom Foundation project "designed to demonstrate unity between evangelical Christianity and a conservative political agenda." See William Martin, *With God on Our Side: The Rise of the Religious Right in America* (New York: Broadway Books, 1996), 152–153.

72. Transcript of Mark-Up Session in the Matter of the National Science Foundation, March 6, 1975, 48–50, Committee on Science and Technology, U. S. House of Representatives, "Committee Mark-Up Session" folder, controversy drawer, EDC.

73. Ibid., 50–52.

74. Interview with Peter Dow, May 19, 2008, Buffalo, New York, conducted by the author.

75. Peter Dow, *Schoolhouse Politics*, 202.

76. H. Guyford Stever to Olin E. Teague, March 17, 1975, p. 1, "NSF Report—Draft" folder, controversy drawer, EDC.

77. J. M. England Interview with Dr. Lowell J. Paige, August 20, 1975, 24–25, "Interview Lowell J. Paige, August 20, 1975" folder, box 44 Interviews with H. Guyford Stever, RG 304, Civilian Records Unit, National Archives II, College Park, MD.

78. Dow, *Schoolhouse Politics*, 206.

79. James J. Kilpatrick, "Teaching Fifth-Graders about Eskimo-Style Sex," *Washington Star*, April 1, 1975, "CLO: MACOS" folder, box 20, NSF/HF; under a different title, James J. Kilpatrick, "Is Eskimo Sex Life a School Subject," *Boston Globe*, April 2, 1975, EDC.

80. Peter B. Dow to Friends of Man: A Course of Study, April 4, 1975, "EDC—Prepare Materials on Controversy" folder, controversy drawer, EDC.

81. John B. Conlan to H. Guyford Stever, April 18, 1975, "CLO: MACOS" folder, box 20, NSF/HF.

82. Congressional Record, April 9, 1975, H2587; Dow, *Schoolhouse Politics*, 211.

83. Congressional Record, April 9, 1975, H2589.

84. Dow, *Schoolhouse Politics*; Nelkin, *Science Textbook Controversies*.

85. Peter B. Dow to Jerome Bruner, April 7, 1975, "Dow-Correspondence" folder, controversy drawer, EDC.

86. Jerome Bruner to Peter Dow, April 12, 1975, "Dow-Correspondence" folder, controversy drawer, EDC.

87. Ibid., 2–3.

88. "Apparatus of Teaching" report, September 16, 1959, 1, 4, 5, WH.

89. Zacharias interview, PSSC, Oral History Collection, as cited by John L. Rudolph, *Scientists in the Classroom: The Cold War Reconstruction of American Science Education* (New York: Palgrave Macmillan, 2002), 100.

90. Statement of Dr. Onalee S. McGraw before the Senate Special Subcommittee on the National Science Foundation, April 21, 1975, "Senate" folder, controversy drawer, EDC; Dow, *Schoolhouse Politics*.

91. Dow, *Schoolhouse Politics*; Nelkin, *Science Textbook Controversies*.

92. Science Curriculum Review Team, NSF, *Pre-College Science Curriculum Activities of the National Science Foundation: Volume I—Findings and Recommendations* (Washington, DC: National Science Foundation, 1975).

93. Dow, *Schoolhouse Politics*, 220–221; Letter from student Ben Kahn, "Let Me Choose," *Middletown Press* (Connecticut), April 23, 1975, "Misc. Other Local Controversies" folder, EDC.

94. Susan Marshner, *Man: A Course of Study—Prototype for Federalized Textbooks?* (Washington, DC: Heritage Foundation, 1975), 35.

95. Ibid., 35, 40.

96. Ibid., 41.

97. Ibid., 42–44.

98. Edwards, *The Power of Ideas*, 19; McGraw, *Secular Humanism and the Schools*.

99. Science Curriculum Implementation Review Group, "Report of the Science Curriculum Implementation Review Group to the Chairman," Committee on Science and Technology," October 1, 1975, attached to J. M. Moudy to Olin E. Teague, October 1, 1975; and "Minority Report of Joanne McCauley Including Dissenting and Additional Views," October 20, 1975, both in "CLO: MACOS" folder, box 20, NSF/HF.

100. Comptroller General of the United States, "Draft of Report to the Chairman, Committee on Science and Technology, Administration of the Science Education Project 'Man: A Course of Study,'" October 14, 1975, "GAO Report—DRAFT" folder, controversy drawer, EDC.

101. Goetz, "The Rise and Fall of MACOS," 519–520; National Council for the Social Studies, "The MACOS Question: Views of 'Man: A Course of Study,' and the Roles of the National Science Foundation and the Federal Government in Curriculum Development and Implementation," June 20, 1975, Accession # 820912, box 1, Executive Director Office Files, 1974–1980, NCSS.

102. Gerard Piel, "Congress Shall Make No Law…," Address to the National Science Teachers Association, March 21, 1976, "Academic Freedom" folder, box 13, Accession # 850001, NCSS.

103. Comments Related to Man: A Course of Study, May 8, 1975 Open Hearing, California State Board of Education, "California" folder, controversy drawer, EDC.

104. Tom Brunelle to Peter Dow, September 17, 1975; attached newspaper article, "Guilford Parents Organize to Discuss School Priorities," September 15, 1975, both in "Misc. Other Local Controversies" folder, controversy drawer, EDC.

105. "Social Studies Course Assailed," *Patriot Ledger*, October 8, 1975; "MACOS Orientation Discussed," *Patriot Ledger*, October 30, 1975; Notes of October 7 Meeting by NC of EDC Staff, 3–4, "Quincy, Massachusetts" folder, controversy drawer, EDC.

106. Tom Morris to Peter Dow, January 6, 1976, and EDC staffer notes of phone call; Majority Report of "The Citizen's Committee for Review of Man: A Course of Study," Collier County Public Schools, November 3, 1975; Minority Report, November 3, 1975; Position Statement (School District);

"Citizens Request for Reconsideration of a Book," all in "Collier, County, Fla." folder, controversy drawer, EDC.

107. Unidentified EDC Staffer to Peter Dow, November 4, 1975, "Quincy, Massachusetts" folder, controversy drawer, EDC.

108. Ibid.

109. Ronald O. Smith, "Response to *Social Education* Asks: What Was One of Your Most Interesting or Significant Experiences during Your Year as President of the National Council for the Social Studies," *SE* 34, no. 7 (November 1970): 812, 868; NCSS, "Minutes: 13th Delegate Assembly, NCSS House of Delegates," *SE* 34, no. 4 (April 1970): 466–471.

110. George H. Archibald, Speaking at the NCSS Wingspread Conference, Wingspread Conference Center, Racine Wisconsin, May 16, 1976, 1, 17, "Wingspread Conference folder," Accession #850625, box 2, NCSS.

111. Ibid., 18–20, 25.

112. Ibid., 24.

113. The controversy and cut in funding meant a gradual disappearance from classrooms. See, for example, Harry F. Wolcott, "The Middlemen of MACOS," *AEQ* 38, no. 2 (June 2007): 195–206.

114. Peter Dow, interview in Charles Laird, *Through These Eyes* (Documentary Educational Resources: Watertown, MA, 2003), DVD.

115. Interview with Jerome Bruner, May 12, 2008, Bruner's study in New York City, conducted by the author; Wolcott, "The Middlemen of MACOS."

6   The Conservative Restoration

1. Edward B. Jenkinson, *Censors in the Classroom* (Carbondale, IL: Southern Illinois University Press, 1979), 2–3. Jenkinson was director of the NCTE Committee Against Censorship.

2. Ibid., 10; from Minutes from a Special Session of the Board of School Trustees of the Warsaw Community Schools, June 20, 1977.

3. Jenkinson, *Censors in the Classroom*, 4–5; *WTU*, June 20, 1977, 1.

4. Jenkinson, *Censors in the Classroom*, 5–6.

5. Ibid., 6–7.

6. Larry Green, "School Book Protest a Burning Issue," *LAT*, June 3, 1978, 1; Stephen Arons, *Compelling Belief: The Culture of American Schooling* (New York: New Press, McGraw-Hill, 1983).

7. Jenkinson, *Censors in the Classroom*, 10–11.

8. Ibid., 8–9.

9. Ibid., 9–10.

10. Donald T. Rogers, *BANNED! Book Censorship in the Schools* (New York: Julian Messner, 1988), 57; Arons, *Compelling Belief*, 9.

11. Jenkinson, *Censors in the Classroom*, 13–14.

12. Arons, *Compelling Belief*.

13. Green, "School Book Protest a Burning Issue," 1.

14. Rogers, *BANNED!*

15. Robert A. Carp, "Censorship Pressure on Social Studies Teachers," *SE*, 32 (May 1968): 487–488, 492.

16. Irving R. Morrissett, "Curriculum Information Network, Fourth Report: Controversies in the Classroom," *SE* 39, no. 4 (April 1975): 246–252.

17. L. B. Woods, "Is Academic Freedom Dead in Public Schools," *PDK* 61, no. 2 (October 1979): 104–106.

18. Fred L. Pincus, "From Equity to Excellence: The Rebirth of Educational Conservatism," *SP* 14, no. 3 (Winter 1984): 50–56.

19. Ben Brodinsky, "The New Right: The Movement and Its Impact," *PDK*, 64, no. 2 (October 1982): 87–94.

20. Connaught C. Marshner, *Blackboard Tyrany* (New Rochelle, NY: Arlington House, 1978).

21. Brodinsky, "The New Right," 90. For an in-depth look at the New Right and its crusade to purify the schools see, Barbara B. Gaddy, T. William Hall, and Robert J. Marzano, *School Wars: Resolving Our Conflicts over Religion and Values* (San Francisco: Jossey-Bass, 1996).

22. Brodinsky, "The New Right," 91–92; Fred L. Pincus, "Book Banning and the New Right: Censorship in the Public Schools," *EF* 49, no. 1 (Fall 1984): 7–21.

23. Brodinsky, "The New Right," 94.

24. Pincus, "Book Banning and the New Right," 52–53.

25. *Report of the Advisory Panel on the Scholastic Aptitude Test Score Decline: On Further Examination* (New York: College Entrance Examination Board, 1977), 27.

26. Ben Brodinsky, "Back to the Basics: The Movement and Its Meaning," *PDK* 58, no. 7 (March 1977): 522.

27. Ibid., 522.

28. Ibid., 523.

29. Ibid., 527.

30. Ibid., 523.

31. Merrill Sheils, "Why Johnny Can't Write," *NW*, December 8, 1975, 58.

32. Merrill Sheils, "Back to Basics in the Schools," *NW*, October 21, 1974, 87–93.

33. Special Issue, "Teaching Basics in Social Studies," *SE* 41, no. 2 (February 1977): 96–121; Barry K. Beyer, "Teaching Basics in Social Studies," *SE* 41, no. 2 (February 1977): 96–104.

34. John P. Lunstrum, ed., Special Issue, "Improving Reading in the Social Studies," *SE* 42, no. 1 (January 1978): 8–31; John P. Lunstrum and Judith L. Irvin, "Integration of Basic Skills Into Social Studies Content," *SE* 45, no. 3 (March 1981): 169.

35. Essentials of Education Statement. *Essentials of Social Studies.* (Washington, DC: National Council for the Social Studies, 1980).

36. Richard Ohman, "The Literacy Crisis is a Fiction, if Not a Hoax," *CHE*, October 25, 1976, 32.

37. See for example, "Can the Schools Be Saved?" *NW*, May 9, 1983, 50–58; "The Bold Quest for Quality," *Time*, October 10, 1983, 58–66.

38. National Commission on Excellence in Education. *A Nation at Risk: The Imperative for Educational Reform* (Washington, DC: US Government Printing Office, 1983).

39. National Commission, *A Nation at Risk*.

40. Task Force on Education for Economic Growth. *Action for Excellence: A Comprehensive Plan to Improve Our Nation's Schools*. (Washington, DC: Twentieth Century Fund Task Force on Federal Elementary and Secondary Education Policy, 1983).

41. Joel Spring, "From Study Hall to Hiring Hall," *PR*, April 1984, 30–31.

42. Milton Goldberg, "The Essential Points of *A Nation at Risk*," *EL* 41, no. 6 (March, 1984): 15–16.

43. Lawrence C. Stedman and Marshall S. Smith, "Weak Arguments, Poor Data, Simplistic Recommendations," in Ronald Gross and Beatrice Gross. eds. *The Great School Debate* (New York: Simon and Schuster, 1985), 83–105.

44. Daniel Tanner, "The American High School at the Crossroads," *EL* 41, no. 6 (March 1984): 4–13; For another critical perspective see, Andrew Hacker, "The Schools Flunk Out," *NYR*, April 12, 1984, 35–40.

45. Peter Brimelow, "What to Do about America's Schools," *Fortune*, September 19, 1983, 60–64.

46. Ernest L. Boyer. *High School: A Report on Secondary Education in America* (Carnegie Foundation for the Advancement of Teaching. New York: Harper, 1983); Theodore R. Sizer. *Horace's Compromise: The Dilemma of the American High School* (Boston, MA: Houghton Mifflin, 1983); John I. Goodlad. *A Place Called School* (New York: McGraw-Hill, 1984).

47. Goodlad, *A Place Called School*.

48. Samuel Bowles and Herbert Gintis, *Schooling in Capitalist America: Educational Reform and the Contradictions of Economic Life* (New York: Basic Books, 1976); Michael Apple, *Ideology and Curriculum* (Boston: Routledge and Keegan Paul, 1979); Stanley Aronowitz and Henry Giroux, *Education Under Siege: The Conservative, Liberal, and Radical Debate over Schooling* (South Hadley, MA: Bergin and Garvey, 1985).

49. Thomas James and David Tyack, "Learning from Past Efforts to Reform the High School," *PDK* 64, no. 6 (February 1983): 400–406; Ronald W. Evans, "Corporate Agendas for the Social Studies: A Critique," *SSRV* 25, no. 1 (Fall, 1985): 17–24.

50. Editor, "Discussion and Debate on New Proposals for the Social Studies Curriculum," *SE* 44, no. 7 (November—December 1980): 592, 652–653.

51. Letter to the Editor, "Real vs. Ideal," *SE* 43, no. 6 (October 1979): 415.

52. Charles Myers, "Diffusion Does Not Equal Instructional Change," *SE* 43, no. 6 (1979): 485, 487–489.

53. Larry Cuban, *How Teachers Taught: Constancy and Change in American Classrooms, 1890–1980* (New York: Longman, 1984).

54. Richard S. Kirkendall, "The Status of History in the Schools," *JAH* 62, no. 2 (1975): 557–570, see 558–561; See also, Hazel W. Hertzberg, "The Teaching of History," in Michael Kammen. ed. *The Past Before Us* (Ithaca, NY: Cornell University Press, 1980).

55. Kirkendall, "The Status of History in the Schools," 565; See also, Richard S. Kirkendall, "More History/Better History," *SE* 40, no. 6 (1976): 446, 449–451; Allan O. Kownslar, "The Status of History: Some Views and Suggestions,"

SE 40, no. 6 (1976): 447–449; Stuart Paul Marcus and Paul Jeffrey Richman, "Is History Irrelevant," *SE* 42, no. 2 (1978): 150–151; Warren L. Hickman, "The Erosion of History," *SE* 43, no. 1 (January 1979): 18–22; Margaret S. Branson, "Introduction: Teaching American History," *SE* 44, no. 6 (October 1980): 453–460; Myron A. Marty, "Doing Something about the Teaching of History: An Agenda for the Eighties," *SE* 44, no. 6 (October 1980): 470–473.

56. Kownslar, "The Status of History," 447–449.

57. Stuart Paul Marcus and Paul Jeffrey Richman, "Is History Irrelevant," *SE* 42, no. 2 (1978): 150–151.

58. Branson, "Introduction," 453–460; Marty, "Doing Something about the Teaching of History," 470–473.

59. Kieran Egan, "Social Studies and the Erosion of Education," *CI* 13, no. 2 (1983): 195–214.

60. Diane Ravitch, "Decline and Fall of History Teaching," *NYT Magazine*, November 17, 1985, 50–53, 101, 117; Lynne V. Cheney, *American Memory: A Report on the Humanities in the Nation's Public Schools* (Washington, DC: National Endowment for the Humanities, 1987); Paul Gagnon, "Why Study History?," *AM* (November, 1988): 43–66; Diane Ravitch and Chester Finn, Jr. *What Do Our 17-Year-Olds Know?: A Report of the First National Assessment of History and Literature* (New York: Harper and Row, 1987). Diane Ravitch's scholarly work during this period was "supported by conservative foundations, principally the John M. Olin foundation." See Diane Ravitch, *The Death and Life of the Great American School System: How Testing and Choice are Undermining Education* (New York: Basic Books, 2010), 12.

61. Diane Ravitch, "The Revival of History: Problems and Progress," Paper presented at the Annual Meeting of the American Educational Research Association, Washington, DC, April 24, 1987, 6; Diane Ravitch, "The Plight of History in America's Schools," in Paul Gagnon, ed. *Historical Literacy: The Case for History in American Education* (New York: Macmillan, 1989).

62. Ravitch, "The Revival of History," 12, 18.

63. Bradley Commission, *Building a History Curriculum: Guidelines for Teaching History in Schools* (Washington, DC: Educational Excellence Network, 1988), 5.

64. Paul Gagnon, ed. *Historical Literacy: The Case for History in American Education* (New York: Macmillan, 1989).

65. Richard E. Gross, "Forward to the Trivia of 1890: The Impending Social Studies Program?" *PDK* 70, no. 1 (September 1988): 47–49.

66. Ronald W. Evans, "Diane Ravitch and the Revival of History: A Critique," *TSS* 80, no. 3 (May/June 1989): 85–88; Ravitch, "The Revival of History," 89–91; "Evans and Ravitch Square Off in the Social Studies," *History Matters!*, 1989.

67. Stephen J. Thornton, "Should We Be Teaching More History?" *TRSE* 18, no. 1 (1990): 53–60.

68. Sid Lester, "An Analytic Critique of the 1987 Framework," *SSR* 28, no. 2 (Winter 1989): 52–61.

69. Duane Campbell, "California Framework," Letter to the Editor, *SE* 52, no. 6 (October 1988): 403.

70. Vince Stehle, "Righting Philanthropy," *NAT*, June 30, 1997, 15–20.
71. George H. Nash, *The Conservative Intellectual Movement in America Since 1945* (New York: Basic Books, 1976), xiii–xiv; Freidrich A. Hayek, *The Road to Serfdom* (Chicago, IL: University of Chicago Press, 1944).
72. Eugene F. Provenzo, *Religious Fundamentalism and American Education: The Battle for the Public Schools* (Albany: SUNY Press, 1990), 88–89; Paul Boyer, "The Evangelical Resurgence in 1970s American Protestantism," in Bruce J. Schulman and Julian E. Zelizer, eds., *Rightward Bound: Making America Conservative in the 1970s* (Cambridge, MA: Harvard University Press, 2008), 29–51; William Martin, *With God on Our Side: The Rise of the Religious Right in America* (New York: Broadway Books, 1996); and Clyde Wilcox and Carin Larson, *Onward Christian Soldiers? The Religious Right in American Politics* (Boulder, CO: Westview Press, 2006).
73. Alice O'Connor, "Financing the Counterrevolution," in Bruce J. Schulman and Julian E. Zelizer, eds., *Rightward Bound: Making America Conservative in the 1970s* (Cambridge, MA: Harvard University Press, 2008), 152–155.
74. John Lawrence Reynolds, *Shadow People: Inside History's Most Notorious Secret Societies* (Toronto: Key Porter Books, 2006).
75. Joseph J. Onosko, "Barriers to the Promotion of Higher-Order Thinking in Social Studies," *TRSE* 19, no. 4 (Fall 1991): 341–366.
76. Cuban, *How Teachers Taught.*
77. David Tyack and Larry Cuban, *Tinkering Toward Utopia: A Century of Public School Reform* (Cambridge, MA: Harvard University Press, 1995).
78. Shirley H. Engle, "Whatever Happened to the Social Studies?" *IJSE* 4, no. 1 (Spring 1989): 51.

7 Can We Transcend the Grammar of Social Studies?

1. Karen B. Wiley and Jeanne Race, *The Status of Pre-college science, mathematics, and social science education: 1955–1975. Volume III: Social Science Education* (Boulder, CO: Social Science Education Consortium, 1977); Iris R. Weiss, *Report of the 1977 National Survey of Science, Mathematics, and Social Studies Education* (Research Triangle Park, NC: Center for Educational Research and Evaluation, 1978); Robert E. Stake and Jack A. Easley, Jr. *Case Studies in Science Education* (Urbana-Champaign, IL: Center for Instructional Research and Curriculum Evaluation, 1978).
2. Largely quoted and adapted from James P. Shaver, "Status in Social Studies and Educational Innovation: Implications of the NSF and the Rand Reports for the ABA Youth Education for Citizenship Committee," A Summary of Comments by James P. Shaver at the October 6, 1979 meeting of the YEFC Committee; James P. Shaver, O. L. Davis, Jr., and Suzanne W. Helburn, "The Status of Social Studies Education: Impressions from Three NSF Studies," *Social Education* 42, no. 2 (February 1979): 150–153.

3. See for example, Gerald Ponder, "The More Things Change … : The Status of Social Studies," *EL* 36, no. 7(April 1979): 515–518; Weiss, *Report of the 1977 National Survey of Science, Mathematics, and Social Studies Education*; Wiley and Race, *The Status of Pre-College Science*; Irving R. Morrissett, and Project SPAN Staff, *The Current State of Social Studies: A Report of Project SPAN* (Boulder, CO: Social Science Education Consortium, 1982); Douglas P. Superka, Sharyl Hawke, and Irving Morrissett, "The Current and Future Status of the Social Studies," *SE* 44, no. 5 (May 1980): 362–369.

4. Larry Cuban, "History of Teaching in Social Studies," in James P. Shaver, ed. *Handbook of Research on Social Studies Teaching and Learning* (New York: Macmillan, 1991).

5. Alan Peshkin, *Growing Up American: Schooling and the Survival of Community* (Chicago: University of Chicago Press, 1978); See also, Alan Peshkin, "Whom Shall the Schools Serve? Some Dilemmas of Local Control in a Rural School District," *CI* 6, no. 3 (1977): 181–204.

6. Superka, Hawke, and Morrissett, "The Current and Future Status of the Social Studies," 368–369.

7. Hertzberg's *Social Studies Reform* was an historical component of Project SPAN. Like others, she largely ignored the importance of the cold war in explaining the nature of the social studies reforms that were attempted during the era of the new social studies.

8. Superka, Hawke, and Morrissett, "The Current and Future Status of the Social Studies."

9. Irving R. Morrissett, "Status of Social Studies: The Mid-1980s," *SE* 50, no. 4 (April/May 1986): 303–310.

10. Michael J. Elliott and Kerry J. Kennedy, "Australian Impressions of Social Studies Theory and Practice in Secondary Schools in the United States," *SE* 43, no. 4 (April 1979): 291–295.

11. Charles Myers, " 'Diffusion' Does Not Equal 'Instructional Change,' " *SE* 43, no. 6 (October 1979): 485, 487–489.

12. Anna S. Ochoa, ed., "A Profile of Social Studies Teachers," *SE* 45, no. 6 (October 1961): 401–421.

13. Stuart B. Palonsky, *900 Shows a Year: A Look at Teaching from a Teacher's Side of the Desk* (New York: Random House, 1986), 173–181.

14. Mark C. Schug, Robert J. Todd, and R. Beery, "Why Kids Don't Like Social Studies," *SE* 48, no. 5 (May 1984): 382–387; Rodney F. Allen, "Letters: Why Kids Really Don't Like Social Studies," *SE* 49, no. 1 (January 1985): 2–3.

15. Howard Mehlinger, "Social Studies: Some Gulfs and Priorities," in Howard Mehlinger and O. L. Davis, eds. *The Social Studies: Eightieth Yearbook of the National Society for the Study of Education* (Chicago, IL: University of Chicago Press, 1981), 244–269; Fred M. Newmann, " Priorities for the Future: Toward a Common Agenda," *SE* 50, no. 4 (April/May 1986): 240–249.

16. Catherine Cornbleth, "What Constrains Meaningful Social Studies Teaching," in Walter C. Parker, ed. *Social Studies Today: Research and Practice* (New York: Routledge, 2009), 215–223; Fred M. Newmann, "Classroom Thoughtfulness and Students' Higher Order Thinking: Common

Indicators and Diverse Social Studies Courses," *TRSE* 19, no. 4 (Fall 1991): 410–433; Geoffrey Scheurman and Fred M. Newmann, "Authentic Intellectual Work in Social Studies: Putting Performance Before Pedagogy," *SE* 62, no. 1 (January 1998): 23–25.

17. J. D. McAulay, "Two Major Problems in the Teaching of Social Studies," *TSS* 51, no. 4 (April 1960): 135–139.

18. Arno A. Bellack, Herbert M. Kliebard, Ronald T. Hyman, and Frank L. Smith, *The Language of the Classroom* (New York: Teachers College Press, 1966); Seymour B. Sarason, *The Culture of the School and the Problem of Change* (Boston: Allyn & Bacon, 1971).

19. James Hoetker and William P. Ahlbrand, Jr., "The Persistence of the Recitation," *AERJ* 6, no. 2 (March 1969): 145–167.

20. Larry Cuban, "Persistent Instruction: The High School Classroom, 1900–1980," *PDK* 64, no. 2 (1982): 113–118; Larry Cuban, *How Teachers Taught: Constancy and Change in American Classrooms, 1890–1980* (New York: Longman, 1984); Cuban, "History of Teaching in Social Studies." Linda M. McNeil, *Contradictions of Control: School Structure and School Knowledge* (New York: Routledge & Kegan Paul, 1986).

21. David Tyack and Larry Cuban, *Tinkering Toward Utopia: A Century of Public School Reform* (Cambridge, MA: Harvard University Press, 1995).

22. Keith C. Barton and Linda S. Levstik, "Why Don't More History Teachers Engage Students in Interpretation? *SE* 67, no. 6 (October 2003): 358–361.

23. Catherine Cornbleth, "What Constrains Meaningful Social Studies Teaching," *SE,* 66, no. 3 (April 2002): 186–190; Diana Hess, *Controversy in the Classroom: The Democratic Power of Discussion* (New York: Routledge, 2009).

24. Diana Hess, "Controversial Issues and Democratic Discourse," in Linda Levstik and Cynthia Tyson, eds., *Handbook of Research in Social Studies Education* (New York: Routledge, 2008), 124–136; S. G. Grant and Cynthia Salinas, Assessment and Accountabilty in Social Studies," in Linda Levstik and Cynthia Tyson, eds., *Handbook of Research in Social Studies Education* (New York: Routledge, 2008): 219–236.

25. Social Studies Inquiry Research Collaborative, "Authentic Intellectual Challenge in Social Studies Classrooms," paper presented at the annual meeting of the College and University Faculty Assembly of the National Council for the Social Studies, Denver, CO, November, 2010, retrieved online at http://www.auburn.edu/ssirc/member.html

26. Edwin P. Fenton, "Reflections on 'the New Social Studies.'" *TSS* 82, no. 3 (May/June 1991): 84–90; Byron G. Massialas, "The 'New Social Studies'— Retrospect and Prospect," *TSS* 83, no. 3 (1992): 120–124.

27. Robert M. Pirsig, *Zen and the Art of Motorcycle Maintenance: An Inquiry into Values* (New York: Morrow, 1974).

28. Herbert M. Kliebard, *Struggle for the American Curriculum, 1893–1958* (Boston: Routledge & Kegan Paul, 1986).

29. Robert E. Stake and Jack A. Easley, Jr., *Case Studies in Science Education: Volume I, The Case Reports* (Urbana-Champaign, IL: Center for Instructional Research and Curriculum Evaluation and Committee on Culture and Cognition, 1978).

30. Cornbleth, "What Constrains Meaningful Social Studies Teaching"; C. Lacey, *The Socialization of Teachers* (London, England: Methuen, 1977); Kenneth M. Zeichner and Jennifer M. Gore, "Teacher Socialization," in W. R. Houston, ed., *Handbook of Research on Teacher Education* (New York: Macmillan, 1990).

31. Stake and Easley, *Case Studies in Science Education*, I-53.

32. Harriet Tyson-Bernstein and Arthur Woodward, "The Great Textbook Machine and Prospects for Reform," *SE* 50, no. 4 (January 1986): 41–45.

33. Frances Fitzgerald, *America Revised: History Schoolbooks in the Twentieth Century* (Boston: Little, Brown, 1979); James R. Loewen, *Lies My Teacher Told Me: Everything Your American History Textbook Got Wrong* (New York: New Press, 1995); Christopher R. Leahy, *Whitewashing War: Historical Myth, Corporate Textbooks, and Possibilities for Democratic Education* (New York: Teachers College Press, 2009).

34. Tyson-Bernstein and Woodward, "The Great Textbook Machine and Prospects for Reform."

35. Wiley and Race, *The Status of Pre-College Science, Mathematics, and Social Science Education*; Weiss, *Report of the 1977 National Survey of Science, Mathematics, and Social Studies Education*; Stake and Easley, *Case Studies in Science Education*; Cuban, "Persistent Instruction"; Larry Cuban, "Persistent Instruction: Another Look at Constancy in the Classroom," *PDK* 68, no. 1 (September 1986): 7–11; Cuban, *How Teachers Taught*.

36. Bellack, Kliebard, Hyman, and Smith, *The Language of the Classroom*; Hoetker and Ahlbrand, "The Persistence of the Recitation."

37. Ibid.; Tyack and Cuban, *Tinkering Toward Utopia*.

38. Tyack and Cuban, *Tinkering Toward Utopia*, 85.

39. McNeil, *Contradictions of Control;* Linda M. McNeil, *Contradictions of School Reform: Educational Costs of Standardized Testing* (New York: Routledge, 2000); Cornbleth, "What Constrains Meaningful Social Studies Teaching."

40. Martin Nystrand, Lawrence Wu, Adam Gamoran, Susie Zeiser, and Daniel Long, "Questions in Time: Investigating the Structure and Dynamics of Unfolding Classroom Discourse," *DP* 35, no. 2 (March 2003): 135–198; Joseph Kahne, Monica Rodriguez, BetsAnn Smith, B., and Keith Thiede, "Developing Citizens for Democracy? Assessing Opportunities to Learn in Chicago's Social Studies Classrooms," *TRSE* 28, no. 3 (Summer 2000): 311–338.

41. Stake and Easley, *Case Studies in Science Education*, 2–11.

42. Jeannie Oakes, *Keeping Track: How Schools Structure Inequality* (New Haven, CT: Yale University Press, 1985); See various publications of Rethinking Schools.

43. Shaver, Davis, and Helburn, "The Status of Social Studies Education"; Shug, "Why Kids Don't Like Social Studies."

44. Robert Slavin, "The Hunterization of America's Schools," *Instructor* 96, no. 8 (April 1987): 56–58, 60; Richard A. Gibboney, *The Stone Trumpet: A Story of Practical School Reform, 1960–1990* (Albany: State University of New York Press, 1994); Richard A. Gibboney, "A Critique of Madeline Hunter's Teaching Model From Dewey's Perspective," *EL* 44, no. 5 (February 1987): 46–50.

45. Stake and Easley, *Case Studies in Science Education*, I-114.
46. Ibid.
47. Fenton, "Reflections on 'The New Social Studies,'" 84–90.
48. Lee F. Anderson, "Barriers to Change in Social Studies," in Irving R. Morrissett, and Project SPAN Staff, *The Current State of Social Studies: A Report of Project SPAN* (Boulder, CO: Social Science Education Consortium, 1982), 265–313.
49. Seymour B. Sarason, *The Culture of the School and the Problem of Change* (Boston: Allyn & Bacon, 1971).
50. Jules Henry, *Culture Against Man* (New York: Random House, 1963), 283.
51. Samuel Bowles and Herbert Gintis, *Schooling in Capitalist America: Educational Reform and the Contradictions of Economic Life* (New York: Basic Books, 1976); Anderson, "Barriers to Change in Social Studies"; "Clockwork," Film by California Newsreel, 1982.
52. Larry Cuban, *The Blackboard and the Bottom Line: Why Schools Can't Be Businesses* (Cambridge, MA: Harvard University Press, 2004).
53. Suzanne W. Helburn, "The Social Studies Curriculum: Status and Potentials for Reform," *TPS*, 8, no. 3 (April 1981): 339–362; Anderson, "Barriers to Change in Social Studies."
54. Edwin Fenton, "Choosing Curriculum Materials: Who and How," Speech to Georgia Council for the Social Studies, March 1, 1974, Savannah, Georgia, 12, "Georgia Council for the Social Sciences: Choosing Curriculum Materials: Who and How" Speech, 1974 folder, box 1, Fenton Papers; Jerome Bruner, Interview conducted by the author, May 12, 2008, New York.
55. Diana Hess, "Discussion in Social Studies: Is It Worth the Trouble?" *SE* 68, no. 2 (2004): 151–155.
56. Henry, *Culture Against Man*, 283–284, 320–321.
57. Peter Levine, "Why Schools and Colleges Often Overlook Civic Development," (2005), http://www.peterlevine.ws/mt/archives/000751.html.
58. Gross, "The Status of the Social Studies," 199.
59. Paul M. Nachtigal, *A Foundation Goes to School: The Ford Foundation Comprehensive School Improvement Program, 1960–1970* (New York: Ford Foundation, 1972).
60. Gerald W. Marker, "Why Schools Abandon the 'New Social Studies' Materials," *TRSE* 7 no. 4 (Winter 1980): 35–57.
61. Edwin P. Fenton, "What Happened to the New Social Studies: A Case Study in Curriculum Reform," Paper presented at the Annual Meeting of the National Council for the Social Studies, Chicago, 1985, 12.
62. Anderson, "Barriers to Change in Social Studies."
63. Bruner interview.
64. Thomas S. Popkewitz, "Latent Values in Discipline-Centered Curriculum," Paper presented at the annual meeting of the National Council for the Social Studies, Atlanta, Georgia, November 26–29, 1975; published under same title, Thomas S. Popkewitz, "Latent Values in Discipline-Centered Curriculum," *TRSE* 5, no. 1 (April 1977): 41–60.

65. Peter W. Greenwood, Dale Mann, and Milbrey W. McLaughlin, *Federal Programs Supporting Educational Change, Vol. III: The Process of Change* (Santa Monica, CA: Rand, 1975).

66. Nachtigal, *A Foundation Goes to School*; Marker, "Why Schools Abandon the 'New Social Studies' Materials."

67. Bruner interview.

68. Fenton, "Reflections on the 'New Social Studies'"; Tyack and Cuban, *Tinkering Toward Utopia*.

69. Lynn R. Nelson and Frederick R. Drake, "Secondary Teachers' Reactions to the New Social Studies," *TRSE* 22, no. 1 (Winter 1994): 44–73.

70. Tyack and Cuban, *Tinkering Toward Utopia*.

71. Bruner interview.

Conclusion: Reflections on Education for Democracy

1. For a thoughtful analysis of the growing influence of the religious right, see Kevin Phillips, *American Theocracy: The Peril and Politics of Radical Religion, Oil, and Borrowed Money in the 21st Century* (New York: Viking, 2006).

2. Freire, *Pedagogy of the Oppressed* (New York: Continuum, 1970); Marcuse, *One-Dimensional Man: Studies in the Ideology of Advanced Industrial Society* (Boston: Beacon Press, 1964).

3. See, for example, Walter Parker, *Teaching Democracy: Unity and Diversity in Public Life* (New York: Teachers College Press, 2003); Diana Hess, *Controversy in the Classroom: The Democratic Power of Discussion* (New York: Routledge, 2009); Shirley H. Engle and Anna S. Ochoa, *Education for Democratic Citizenship: Decision Making in the Social Studies* (New York: Teachers College Press, 1988); Amy Gutmann, *Democratic Education* (Princeton, NJ: Princeton University Press, 1987); John Dewey, *Democracy and Education: An Introduction to the Philosophy of Education* (New York: Macmillan, 1916).

4. For less than hopeful assessments of the prospects for significant change see for example, James M. Becker, "Prospect for Change in Social Studies," *Social Education*, 29 (1965): 20–22; Seymour B. Sarason, *The Culture of the School and the Problem of Change* (Boston: Allyn & Bacon, 1971); James P. Shaver, "Lessons from the Past: The Future of an Issues-Centered Social Studies Curriculum, *The Social Studies* 80, no. 5 (1989): 192–196; Howard Mehlinger, "Social Studies: Some Gulfs and Priorities," in Howard Mehlinger and O. L. Davis, eds., *The Social Studies: Eightieth Yearbook of the National Society for the Study of Education* (Chicago, IL: University of Chicago Press, 1981), 244–269; John Haas, "Is Social Studies Impervious to Change," *The Social Studies* 77, no. 2 (1986): 61–77.

5. Jerome Bruner interview, conducted by the author, May 12, 2008, at Bruner's study, New York.

6. David Tyack, *Seeking Common Ground: Public Schools in a Diverse Society* (Cambridge, MA: Harvard University Press, 2003).

7. Bruner interview; Harry F. Wolcott, "The Middlemen of Macos," *AEQ* 38, no. 2 (June 2007): 195–206.

8. Michael Cole, "What's Culture Got to Do With It? Educational Research as a Necessarily Interdisciplinary Enterprise," *ER* 39, no. 6 (August/September 2010): 461–470.

9. Kliebard, *The Struggle for the American Curriculum, 1893-1955* (Boston: Routledge and Keegan Paul, 1986), 29.

10. James P. Shaver, "A Critical View of the Social Studies Profession," *SE* 41, no. 4 (April 1977): 300–307.

11. For an overview see, Ronald W. Evans and David W. Saxe, eds., *Handbook on Teaching Social Issues* (Washington, DC: National Council for the Social Studies, Bulletin #93, 1996).

12. See especially, Jerome Bruner, *The Process of Education* (Cambridge, MA: Harvard University Press, 1960); Edwin P. Fenton, *The New Social Studies* (New York: Holt, Rinehart and Winston, 1967); Edwin P. Fenton, *Teaching the New Social Studies in Secondary Schools: An Inductive Approach* (New York: Holt, Rinehart and Winston, 1966); Donald W. Oliver and James P. Shaver, *Teaching Public Issues in the High School* (Boston: Houghton Mifflin, 1966); and High School Geography Project and Sociological Resources for the Social Studies, *Experiences in Inquiry: HSGP and SRSS* (Boston: Allyn and Bacon, 1974).

13. On academic freedom and related issues see Jean E. Brown, ed. *Preserving Intellectual Freedom: Fighting Censorship in Our Schools* (Urbana, IL: National Council of Teachers of English, 1994); Harmon Zeigler, *The Political Life of American Teachers* (Englewood Cliffs, NJ: Prentice-Hall, 1967); Howard Beale, *Are American Teachers Free? An Analysis of the Restraints upon the Freedom of Teaching in American Schools* (Chicago: Charles Scribners' Sons, 1936); "Academic Freedom Forum," *OAH Newsletter* 33, no. 2 (May 2005): 1–16; Joan DelFattore, *Knowledge in the Making: Academic Freedom and Free Speech in America's Schools and Universities* (New Haven, CT: Yale University Press, 2010); "Academic Freedom and the Social Studies Teacher," http://www.socialstudies.org/positions/academicfreedom, accessed 9/15/2010; and Jack L. Nelson with Carole Hahn, "The Need for Courage in American Schools: Cases and Causes," *SE*, no. 4 (November/December 2010): 298–303.

14. Jim Carnes, *Us and Them: A History of Intolerance in America* (Montgomery, AL: Teaching Tolerance, 1995); Karen Armstrong, *The Battle for God* (New York: Ballantine, 2000).

15. Harold O. Rugg, *That Men May Understand: An American in the Long Armistice* (New York: Doubleday and Doran, 1941) xiv–xv.

16. Bruner interview.

17. Stephanie van Hover, David Hicks, Jeremy Stoddard, and Melissa Lisanti, "From a Roar to a Murmur: Virginia's History & Social Science Standards, 1995–2009," *TRSE* 38, no. 1 (Winter 2010): 80–113.

Index

abortion, 126, 155, 186

academic freedom, 2, 83–88, 97, 99, 104, 119, 131, 137, 141, 144, 146, 153, 155, 179, 185, 197, 207–210, 214

academics, 67, 68, 84, 155, 207, 214

accountability, 2, 6, 57, 79, 133, 137, 162, 195, 200, 208

Action for Excellence, 167

activism, 2, 28, 29, 57, 58, 67, 79, 83, 121, 123, 126, 159, 178–182, 207, 210

activities, 21, 33–34, 40, 55, 61–64, 77, 84, 92, 95, 97, 102, 120, 133, 139, 141, 159, 160, 181, 191, 198

Adelson, Joseph, 159

administration, 19, 34, 35, 43, 57, 65, 86, 122, 151, 168, 199, 200, 201

administrators, 40, 46, 48, 72, 77, 83, 86, 88, 96, 102, 151, 155, 161, 168, 191, 196, 197, 198, 199, 200, 206, 212

adoption(s), 51, 68, 91, 92, 93, 142, 154, 177, 187, 195, 196, 197, 198, 203

affective, 12, 23, 37, 53, 63, 187

Africa, 29, 56

Ahern, Francis, 85

Ahlbrand, William P., 188, 193

Air Research and Development Command, 15

Alabama, 125

Alaska, 49

alienation, 36, 40, 50, 60, 70, 142, 204

Alpert, Richard, 15

alternative schools, 38, 60–63

American Civil Liberties Union (ACLU), 155

American Collegiate Testing Program (ACT), 165

American Enterprise Institute (AEI), 123, 127, 159

American Historical Association (AHA), 50

American Legion, 154

American Library Association's Office for Intellectual Freedom, 153

American Memory, 174

American Opinion, 122

American Opinion Bookstores, 114, 122–123

American Party, 3, 118, 125, 143

American Political Behavior, 203

Americanism, 87, 89, 115, 154

Americans, The, 86–90

Amherst Project, 21

Anaheim, 116, 121

Anaheim Bulletin, 116, 121

analogy, 17, 136

"An Andalusian Dog," 84

Anderson, Vernon, 89

Anglo, 34

Angus, David, 56
animals, 99, 101, 108–112, 116, 128, 139
announcement of "project social studies," 20, 21
Annunzio, Frank, 133
anthropologists, 80, 99, 202. *See also* DeVore, Henry, Oliver (Douglas)
anthropology, 21, 131, 176, 177, 187–188
anti-communism, 14, 122, 178
antiwar, 28, 30, 38, 47, 57, 73, 126, 207
anxieties, 9, 90, 128, 133, 139, 170, 171
Anyon, Jean, 71
apathy, 34, 48, 109, 180, 201
apparatus (of teaching), 17, 135
Apple, Michael, 70, 72, 169
appropriations bill, 127, 128, 131, 141
aptitudes, 61, 160, 199
Archibald, George H., 118, 122, 127, 129, 144, 145, 146
Arctic, 112, 128
Arizona, 91, 107, 108, 110, 113, 114, 115, 118, 127, 135
Arizona Republic, 118
Armor, David, 156
Aronowitz, Stanley, 169
arts, 48, 63, 64, 92, 94, 166
Asante, Molefi K., 64
Ashford, John, 127
Asia, 29, 56
Asian Pacific, 27, 32
assassination, 28, 32
assessments, 41, 78, 164, 174, 179, 188–189, 204
assimilation, 66, 108
associations, professional, 50, 92–96, 106, 122, 151–155. *See also specific associations*: AHA, NEA, Kanawha County

Association of Classroom Teachers, NAM, WCEA, Indiana State Teachers Association, American Library Association's Office for Intellectual Freedom
associations (other). *See specific associations*: PTA, NAACP, YWCA
assumptions, 12, 16, 25, 33, 42, 55, 61, 74, 91, 178, 191, 201, 204–205
atheism, 92, 103, 117, 123, 126
Atlanta, 84, 88, 144
Atlanta Constitution, 88
Atlantic Monthly, 174
atomic bomb, 10, 48
attitudes, 19, 32, 42, 47–52, 61, 65, 69, 91, 106, 107, 113, 128–129, 134, 156, 173, 192, 199
attorney, 149, 153
audiovisual, 64, 78
Austin, Texas, 85, 120
Australia, 144, 190
authentic, 193, 195, 199, 208, 214, 215
authoritarian, 28, 42
avante-garde, 57, 59, 210

baboon, 108, 109, 128
back-to-basics, 77, 79, 113, 149, 156, 159, 160–171, 178, 180, 207
backlash, 125, 156, 159
Balkanize, 65
ban, 161. *See also* academic freedom
Baptists, 93, 100–103, 109, 122
Barr, Burton, 110
Barr, Robert D., 63, 110
barriers to reform, 63, 198, 202
Barth, Roland S., 61, 62
Barton, Keith, 194
Barzun, Jacques, 124

basics, 3, 77, 79, 87, 113, 117,
    118, 124, 145, 149, 156, 159,
    160–171, 178, 180, 207. *See
    also* back-to-basics, Council for
    Basic Education
Bauman amendment, 133
Becker, James, 23, 189
behaviorism, 29, 56, 57, 62, 107,
    116, 119, 200. *See also* Skinner
beliefs, 18, 24, 42, 53, 71, 91, 96, 97,
    103–107, 113, 118, 128, 139,
    164, 179–181
The Bell Jar, 151, 168
Bellack, Arno, 193
Bellevue, Washington, 114
Benjamin, James M., 77, 78, 84
Bennett, William J., 65, 174
Berger, Evelyn, 64
Berkeley, California, 144
Bestor, Arthur E., 10, 40, 124, 160
Beyer, Barry K., 163, 164
Bible, 101, 119, 157, 159
Bigelow, Bill, 72
bigotry, 65
Bingham, Mary, 124
biologists, 15
Birch Lane Elementary, 142
Birchers (John Birch Society), 3, 49,
    91, 92, 96, 106, 114, 118–123,
    142, 143, 154
Blacks, 27, 30, 31, 32, 33, 34, 36,
    48, 49, 84, 85, 93, 150
Black Panthers, 49
Black Power, 30
Black Voices, 84
blindfolded games, 158
blood, 1, 36, 108, 109, 215
blueprint, 20
Blum, John Morton, 15
Boise, Idaho, 118
bombings, 94–96
bookstores, 41, 56, 91, 114, 126
boredom, 19, 201
Boston, 17, 40, 142, 143

Bowles, Samuel, 69, 70, 169
Boyer, Ernest, 168
Bradley, Harry, 122, 175–179
Bradley Commission on History in
    the Schools, 175–178
Bradley Foundation (Lynde and
    Harry), 177, 179
Bragg, Dr. Charles, 150
brains, 13, 14, 17, 24
brainwashing, 14, 40
Brainwashing in the High School, 14
Brameld, Theodore, 35, 36
Britain, 60
British infant school, 59
Brown, Richard, 49
Bruner, Jerome S., 14–18, 21, 24,
    40, 62, 99, 106–115, 119,
    124, 132–139, 147, 202, 205,
    206–216. *See also* Endicott
    House Conference, *Process of
    Education*, Woods Hole
Buckley, William F., 179
Building a History Curriculum, 175
Bunuel, Luis, 84
bureaucracy, 37, 43, 44, 125, 137,
    145, 198, 201
Burlington, Vermont, 115–117
Burlington Free Press, 117
Burnau, Teresa, 150, 151
Burns, Daniel, 119, 236
Bush, George H. W., 65
business, 2, 5, 11, 79, 95, 118, 126,
    156, 159, 167, 168, 170, 179,
    182, 200, 201, 207, 208, 211,
    215
Business and Professional People's
    Alliance for Better Textbooks, 95
business mentality, 208, 211
busing, 126, 142
bypass, 12, 25, 40, 200

Cain, Richard W., 109
California, 50, 66, 68, 116, 130,
    142, 143, 174–177

Callaway, Luke, 84
Cambridge, Massachusettts, 19, 131
Campbell, Duane, 177
Campbell, Edwin, 138, 177, 243
Canada, 116, 173
cannibalism, 108, 116
canon (literary), 64
capitalism, 43, 69, 70, 80, 169, 200,
    202, 212
career, 56, 57, 79, 152, 167, 171,
    173, 185, 197
Carlsen, Robert, 46, 47
Carmichael, Stokeley, 30, 31
Carnegie Foundation, 12, 20
Carnegie Institute of Technology,
    18, 19
Carnegie Mellon Project, 186, 203
Carnegie unit, 51, 181
Carpenter, John, 49
Castle Rock Foundation (Coors),
    121
Cato Institute, 179
CBE Bulletin, 124, 137
CBS television, 95
censorship, 5, 86, 90, 93, 102, 129,
    133, 144, 152–158, 185, 186,
    192
Central Intelligence Agency (CIA),
    10, 11, 204, 217
centrist conservatives, 156, 159, 161
certification of teachers, 172, 190,
    200, 205
Chamber of Commerce, 11
Chapel, William I., 150
Charleston, West Virginia, 92, 93
Charleston Daily Mail, 93
Charleston Gazette, The, 93
Chausse, Peggy, 115, 236
Cheney, Lynne, 174
Cherryholmes, Cleo, 72
Child Seducers, The, 116, 121
child-centeredness, 78
chimpanzee, 128
Chisholm, Jeanne S., 112

Christianity, 93, 101, 103, 106, 116,
    143
Chronicle of Higher Education, 137
chronological, 90, 172, 175, 176,
    190
churches, 2, 4, 5, 93, 100–105, 109,
    116, 117, 119, 120, 126, 142,
    149, 150, 157, 195
citizens, 1–3, 11, 25, 73, 78, 88,
    94–97, 100, 106, 115, 117,
    123–127, 132, 133, 142–145,
    151, 152, 176, 182, 201, 214
Citizens for Decency Through Law,
    96
Citizens for Moral Education
    (CME), 100–105
Citizens United for Responsible
    Education (CURE), 106, 107
citizenship, 21, 56, 167, 170, 171,
    174, 182, 186, 194, 201
civics, 65, 116, 158, 182, 196, 202,
    212, 213
civil rights, 25, 27, 36, 40, 57, 59,
    64, 68, 73, 123, 126, 204, 207
Clark, Todd, 96
classroom practices, 2, 43, 177,
    186–187, 195, 198–199, 200,
    203, 209–213
Cleaver, Eldridge, 92
clinics, 33–35, 61
cognitive, 12, 17, 23, 53, 55, 63,
    119, 187
cold war, 5, 9–20, 24, 42, 48, 109,
    189, 207
Coleman, James, 159
colleges, 18, 47, 67, 76, 79, 84, 88,
    145, 150, 153, 157, 160, 162,
    165, 171, 172, 214
Collier County, Florida, 143
Colorado, 144
Columbia County, Florida, 103, 114,
    139
Columbia University, 139
columnist, 119, 121, 131, 159

Commentary, 159

commercial publishers, 100, 129, 137, 189, 206

commissions, 60, 93, 165, 167, 168, 169, 175, 178. *See also specific commissions*: Bradley Commission on History in the Schools, National Commission on Excellence in Education, Plowden Commission, West Virginia Human Rights Commission

communism, 9, 10, 14, 17, 97, 101, 103, 110, 117, 122, 123, 143, 158, 179

communities, 31–34, 45, 61, 62, 68, 85, 86, 93–96, 110, 114, 118, 128, 129, 145, 146, 149, 151–155, 159, 188, 197, 205, 215

competency, 57, 79, 113, 160, 161, 162, 167, 189

competition, 10, 14, 128, 129, 166, 167, 190, 211

complacency, 28

complaints, 15, 35, 76, 77, 78, 84, 85, 86, 91, 103, 105, 107, 114, 115, 120, 127, 143, 149, 151, 160, 162, 168, 172, 190

compulsory, 38, 39, 40, 43, 172

Compulsory Miseducation, 39–40

computer, 57, 166, 167, 198

Conant, James B., 39

concepts, 2, 13, 16, 24, 27, 29, 32, 45, 47, 48, 54, 56, 63, 74, 76, 79, 103, 106, 117, 136, 160, 161, 171, 190, 193, 195, 201, 203, 204, 205, 206, 214

conceptual, 19, 24, 27, 165, 170, 173, 188

conference, 14–20, 22, 29, 35, 36, 85, 134, 144–145, 191
    Endicott House, 19–20
    Wingspread, 144–145

Woods Hole, 15–20, 135

Conflict and Change, 154

conformity, 27, 38, 39, 60, 67, 188

confrontations, 4, 28, 29, 52, 100, 105, 125, 204, 205

Congress, US, 3, 10, 97, 119, 123–138, 141

congressional, 119, 129–142, 144

Congressmen, 118, 122–127, 132, 135, 139, 144, 146

Conlan, Jocko, 127

Conlan, John B., 118, 122–146

Conlan amendment, 128–133, 141

conscientization, 69

consensus, 3, 15, 20, 23, 156, 161, 165, 182, 213, 215

conservative restoration, 1, 92, 149–182, 207, 209, 212, 214

conservatives, 99, 123, 125–126, 141–143, 149–181, 202, 214–215

conspiracy, 83–97, 117, 122, 179, 180, 202

The Conspirators: Men Against God, 116

constancy (classroom), 2, 181, 188, 192–196, 209–215

Constitution, US, 46, 88, 122

constraints, 1–6, 180, 181, 194, 197, 202, 206, 209–216

constructivism, 208

consumerism, 56, 76, 78, 85, 171

context, 5, 9, 10, 13, 18, 21, 22, 94, 115, 143, 171, 196, 202–212

"continuum from winners to losers," 63

controversies
    Fenton textbook controversy, 86–91
    Kanawha County, West Virginia, 91–97
    MACOS controversy, 99–147
    Warsaw, Indiana, 149–153

conventional, 45, 169, 181, 191, 206

Cooperative Research Program, 15
Coors, Joseph, 121, 123, 179
Corinth, New York, 117
Cornbleth, Catherine, 194
Cornell, Marvin, 108, 110, 111
corporations, 14, 15, 69, 123, 145, 153
Correll, Shirley, 143
Council for Basic Education (CBE), 3, 118, 124
councils, 3, 22, 28, 83, 84, 87, 102, 118, 121, 122, 124, 141, 145, 155, 160, 215. *See also specific councils*: CBE, NCHE, NCSS
counterculture, 27, 40, 43, 47, 57, 61, 74
countersocialization, 188, 201, 211
Counts, George S., 213
course offerings, 28, 45–51, 56, 75, 76, 185, 192
coverage, 11, 88, 93, 97, 180, 194–197, 199, 210–215
Cox, C. Benjamin, 73
creation myths, 108
creationism, 156, 157, 186
creativity, 99, 162, 213
credentials, 172, 200, 202
crisis, 13, 14, 20, 28, 38, 56, 60, 96, 114, 156, 164–167, 172–174, 178. *See also* crisis mentality, literacy crisis, *Nation at Risk*, Sputnik
Crisis in the Classroom, 60
crisis mentality, 14
critical pedagogy, 68–72
critics
    of MACOS, 119–127
    of new social studies, 23–24
    of newer social studies, 155–165
    of progressive education, 9–10
Cronbach, Lee, 15
crusade, 48, 74, 88, 93, 97, 149, 172
Cuban, Larry, 20, 171, 181, 188, 194, 198, 206

culture, 1–4, 13, 27, 30–32, 38, 41, 49, 58, 64–66, 70, 73, 75, 78, 80, 97, 99, 104–107, 112, 116, 126, 131, 133, 138–139, 155, 159, 175, 180–185, 193–196, 200–205, 212
    cultural pluralism, 65–67
    culture of the school, 193–204
    Netsilik culture, 99, 105–116, 126, 128, 132, 139, 142
curiosity, 19, 38, 59, 61, 116, 164, 201
curriculum
    curriculum politics, 1–4, 188, 204, 209–216
    curriculum reform, 2, 11–20, 40, 129, 132, 140, 195–196, 207, 209
Curriculum Development Associates (CDA), 100, 105, 137, 138, 141
cyclical, 53, 208

Dali, Salvador, 84
Dallas, Texas, 76, 141
Daughters of the American Revolution, 154
Davie, Donald, 115, 117
Davis, California, 142
Davis, Carl, 152
Davis, O. L., 85, 186, 188
De Kalb, Illinois, 143
death, 37, 40, 120
Death at an Early Age, 37, 40
Debating P. C., 67
decision making, 29, 54, 56, 63, 83, 156, 171, 186, 211
deconstructionists, 67
defense, 3, 11, 13, 67, 72, 78, 85, 89, 102, 115, 133, 136, 140, 141, 144, 146, 151, 155
dehumanizing, 63, 69
deluge of attacks, 10, 39
democracy, 16, 43, 56–58, 78, 88, 101, 140, 143, 182, 185, 194, 196, 199, 209–211, 214, 216

democratic, 1, 5, 27, 49, 60, 72, 78,
    89, 91, 129, 135, 164, 173, 175,
    194, 199, 211, 215
Democratic Education, 72
deposits, 69
depth, 1, 3, 6, 16, 19, 20, 32, 34,
    48–49, 51, 106–107, 123, 146,
    169, 170, 192, 215
deregulation, 123
Derrida, Jacques, 68
deschooling, 40, 41, 44, 60, 61
Deschooling Society, 38, 41
desegregation, 144
*Design for Social Education in the
    Open Classroom, A*, 63–64
detachment, 36, 205
developmental, 21, 150
devil, 84, 134
DeVore, Irven, 99
Dewey, John, 3, 54, 55, 60, 61, 68,
    116, 121, 213, 216, 247, 249
dialogue, 53, 68, 69, 71, 112, 145
differentiated, 39, 56, 57, 75, 199
diffusion, 22, 64, 73, 171, 190
DiFrancesco, Dr. Armand, 139
dilemmas, 1, 2, 6, 22, 35, 40, 55, 80,
    131, 170, 171, 192, 198, 205,
    209–216
"directionlessness," 171
directorate, 128, 130, 145, 179,
    180
"dirty books," 94, 125
"dirty words," 151, 158
disadvantaged, 170, 204
discipline, 79, 80, 161
discourse, 64, 65, 70, 71, 133, 181,
    198, 199
discovery, 12, 16, 23, 139, 207
discrimination, 33, 35, 48
discussion, 1, 17, 34–35, 41, 49,
    55, 63, 80, 84–87, 101–104,
    110, 118, 120, 126–129,
    139–141, 145, 158, 170,
    187–189, 194, 195, 199, 202,
    204, 211

dismissals, 84–85, 151–153
dissemination, 20, 22, 34, 45, 47,
    101, 102, 133, 137
dissent, 49, 60, 87, 104, 140
distribution, 146, 158
districts, 22, 45, 49, 51, 59, 61, 76,
    90, 94, 95, 101, 105, 106, 107,
    113, 115, 128–129, 139, 144,
    149, 150–153, 160, 161, 187,
    189, 197, 206
Disuniting of America, The,
    66–67
diversity, 21, 64, 65, 131, 134, 136,
    156, 189
divinity, 158
Dixie, 125
docility, 41, 60, 167
Doeller, Thomas, 111
dollars, 13, 22, 48, 106, 120, 142
Dornan, Robert (Bob), 98
Dow, Peter, 102–119, 129–141, 147,
    182
Down These Mean Streets, 154
"drilling children," 80, 201, 202,
    211
"drivenness," 80, 202
D'Souza, Dinesh, 67
DuBois, W. E. B., 32
dumbing-down, 78
Dupont, Joann, 151
DuShane Fund, 155
dynamited, 95
dysfunctional, 2, 37, 63, 196

Eagle Forum, 159
Eames, Charles, 135
ecology, 56, 64, 73
economics, 11, 18, 24, 67, 84, 167,
    176, 177, 185, 189, 201,
    202
economists, 24, 156
ecumenical, 215
editorials, 51, 93, 151, 152
Edmundson, Mark, 67
Education and Freedom, 13

Education Development Center
    (EDC; later ESI), 21, 100, 105,
    114, 115, 118, 124, 132–138,
    141–144
Education Under Siege, 169
Educational Advisory Committee of
    the NAM, 122
Educational Services Incorporated
    (ESI; later EDC), 14, 19, 20, 99,
    100
Educational Testing Service (ETS),
    165, 172
Educational Wastelands, 10
educationists, 10, 145, 174
Educator, The, 121
efficiency, 3, 4, 5, 57, 164, 169, 175,
    194, 200, 201, 211, 213
Egan, Kieran, 173
Eisenhower, Dwight D., 11
elections, 48, 92, 156
electives, 47–51, 75–78, 104, 150,
    159, 161, 169, 185, 204
elementary, 18, 40, 46, 64, 95, 100,
    106, 108, 119, 142, 149, 160,
    185, 203
elites, 25, 43, 70, 97, 106, 165
Elliott, Michael, 190
Ellsworth, Elizabeth, 71
emancipation, 70–72
embalming, 36
embryonic democracy, 199
empire, 2, 32, 195
empowerment, 179, 194
enculturation, 201
Endicott House Conference, 19, 20
engagement, 29, 192, 215
England, 38, 62
Engle, Shirley H., 54, 63, 73, 182
enthusiasm, 22, 47, 50, 52, 54, 60,
    75, 114
entrenched dilemmas, 1, 2, 31, 68,
    74, 176, 181, 207, 209, 211, 212
environmental, 29, 45, 50, 56, 69,
    73, 76, 84, 119, 123, 136, 189,
    205

Episcopal, 93
epistemologies, 72
equality, 27, 30, 32, 69, 75, 127,
    152, 178, 182, 205–207
equity, 65, 156, 159, 170
Eskimos (Netsilik), 99, 106, 107,
    116, 117, 128–132, 142
establishment, 5, 18, 28, 30, 40, 42,
    79, 106, 166, 179, 200
ethnicity, 57, 66
ethnocentrism, 65, 131, 136
ethnographic, 188
Etzioni, Amitai, 62
Europe(an), 14, 17, 59, 65–71
evaluations, 21, 35, 44, 51, 90, 110,
    111, 141, 206
evangelical, 5, 126, 178, 179, 180,
    238
Evans, Ronald W., 176
evidence, 10, 18, 28, 35, 51, 57, 75,
    76, 88, 96, 97, 114, 129, 153,
    164–166, 172, 176, 188, 193–
    196, 199, 203, 211
evolution, 9, 66, 69, 99–103, 107–
    108, 117–120, 126, 158, 186,
    204
examination, 34, 39, 71, 120, 139
excellence, 37, 97, 105, 156, 165,
    167, 168, 170, 178, 202
expectations, 6, 25, 31, 35, 63, 172,
    180, 190, 192, 195–198, 203,
    206, 210
experimentation, 3, 44, 51, 52, 75,
    80, 110, 119, 140, 146, 156,
    159, 206
exploitation, 80
extracurricular, 95
extremism, 49, 96, 105, 156
Extremism—USA, 49

facts, 16, 91, 94, 103, 107, 108, 124,
    145, 161, 164, 174
Facts About Sex for Today's Youth,
    94
fads, 74, 157, 160, 206

faith, 24, 103, 105, 112
Falwell, Jerry, 156
families, 87, 92, 96, 104, 120–123, 128, 131, 139, 145, 150–162, 179–180, 185
fanatical, 93, 112
Fantini, Mario, 63
Featherstone, Joseph, 60, 62
federal, 47, 106, 132, 133, 138, 145
federation of subjects, 18
Feldmesser, Robert, 19, 20
feminist, 68, 71, 72, 126
Fenocchio, Floyd, 142
Fenton, Edwin P. (Ted), 2, 18–21, 32, 40, 49, 54, 55, 86–91, 97, 106, 182, 202, 213
    and Carnegie Mellon Project, 18–19, 186, 203
    and Georgia textbook controversy, 86–96
    on "national conspiracy," 91
ferment, 22, 37
Feulner, Edwin, 123
Fike, Elmer, 95
filiopietism, 66
filmstrips, 99
financial, 3, 62, 99, 120, 127, 138, 141, 154, 159
Finland, 144
Finn, Chester E., 159, 174
Fitzgerald, Frances, 173
Florida, 100, 102, 103, 143, 144
Florida Action Committee for Education (FACE), 143
Florida Times-Union, 103
Fogarty, John, 86
Ford Foundation, 12, 20
Fortune, 168
Foucault, Michel, 68, 80
foundations, 3, 10, 12, 14, 20, 21, 53, 83, 95–98, 100, 112, 118–127, 138–141, 144, 156, 175–179, 182, 186, 207, 209, 213. See also AEI, Carnegie, Castle Rock, Cato, Ford,

Heritage, Hudson, JM, Koch, Manhattan, Olin, Scaife, Smith Richardson
Fraenkel, Jack, 55
fragmentation, 28, 66
framework, 44, 51, 66, 76, 77, 97, 169, 175–177, 194
Frankfurt school, 68
Free and the Brave, The, 111
free enterprise, 157–159, 179, 180, 185, 189
free schools, 60–63
freedom, 1–4, 13, 17, 27–28, 39, 44, 60–62, 74, 79, 80–91, 97, 99, 104, 106, 111, 117, 119, 131–132, 137, 141, 144–146, 153–155, 185, 197, 207–216. See also academic freedom
Freire, Paulo, 69
"frills," 161
frontier of knowledge, 16
Fulbright, 127
Fulton County, Georgia, 87
fundamentalism, 92–98, 100, 103, 126, 146, 149, 152, 156, 157, 209
futurism, 29, 56, 170

Gabler, Mel and Norma, 3, 92, 95, 115–121, 142, 153–159
Gadamer, Hans-Georg, 68
Gagne, Robert, 15
Gagnon, Paul, 174, 175
Gallup poll, 162
Gardner, David P., 168
Gardner, Eileen, 156
Gates, Henry Louis, 64
Gay rights, 27, 73, 85
gender, 27, 30, 65, 72, 201
General Accounting Office (GAO), 138, 141
General Accounting Office (GAO) investigation, 138–141
generalizations, 23, 171
Genesis, 108

genocide, 108
geography, 10, 21, 140, 155, 158, 171–177, 182, 185, 187, 196, 203, 212, 213
Georgetown University, 121
Georgia, 2, 84–91, 97, 106, 144
ghetto, 37
Giamatti, A. Bartlett, 168
Gibson, Emily, 32
gifted, 12, 14
Gilder, George, 156
gimmicks, 77
Gintis, Herbert, 69, 70, 169
girls, 89, 109, 139, 151, 158
Giroux, Henry, 71, 72, 169
Glazer, Nathan, 159
Glenn, Rev. Donald, 100–105, 143
glorification, 40
Go Ask Alice, 151
goals, 4, 16, 23, 40, 44, 51–54, 62, 66, 68, 108, 117–118, 125, 135–139, 167, 176–177, 187, 194
Godless, 100, 111, 123
Godly, 125
Good, John M., 21, 150, 167
Goodlad, John I., 168, 169
Goodman, John, 38, 39, 40, 60
gory, 128, 139, 142
Gothic, 150
government, 2, 5, 10–11, 15, 17, 24, 29, 38, 44, 46, 51, 75, 88, 90, 106–107, 116, 120, 122–141, 145–146, 150, 156, 158, 159, 166, 175, 178–179, 185, 187, 190, 198, 207
governor, 125, 168
Graley, Rev. Ezra, 124
grammar of schooling, 25, 180, 181, 194, 198, 206
grammar of social studies, 1, 4, 185–216
Gramsci, Antonio, 68
Grand Island, Nebraska, 85

graphic, 99, 128
Greeley, Colorado, 144
Gross, Richard E., 23, 176, 185–186
Gross, Ronald, 43
Growing Up Absurd, 38, 39
guidelines, 12, 44–46, 64, 96, 101, 105, 107, 118, 189
Guilford, New Hampshire, 142
Gulf Oil, 123
"gulfs" in social studies, 192
gunfire, 94, 95
Gutman, Amy, 72

Haas, John, 203
Habermas, Jurgen, 68
Hahn, Carole, 185, 186
Hale, Nathan, 120
Halsey, Van, 21
Hamilton, Charles V., 30, 31
Hampton, Virginia, 144
Handbook of Research on Multicultural Education, 64
"handmaidens" to socializing purpose, 174
Hare, Nathan, 32
Harlan, Louis, 32
Harlem renaissance, 50
Harrison, Robert, 102–105
Hartwell, Project, 17, 135
Harvard, 19, 21, 55, 99, 100, 119, 127, 135, 186, 203
Harvard Project, 21, 203
Hatch, Orrin, 156
Hatter, M. E., 108
Hayek, Freidrich, 178
hegemony, 66, 70, 202
Helburn, Suzanne W., 186, 188
Heller, Joseph, 154
Helms, Jesse, 156
helter-skelter, 79
Hemingway, Earnest, 42
Hempstead, New York, 143
Henry, Jules, 80, 201, 202
Hentoff, Nat, 37, 41, 87

heritage, 3, 32, 65, 77, 95–98, 104,
    117–119, 121–124, 127, 138,
    140, 145, 156, 179. *See also*
    Heritage Foundation
Herndon, James, 37, 41, 60
heroes, 66
herring gull, 65, 128
Hertzberg, Hazel W., 32, 33
Hess, Diana, 194
heterosexual, 155
hierarchy, 70
High School, 168
High School Geography Project
    (HSGP), 186, 203
hippie-yippie philosophy, 100, 101
historians, 3, 15–19, 24, 32, 49, 53,
    56, 66, 96, 124, 171–177, 180,
    193
Historical Literacy, 175
history (American), 9, 28, 31–32,
    46, 51–54, 86, 90, 107, 145,
    172–174. *See also* Amherst
    Project, Brown, Carnegie
    Mellon Project, Fenton, Yale-
    New Haven History Education
    Project
history (world), 19. *See also* Fenton,
    32 Problems in World History
history teaching, 171–174
Hobbs, Max E., 149
hodgepodge, 79
Hoetker, James, 188, 193
holiday curriculum, 196
holocaust, 10, 79
Holt, John, 37, 41, 53, 60
Holt, Marjorie, 127
Holt, Rinehart and Winston, 89
homework, 43, 88, 159, 160, 166
homosexuality, 155
Honig, Bill, 174
Horace's Compromise, 168, 169
Horan, Rev. Marvin, 94, 96
"Horror flicks," 137
hostility, 33, 86, 96, 103, 105, 182

House of Representatives, U. S., 19,
    20, 29, 46, 106, 110, 122, 127,
    131, 133, 136
housewives, 115, 119, 150
Houston, Texas, 115
How Children Fail, 37, 41
How Children Learn, 37
How Teachers Taught, 171
*How to Survive in Your Native
    Land*, 41
Howe, Leland W., 150
Hudson Institute, 179
Human Events, 106, 114, 121
humanism, 30, 39, 74–80, 97, 100,
    103, 107, 111, 116–117,
    120–121, 126, 137, 140, 143,
    152, 156–158
Humanist Manifesto, 29, 121
humanistic, 2, 33, 43, 46, 51, 55–57,
    62, 63, 73, 77–78, 83, 100, 116,
    120, 121, 140
humanities, 14, 19, 65, 174, 177
hunches, 16
Hunt, Maurice P., 73, 80
Hunter, Madeline, 199
"Hunterized," 199

Idaho, 86, 118, 144
ideals, 27, 28, 44, 67, 87
ideologies, 13, 61, 65, 70, 71,
    106, 145, 169, 173, 178, 179,
    201
Ideology and Curriculum, 70
Illiberal Education, 67
Illich, Ivan, 38, 41
Illinois, 11, 12, 133, 143
Illinois Math (UICSM), 11, 12
imagination, 20, 39, 73, 175
impediments, 180, 193
implementation, 12, 13, 32, 84, 107,
    115, 127, 128, 130, 133, 138,
    141, 160, 206
imposition, 2, 40, 41, 55, 70, 132,
    182, 196–197, 208–211

improvements, 2, 3, 4, 11–14, 36, 44, 79, 83, 135, 160, 164, 188, 195, 209, 212–214

inclusion, 18, 19, 65, 66, 87, 99, 161, 176

inculcation, 128, 164, 173, 188, 201

Indiana, 122, 149, 150, 151, 152, 217

Indiana Civil Liberties Union (ICLU), 152, 153

Indiana State Teachers Association, 152

Indianapolis, Indiana, 122

Indians, 30–33

indifference, 31, 192, 201

individualized, 47, 57, 62, 149

Individually Guided Instruction (IGE), 149

indoctrination, 58, 65, 72, 88, 92, 97, 116–118, 121, 182

inductive reasoning, 21, 23

industrialists, 2, 10, 12, 24, 41, 49, 52, 67, 80, 98, 122, 128–129, 162, 166–167, 195, 201–202, 211

inequality, 30, 70

infanticide, 108, 112, 116, 128

inflammatory, 104, 127, 166

infusion, 46, 49, 159, 163

initiatives, 75, 140, 146, 170, 171, 177, 213, 215

injustice, 31, 33, 45, 57, 145

innate, 38, 59, 61

innovations, 2, 4, 10, 12, 22–23, 29, 45, 51–52, 56–62, 74, 80, 97, 105, 113–115, 120, 125, 132, 135–137, 146–147, 155, 159, 161, 163, 170, 178, 182, 187, 195–201, 207–213

innuendos, 108, 112, 134

inquiry, 1–5, 12, 16–19, 20–25, 29, 32, 37, 42, 45, 49–56, 74, 83, 86, 89, 91, 96, 113, 120, 121, 124, 138, 142, 145, 146,

157, 159, 171–174, 178, 187, 193–216

institutes for teachers, 10, 85

institution of schools, 28, 41, 70, 203, 206, 212

institutional obstacles, 1, 180, 189

instruction, 6, 12–13, 17, 20, 24, 27, 57, 60, 62, 75–76, 85, 87, 124, 133, 149–150, 157, 160–164, 169, 174, 176, 180–181, 187–201, 205–209, 211–215

integration, 30, 55, 60, 63, 66, 164, 172, 205

intellectual, 1–3, 10, 13, 16, 18, 21, 40, 43, 55, 60, 66, 70–72, 77–78, 103–107, 121–125, 131, 134, 140, 153, 159, 173, 178–179, 195, 200–209, 214

intellectual snobs, 125

intelligence, 10, 17, 66, 109, 113, 122, 135, 158

interdisciplinary, 75, 145, 155, 169, 214

interest, 60, 159

interpretation, 32, 89, 169, 186, 193, 194, 198, 199, 210

intolerance, 65, 67, 214

intuition, 16, 17, 72

Iowa, 47, 144

iron curtain, 17

irony, 23, 56–57, 66, 83, 119, 124, 142, 201

irrelevance, 31, 38, 41, 53–54, 59, 60, 173, 211

Israel, 89

issues, 1–5, 21–22, 25, 27–37, 44–51, 54, 57–58, 69, 72–85, 88, 96–97, 106, 121, 126, 130, 133, 137–138, 141–144, 147, 155–156, 160, 169–172, 177–178, 186, 190–198, 203, 207–216

Jackson, Kenneth T., 175

Jackson, Richard, 109, 175

Japan, 10, 170
Jehovah's Witness, 154
JM Foundation, 179
Johnson Foundation, 144
Jones, Richard, 139
Jonesboro, Georgia, 87
Journal of American History, 172
journalists, 3, 124
joy, 41
joyless, 60
Judeo-Christian, 106, 108
"junior" historian or social scientist, 15, 18, 142
justice, 4, 27, 57–58, 73–75, 165, 213

Kahn, Ben, 138
Kammen, Michael, 175
Kanawha County, West Virginia, 91–98, 124, 146, 149, 153
Kanawha County Association of Classroom Teachers, 95
Kansas, 46, 48, 51
Keller, Charles R., 18
Kennedy, John F., 19, 87, 136, 142, 190
Kesey, Ken, 86
Kigtak, 131
Killian, James, 11
Kilpatrick, James J., 60, 87–90, 119, 131, 132, 213
Kimball, Roger, 67
kindergarten, 108, 175
King, Dr. Martin Luther, 28, 31, 144
King, Rev. Frank, 104
Kirk, Russell, 156
Kirkendall, Richard S., 172
Kirschenbaum, Howard, 150
knowledge, 4, 15–16, 25, 32, 33, 42–44, 49, 52–53, 65, 69, 70–77, 88, 91, 105, 108, 153, 161, 164, 171–175, 180–181, 187–188, 194, 198, 205, 214
Koch, Fred, 122, 179
Kohl, Herbert, 40, 41

Kohlberg, Lawrence, 55
Kownslar, Allan O., 52–54, 78, 172–173
Kozol, Jonathan, 37, 40, 60
Krug, Mark, 24, 153
Ku Klux Klan, 49, 95, 96
Kubie, Lawrence, 139

Ladson-Billings, Gloria, 64, 67
Laffer, Arthur, 156
Laidlaw Brothers, 120
Lake City, Florida, 100–105, 114, 143
lament, 24, 66, 135, 141, 161, 167
language arts, 48, 64, 92, 94
languages, foreign, 21, 42, 124, 163
Latinos, 27, 32, 162
law-related education (LRE), 56
laws, 34, 46, 56, 87, 90, 92, 96, 104, 108, 112, 127, 131, 141, 151, 154, 160, 170, 177, 180, 185, 186
lawsuits, 110, 152–153
lax, 138, 160, 163
leaders, 3, 15, 24–25, 30, 43, 73, 96, 110–111, 126, 146, 157, 160, 167–168, 192
leadership, 15, 17, 19, 21, 35, 73, 115, 118, 121, 125, 138, 160, 201
Leake, Al, 87, 89–91
leftist, 65, 100
legislative, 110, 111, 118, 122–127, 133, 144, 157, 160, 162
legitimate, 63, 70, 71, 92, 107, 137, 205
LeHay, Timothy, 156
Leinwand, Gerald, 35–37
lessons, 1, 4, 36, 38, 43, 54, 89, 131, 158, 213
Lester, Sid, 176
Leuchtenburg, William E., 175
Levstik, Linda, 194
Lewis, Frank, 111
Lewis, Rev. James, 93

Libby, Mrs., 142
libelous, 134
liberalism, 96, 123, 143, 162, 169, 178
liberation, 27, 31, 69, 72, 85, 126
libertarians, 178
liberties, 36, 49, 120, 123, 152, 155
libraries, 95, 153–157, 189
life-adjustment education, 39, 124
lifelessness, 39, 197
limitations, 13, 78, 80, 120, 146, 199, 206
Lincoln, Nebraska, 144
Lindamood, Rev. Samuel J., 112
literacy, 53, 65, 69, 156, 163, 164, 165, 167, 175
literacy crisis, 156, 164–165
literacy hoax, 164
literature, 30, 37–38, 41, 46–47, 52, 56, 63, 65, 79, 84, 92, 123–126, 131, 150, 158, 165, 174, 176, 199, 208
litigation, 153, 154
lobbying, 179
localized controversies, 91, 117, 132, 142, 144
lockstep, 46
Loewen, James W., 154
logical, 2, 24, 39, 50, 53, 72, 78, 123, 136, 146, 182, 195
Longstreet, Wilma, 63
Longview, Texas, 92, 115
loosely coupled, 196, 200
Lorand, Dr. Rhoda, 139
Los Angeles Times (LAT), 86
Lowry, Sharon, 152
Luke, Carmen, 71, 84
luminaries, 15, 182
Lunstrum, John, 102
Lykes, Rev. Phillip, 102, 103
Lynch, Quintilla, 101
Lynd, Robert S., 188

MacDonald, J. F., 110
Madison, Wisconsin, 84, 107, 109, 110, 111, 113, 167

magazines, 13, 67, 114, 137, 156, 158, 173
Magruder textbook, 88
mainstream, 24, 30, 32, 65, 68, 72, 79, 99, 123, 156, 168, 169
majority, 21–22, 34, 67, 72, 78, 105, 110, 140, 158, 162, 168, 187, 191, 195, 204, 205
Making the Grade, 167
Malcolm X, 31, 32, 92
Male and Female Under 18, 154
males, 65, 154
Man: A Course of Study (MACOS), 2–3, 20–21, 83, 99, 100–149, 186, 189, 203, 212, 213
mandates, 68, 76, 90, 181, 185, 189, 190, 197, 215
Manhattan Institute, 179
Manhattan Project, 17
manpower, 5, 9, 10, 11, 12, 13, 15, 17, 24, 74, 204, 207
Mansfield, 188
Manson, Gary, 44, 92
Marcuse, Herbert, 80
marijuana, 74
Marin County, California, 50
Marks, Robert E., 104
Marshner, Susan, 139
Martin, Edward, 115
Marxism, 68, 71, 116
Maryland, 105, 121, 127
Massachusetts, 11, 15, 122, 142, 143, 154
Massachusetts Institute of Technology (MIT), 11, 12, 15, 17
Massialas, Byron G., 23, 73
mastery, 16, 71, 160, 161
masturbation, 150
materials (classroom), 29, 99, 150, 186. *See also* Amherst, Carnegie Mellon, Fenton, Harvard, HSGP, MACOS, new social studies, Public Issues Series, projects, SRSS, Taba

mathematics, 9–15, 18, 21, 42, 124, 141, 160, 166, 167, 186, 190, 202, 207, 208
McAulay, J. D., 141
McCarthyism, 10
McCaughey, Mrs. Rosanne, 114
McCauley, Joanne, 141
McGraw, Dr. Onalee S., 106–107, 114, 118–124, 136–140, 156
McLaren, Peter, 71
McNeil, Linda, 194
McNeill, William H., 175
Mead, Dr. Margaret, 131
meaningful learning, 193–202, 209–215
media, 11, 35, 49, 57, 64, 86, 91, 93, 97, 110, 125, 127, 131, 137–138, 142, 144, 163, 165, 173, 197. See also *Anaheim Bulletin, Arizona Republic, Burlington Free Press,* CBS, *Florida Times-Union, Los Angeles Times, Newsweek,* NBC, *New York Times,* radio, *Time, Times-Union* (Warsaw), Today, *Wall Street Journal,* WCHS, WCR, *Weekly American News*
mediocrity, 14, 162, 166–167
meetings, 14, 19, 36, 86, 91, 95, 103, 108–109, 114, 140, 143
Mehlinger, Howard, 192
meliorists, 3, 44, 73, 204
memorization, 52, 69, 78, 89, 173, 174, 185
men, 66, 95, 116–117, 131, 135, 152, 191
Metcalf, Lawrence, 73, 80
meteoric rise, 61, 73
Methodist, 110
methods, 12–13, 19, 23, 29, 31, 38, 41–42, 45, 50, 54, 56, 59, 71, 74–78, 84–85, 89, 107, 116, 124, 139, 160, 169, 172–173, 176, 187–190, 195, 200–201, 210
Michigan, 47

Middletown, 188
midwestern, 76, 154
milieu, 10, 16, 39
militancy, 28, 36, 88, 154, 178
militarism, 40, 43, 159
Millet, Kate, 94
Millis, John, 101
Milwaukee, Wisconsin, 143
mindlessness, 60, 213
mindnumbing, 39, 173
minds, 10, 12, 17, 49, 104, 107, 109, 116, 119, 134–136
miners, 95, 96
minicourses, 28, 41, 46–52, 56–57, 62, 74–76, 189, 196, 210
minimum competency tests, 160
minorities, 28–35, 50–51, 56, 85–86, 104, 122, 130, 135, 141, 145, 180, 186
minutiae, 52
Mirel, Jeffrey, 56
misconceptions, 42
miseducation, 38
missiles, 20
Mississippi, 84, 154
Missouri, 51, 129, 144
modal pattern, 189, 196
modernist, 71, 80
molesting, 157
money, 10, 24, 125, 182, 207, 213
monkey trial, 152
monolithic, 33, 68, 106
monopolies, 39, 168
Montgomery County, Maryland, 105–107, 121
Montrose Baptist Church, 100
Moore, Alice, 92–97
Moral Majority, 158
morality, 55, 88, 92, 100, 124, 129, 158, 159, 160, 213
moratorium, 42, 130
Morris, Tom, 143
Morrissett, Irving, 189
Morristown, Vermont, 116–117
Morse, William, 143

Mosher, Charles, 129, 133
motivation, 16, 17, 18, 24, 50, 51, 88, 132, 216
motivations of reformers, 18
MOTOREDE (Movement to Restore Decency), 92
Moudy, James, 138, 140
movements. *See specific movements*: antiwar, Black Power, civil rights, Gay rights, multicultural education, new social studies, newer social studies, peace, women
Movie Aids for Teaching Physics in High School, 11
Moynihan, Daniel P., 159
multiculturalism, 27, 30, 32, 59, 64–67, 92
multiculturalists, 30, 65–67, 73
multidisciplinary, 172
multiracial, 92
Musselman, Phyllis, 107–115
Myers, Donald A., 62
myths, 54, 99, 106, 108, 180

naivete of reformers, 72, 74, 147, 206
Naples, Florida, 143, 144
narrative, 69, 174, 176
Nation at Risk, A, 165–167
National Academy of Sciences (NAS), 14
National Assessment of Educational Progress (NAEP), 164
National Association for the Advancement of Colored People (NAACP), 93, 154
National Association of Manufacturers (NAM), 122
National Commission on Excellence in Education, 165–170
National Council for History Education (NCHE), 217
National Council for the Social Studies (NCSS), 22, 28–36, 44, 52, 64, 83, 141–146, 155, 164, 182, 215
National Defense Education Act (NDEA), 13, 14, 85
National Education Association (NEA), 88, 92, 96, 106, 145, 155, 157, 182
National Enquirer, 137
National Review, 161, 179
National Science Foundation (NSF), 10–15, 20–22, 100, 103, 105, 119, 124–141, 186–188, 203, 209
national security, 5, 10–17, 42, 95, 202, 208
Nation's Business, 11
native, 27, 28, 32, 41
nature, 4, 16, 21, 31, 60, 68, 74, 91, 105, 116, 133, 147, 190, 195, 201–208, 212
Navy, 17
NBC television, 137
NCSS Curriculum Guidelines (1971), 44–46
Nebraska, 51, 85, 144
needs, 188
Negro, 31, 36
Neill, A. S., 38, 39
neoconservatives, 5, 64, 65, 124, 156, 159, 160, 168, 169, 174, 178, 180
neoefficiency, 79
neo-Marxist, 68
Netsilik, 99, 105–108, 112, 116, 126, 128, 132, 139, 142
neutrality, 16, 43, 107, 112
Nevins, Allan, 10, 172, 175
New Hampshire, 142, 143
New Jersey, 118, 127, 143
New Republic, 60
new social studies, 1–6, 9–25
new wave critics, 29, 37–39, 57, 59, 60, 63, 73–75, 79–80, 210. *See also* Goodman, Hentoff,

Herndon, Holt, Kozol, Neill, Postman, Reimer, Weingartner
New York Times, 11, 137, 174
New Yorker, 173
newer social studies, 27–57, 72, 203
Newmann, Fred M., 23, 73, 192, 193
newspapers, 88, 91, 94, 106, 108, 115, 121, 126, 132–137, 150–152
Newsweek, 67, 137, 163
Niblack school, 100–104
nihilists, 67
Noble, Edward, 123
nonacademic, 76, 159
nonbelievers, 179
noncurriculum, 35, 36, 57
nongraded, 46, 47, 61
North Dakota, 61–63
northeastern liberal establishment, 180

objectives, 23, 29, 44, 45, 49, 56, 57, 70, 113, 157, 163, 187, 200, 206
obscene, 92, 151
"Observation, Evidence, the Basis for Belief," 18
obstacles, 1, 4, 25, 180, 189, 206, 212
Ochoa, Anna S., 44
Office of Defense Mobilization (ODM), 11, 217
Office of Education. *See* USOE
O'Hara, Mrs. Richard, 114
Ohio, 127, 129, 154
Ohman, 164, 165, 241
Olin foundation, 129, 138, 179
Oliver, Donald, 21, 54, 73
Oliver, Douglas, 99
omnipotence, 13
One Flew Over the Cuckoo's Nest, 86
open schools, 60–64, 163

opposition, 30, 52, 67, 70, 72, 90–96, 103, 106, 107, 110–114, 118–119, 143
oppression, 27, 30, 31, 32, 38, 40, 59, 65, 66, 69, 72, 73, 74, 75, 80, 211
optimism, 70, 74, 79, 155, 188
Orange, California, 144
Organization of American Historians (OAH), 172
orientations, 21–25, 35–38, 45, 68, 72, 80, 160, 177, 187, 201–204, 208–211
origins, 2, 5, 9–10, 13, 21–24, 46, 73, 105, 146, 155, 178, 203–208
Orlando, Florida, 102
orthodoxy, 62
Our Children Are Dying, 37
Our Nation's Story, 120
Our Working World, 18
outcomes, 51, 95, 113, 144
Owyhee Elementary School, 119
Oxford University, 134

Paige, Lowell, 130
Palonsky, Stuart, 191, 192
pamphlets, 95, 121, 140, 157, 175
panacea, 55
paradox, 171, 204
Parent Teacher Association (PTA), 93, 100
parents, 39, 86, 93–96, 115, 162
Parker, Walter, 4
particularists, 65–66
pastor, 101, 102, 104
patriarchal, 72
patriotism, 97, 120, 126, 154, 158, 160, 161
Patton, John E., 118
peace education, 185
pedagogy, 29, 41, 59, 66–72, 80, 99, 146–147, 157, 169, 172, 181, 195, 207–216
Pedagogy of the Oppressed, 69

pendulum, 3, 162, 178
Pennsylvania, 143
perennialist, 168
permissiveness, 124, 128, 162, 163
persistence, 51, 112, 169, 181, 188, 192–199, 206, 209–211
Peshkin, Alan, 188
phenomenology, 71
Phi Delta Kappan, 137
Philadelphia, 134
philanthropic, 177
philosophers. *See* Derrida, Dewey, Foucault, Gadamer, Gramsci, Habermas
philosophy, 38, 47, 49, 80, 85, 87, 92, 100–107, 111, 117, 126, 140, 152, 159, 168, 177, 181, 205, 206
phobia, 128, 139
Phoenix, Arizona, 107–115, 127, 134, 146
Physical Science Study Committee (PSSC), 12, 14, 18
physicists, 12, 15, 18. *See also* Killian, Waterman, Zacharias
physics, 11, 18
Piaget, Jean, 55
Piazza, Elizabeth, 102
picketing, 94, 95
Piel, Gerard, 140, 141
Pinar, William F., 71
Pine Ridge Middle School, 143
"pissin match with a skunk," 130
Pittman, Silas, 102
Pittsburgh, Pennsylvania, 18, 91
Place Called School, A, 168
plaintiffs, 153
playacting, 142
Playboy, 84
Plowden Commission, 60
pluralism, 66, 194
pluribus v. unum, 65, 66
poetry, 64, 158
polemical, 87, 124, 167, 176–177

policies, 11, 13, 30, 38, 76, 83, 122–125, 137, 149, 150, 152, 156, 160–162, 167–168, 177, 179, 214
politics, 1, 2, 4, 16, 40, 48, 57, 67, 85, 94, 124–125, 155–158, 174, 179–188, 203–216
population studies, 29, 45, 56, 145, 177
pornographic, 92, 101–102, 155
post-holing, 20, 99
postindustrial, 212
postinquiry, 37
Postman, Neil, 38, 41, 42, 53
postmodernism, 68, 71
postmortems, 185–192
poststructuralist, 35, 68, 71
potpourri, 170
poverty, 30, 31, 36, 45, 56
power, 27, 30, 31, 36, 49
pragmatism, 98, 116
prayer, 104, 157, 186
prejudice, 33, 48, 84
premarital sex, 150
premise, 16, 65, 165
Presbyterian, 104
presentist, 29, 79
preservice teacher education, 18
preserving, 70, 74, 83, 124, 159
president, 11, 19, 46, 100, 112, 114, 118, 138, 151, 165, 168. *See also* Bush, Eisenhower, Kennedy, Reagan
President's Science Advisory Committee (PSAC), 19, 217
press, 117, 137, 151
pressures, 1, 40, 117, 128, 154, 164, 186
prestigious, 2, 40
primitive, 128
principal, 48, 110, 118, 142, 143, 150
principles, 15, 22, 44, 45, 55, 61, 66, 97, 135, 136, 156, 160, 201, 215

prison, 80, 96
privileged, 34, 72, 214
problem solving, 35, 64
problems approach, 37
Process of Education, The, 15, 24
Pro-Family Forum, 157–158
profanity, 92, 151
professional associations. *See*
    associations, specific group
professors, 25, 40, 45, 49, 67, 85,
    88, 102, 162, 164, 175–177,
    187, 191, 192, 200, 206
programmed instruction, 57
progressive education, 1–2, 9–10,
    13, 29, 39, 43, 47, 57, 61, 121,
    124, 141–142, 145, 171, 182,
    213
  critical pedagogy, 68–72
  critiques of, 9–10
  demise of, 9–10
  leaders of, 3, 9–10, 54, 213
  new progressivism, 35–61
  similarity to Bruner, 213, 216
  social reconstruction, 2–3, 35–46,
    71–73
*Progressive Education is
    REDucation*, 10
Project APEX, 47, 150
Project Troy, 17, 135
projects, 14, 17, 20–21, 23, 47, 49,
    135, 186–189, 203
promiscuity, 109, 128
proof, 23, 25, 50, 130, 205
propaganda, 4, 14, 17, 72, 122, 124,
    157
proselytizing, 72
prostitution, 155
Protestant, 159
protesters, 94, 95, 126, 146, 154
provocative, 43, 85, 112, 133, 173,
    182, 192
Proxmire, William, 135
"psychic manipulation," 116
psychological warfare, 109, 115,
    134–136

psychologists, 15, 55, 119, 134,
    139. *See also* Alpert, Bruner,
    Cronbach, Gagne, Piaget,
    Skinner
psychology, 14, 15, 40, 63, 107, 115,
    139, 173, 176–177
Public Interest, 159
Public Issues Series, 203
publications, 12, 19, 22, 39, 64, 72,
    121–122, 124, 140, 151, 163,
    165, 169, 174, 178–179
publishers, 89, 90, 100, 120,
    137–141, 153
punishment, 55, 58, 80, 160
Purdue University, 18
purposes, 5, 23, 33, 44, 60, 74, 97,
    101, 103, 109, 112–113, 132,
    136, 174, 182, 194, 201–206,
    211, 215

quackery, 2, 10, 195
Quackery in the Public Schools, 10
questionnaire, 105, 110, 154
Quigley, Charles, 94
Quincy, Massachusetts, 142, 143

racial, 30, 35, 38, 45, 66, 84, 123,
    133
racism, 30–35, 40, 43, 45, 56, 66,
    74, 144, 161
radiation lab, 17
radicals, 27, 46, 61, 67–68, 145
radio, 17, 101–103, 112, 125–126,
    157
rallies, 94–97, 146, 152
Ramada Inn, Burlington, Vermont,
    115–116
Rand Corporation, 15, 206
Raths, Louis E., 54
rationales, 12, 18, 24–25, 44–48, 78,
    112, 173, 195, 200–206, 213
Ravitch, Diane, 65–67, 159,
    174–177
Reader's Digest, 137
readiness, 16

Reagan, Ronald, 122, 156, 165, 168, 171
realities, 38, 43–45, 54, 112, 147, 154, 178, 180, 187, 190–191, 195, 199, 201, 204–205
rebellion, 25–30, 38, 59, 80, 204
rebels, 73, 80
recapitulation, 16, 56, 60
receptacles, students as, 69
recitation, 160, 171, 187–189, 193, 198, 199, 209–211
reconceptualist, 68
reconstructionism, 2–3, 25, 35–37, 43–44, 56–59, 68, 71–73, 207–208, 213
reconstructionists, 2–3, 25, 35, 43–44, 56, 73, 207, 213
Reconstructive Approach to Problem Solving, A, 37
red, 48
red baiting, 10, 13
red herring, 65
reflective, 3, 42, 105, 178, 197, 200, 213
reformers, 12, 18, 25, 40, 55, 75, 135, 146, 176, 180, 189, 191, 193, 196, 200, 201, 204–207, 211, 213. *See also* Bruner, Fenton, progressives, Ravitch, reconstructionists
reforms. *See* accountability, back-to-basics, conservative restoration, humanistic, new social studies, newer social studies, revival of history
regimentation, 40, 41
Reimer, Everett, 38
relativism, 92, 178
relevance, 2, 6, 19, 28–31, 35, 42–43, 48–57, 63, 74–79, 120, 163, 175–176, 192, 196, 199, 207, 210, 216
religions, 66, 92, 110, 120, 124, 154, 158–159

reporter, 114, 116, 117, 121, 153
reports, 21, 145, 160, 167, 169, 174. *See also specific reports: Action for Excellence*, CIA, manpower, *Nation at Risk*, NCSS, NEA (Kanawha), OAH, ODM, *Process of Education*, status studies
representatives, 30, 95, 105–106, 110, 126–127, 168
repression, 28, 32, 70
reproduction theory, 69–73, 101, 202
Republicans, 123–129, 154
requirements, 11, 37, 42–43, 48, 51, 62, 68, 75, 77, 159, 172, 174, 185, 189, 190
research, 12, 14–17, 51, 64, 72, 117, 121–122, 164
researchers, 23, 75–78, 165, 168, 187, 189, 194–195, 206, 210
resegregation, 66
resistance, 34, 52, 70, 126, 127, 144, 156, 200, 207–208, 212, 215
resources, 3, 11, 13, 21, 43–44, 121, 145–146, 178, 197
restructuring, 37, 46, 52, 161, 169
Reusswig, James M., 107
revival of history, 155–156, 171–181
revival of progressivism, 35–37
revolutionary, 13, 21, 28, 30, 43–44, 51, 56, 60, 67, 204
revolutions, 5–6, 18, 21, 29, 36–37, 44, 48, 60, 74, 84, 87, 116, 123, 154, 179, 195, 207
rhetoric, 3–5, 16, 25, 27, 35, 44, 60, 64, 72–75, 125, 169, 186, 196, 199, 202, 207, 213
Rhoton, Dow, 108, 113
Rickover, Vice Admiral Hyman, 13, 15, 124
right (political), 156–159, 178–180

rigorous, 13, 40, 138, 140, 166, 173
rioting, 28
Road to Serfdom, The, 178
Robinson, Donald, 23
Rochester, New York, 85
role playing, 33, 109, 139–142, 145, 158
romanticized, 28, 43, 74, 79
Root, E. Merrill, 14
Roselle, Daniel, 29
Roszak, Theodore, 43
rote learning, 162, 169, 182
Rousseauian, 38, 39, 59
Rudolph, John, 136
Rugg, Harold O., 9–10, 52, 60, 126, 182, 213, 215
Russians, 11, 13, 88, 170

Sacramento State University, 177
Saigon, 137
Saint Jerome, 73
Sallis, James, 154
San Jose State University, 176
Sarason, Seymour B., 193
Satan, 117
satellite, 13
Saturday Review, 18
Saye, John, 195
Scaife, Richard, 123, 179
scapegoat, 96, 157, 167, 176, 180
Schlafly, Phyllis, 159
Schlesinger, Arthur M., 65–67
"scholacentric," 24
scholarship, 2, 24, 54, 67, 68, 71, 72, 123, 195
Scholastic Aptitude Test (SAT), 160, 164
school board, 84–94, 102, 104, 110–114, 118, 130, 142, 150, 151, 160
School is Dead, 38
Schooling in Capitalist America, 69
schools
    elementary, 100, 106, 119, 149

high school, 11, 14, 19, 21, 28, 40, 46–51, 56, 61–62, 75–78, 84–85, 94, 108, 150, 154, 160–162, 166–168, 181, 185, 203
    middle, 143
    secondary schools, 14, 21, 46, 59, 160, 163, 172, 181, 189, 190
    as a "vast mental hospital for the psychic manipulation of the young," 116
Schroeder High School, 85
sciences, 2–5, 9–22
scientific, 11, 16, 18, 20, 103, 107, 132, 137, 140, 141, 154, 205, 208
Scientific American, 137, 141
scientists, 10–18, 23–24, 29, 116, 142, 177, 187, 201, 207. *See also* Killian, Waterman, Zacharias
Scopes monkey trial, 152
scrambling of history, geography, and government, 10
seatwork, 171, 188, 204
Second Rate Brains, 14
Secretary of Education, US, 65, 168, 174
secular, 97, 116, 121, 125–126, 137, 140, 152, 156–157, 179
secular humanism, 97, 116, 121, 126, 140, 152, 156–157
seedtime (for conservative reform), 179
segregation, 34, 125
seminal, 38, 69
Senate, 122, 127, 134, 136
senators, 90, 106, 127, 131, 135–136, 156
Senesh, Lawrence, 18, 20, 203
senilicide, 99, 108, 128
senior citizens, 151
sensitivity training, 56, 121
sensual philosophy, 100

sex, 76, 92, 94, 101, 102, 104, 107,
    108, 116, 120, 121, 126, 132,
    134, 150, 154, 155, 161
sexism, 30, 40, 43, 66
Sexual Politics, 94
sexuality, 51, 94, 128, 139
Sexuality Information and Education
    Council of the United States
    (SIECUS), 102, 121
shackles, 73, 80
Shaver, James P., 24, 73, 186, 188
"shockproof crap detctor," 42
"shoddy stuff," 12
Shofstall, Weldon, 110
shootings, 94
Silberman, Charles E., 38, 53, 60, 62
Simon, Frank, 37
Simon, Sidney B., 54, 150
simulations, 1, 29, 34–35, 49, 56,
    63, 78, 80, 189, 203
Sizer, Theodore, 168–169
skills, 4, 11, 13, 17–18, 32, 42, 44,
    49, 50, 53, 64–65, 71, 77, 91,
    97, 106–108, 124, 149, 153,
    157, 160–173
Skinner, B. F., 111, 119
slaughter of animals, 128, 139
"slaughter the sacred cow of
    history," 19
smear tactics, 103
Smith, C. J., 150–151
Smith, Horace, 169
Smith, Marshall S., 167
Smith, Mortimer, 124
Smith Richardson, 179
smut, 125
social class, 69, 77
social efficiency, 3, 5, 57, 164, 170,
    175, 201, 211
Social Frontier, The, 71
social problems, 22, 28, 45, 56, 202
social sciences. *See specific social
    science*
"social stew," 10

social studies
    classroom practice in, 186–192
    definitions for, 3, 213
    grammar of, 192–202, 209–211
    interest groups, 3, 213
Social Studies Education: Priorities,
    Practices, and Needs (SPAN),
    188–189
*Social Studies in the Open
    Classroom*, 64
Social Studies Wars, The, 3
socialism, 10, 14, 100, 110, 162
socialization, 69, 106, 117, 169,
    171–174, 182, 188, 197, 201,
    205, 211
sociodramas, 158
Sociological Resources for the Social
    Studies (SRSS), 21, 186, 203
sociologists, 19, 40
sociology, 21, 158, 174, 176–177,
    203, 205
Socratic dialogue, 1, 53, 145
sorting function, 75, 181, 199, 205
souls, 38, 106, 116, 117, 170
South Orange, New Jersey, 118
South Shore Citizens Against Forced
    Busing, 142
"southernization" of politics, 125
Soviet Union, 10–14, 17, 132, 152,
    155
Sowell, Thomas, 65, 156
speakout, 29
spiritual, 41, 106, 145
Spock, Dr. Benjamin, 84, 162
Spring, Joel, 167
springboard, 34
Springbrook School, 118
Sputnik, 13–15, 52, 166, 204
St. Anthony, Idaho, 86
St. Botolph Club, 17
stabbing, 108
stability, 75, 76, 197, 199, 201
Stakhanov movement, 10
Stalin Prizes, 10

standardized, 149, 165–166, 172, 197, 215
standards, 1, 14, 31, 40, 66, 70, 113, 124, 156, 159–165, 173, 175, 180, 182, 189, 197, 200–201, 208–216
Stanley, William B., 72, 169
Starpower, 34
state departments of education, 22, 142, 162
states. *See specific state*
status studies, 186–191
Stedman, Lawrence C., 167
Steinbacher, John, 3, 116–118, 121
Stepford Wives, The, 150
stereotypes, 32, 33, 54
sterile, 52, 60
Sterzing, Keith, 84–85
Stever, H. Guyford, 129–132, 138
Stewart, Potter, 124
stifling, 1, 5, 39, 215–216
straightjacket, 36
strands, 3, 213
strategies, 13, 35, 55, 65, 132, 144, 163, 198, 200, 206
stratification, 70, 201, 205
structuralism, 24, 68, 71, 181, 205
structure, social and economic, 37, 69, 70, 79, 181–182
structure-of-the-disciplines, 12–24, 207–208, 213
Stuart, Logan, 112, 113
student attitudes, 52, 199
student interest, 16, 43, 46, 48, 51, 74, 77–78, 192, 204
Students for a Democratic Society (SDS), 49
subcommittee hearings, 128, 136
subconscious, 35, 119
subliminal, 119, 136
subsidize, 107, 128, 137
suburban, 34, 84, 85, 150
subversive, 38, 41, 43

successes, 11, 13, 31, 52, 100, 115, 141, 180, 190, 202–206, 211, 213
Sugarland, Texas, 84
Summe, Anne, 151
Summerhill, 38, 39, 59
Summers, J. H., 89
superficial, 30, 195
superintendents, 76, 87, 90, 95, 102, 107–108, 119–120, 149–150, 174
superstitions, 42
supervision, 43, 90, 131, 187, 191, 199
suppress, 41
Supreme Court, 101
surrealism, 84
surveillance, 80
survival, 41, 53, 83, 108, 131, 145
suspension, 88
sustained, 181, 197, 203, 210, 212
Symington, James, 129, 133
systems, 4, 14, 17, 57, 69, 107, 109, 123, 132–136, 157, 188, 215
    economic, 201, 215
    school, 85, 116, 132, 157, 167, 182, 188, 199
    social, 69, 198, 200
systems analysis, 17, 135–136

Taba, Hilda, 186, 203
Taba Social Studies Program, 186, 203
tabloids, 106, 156
taboos, 99
talented education, 12, 170
Tamalpais High School, 50
Tanner, Daniel, 168
taxpayers, 106, 109, 128, 137, 145, 146, 163
Taylorism, 201
teacher certification, 172, 190, 200, 205

teacher education, 18, 20, 64, 196, 200, 212

teacher-proof, 23, 25, 205

Teaching American History: The Quest for Relevancy, 52–54

Teaching as a Subversive Activity, 41–44

teaching practices, 42, 200, 206

Teague, Olin, 129, 138, 141

techniques, 2, 12–13, 16, 29, 35, 50, 52, 109, 115, 136, 187, 189, 206

technocratic, 40, 41, 80, 200

technology, 11, 16, 18, 40, 80, 99, 119, 127, 135, 166, 197, 211, 212

television, 93, 95, 126, 137, 157, 162. *See also* CBS, NBC, Today show

Tenured Radicals, 67

testing, 160, 164, 165, 169

Texas, 76, 77, 84, 85, 92, 115, 119, 129, 138, 157

textbook criticism, 122, 127, 141, 156

  controversies, 9, 86, 91, 97, 106, 149

  use in teaching, 197–198

thematic approach, 48, 49

theories, 4, 5, 25, 44–45, 54–55, 59–61, 66–72, 106, 118, 122, 132, 139, 159, 168–169, 171, 190–195, 200, 205, 210–213

36 Children, 40

32 Problems in World History, 19

Thompson, Bennie G., 84

Thornton, Stephen J., 176

threats, 2, 10, 95, 99, 129, 134, 145, 151–152, 179, 195

tide of mediocrity, 166–167

Time, 67

Times-Union (Warsaw), 150, 152

Today show, 91

Toffler, Alvin, 53

tolerance, 62, 79, 97

"tot sociology," 174

totalitarian, 17, 117

Tovey, Susan, 118

traditionalists, 67, 99, 181

traditions, 2–3, 23, 29, 35, 37, 44, 66, 73, 177, 180, 195, 196

training, 11, 118

transmission, 5, 15, 99, 113, 159, 180, 201

trends in schoools, 46, 59–79

tribalization, 66

trivial, 60, 76

truths, 17, 28, 43, 67, 70, 112, 116, 135, 179, 197

Tucker, Jan, 44

Tunsil, Joyce, 101

Ture, Kwame (previously Stokeley Carmichael), 30

Tyack, David, 181, 194, 198, 206

typical classroom, 38, 76, 97. *See also* classroom practices, grammar

ultraconservative, 3, 5, 92, 113, 118, 119, 121, 122, 124, 126

ultrafundamentalists, 179

undemocratic, 177, 199, 206

underlying, 67, 74, 77–78, 124, 165, 175, 177, 187, 202

  assumptions, 74, 117

  causes, 67, 124, 165, 177

  goal, 187

  intent, 175

  structure, 202

  theme, 77, 78

Underwood, Kenneth, 95

unequal, 69, 70

"unfreedom," 80, 211

ungodly, 93

unholy, 174

unions, 44, 157

United States Office of Education (USOE), 12, 14, 15, 21, 22, 50,

92, 157, 165, 186, 209. *See also*
    Cooperative Research Program,
    NDEA, NSF, Project Social
    Studies
units, 4, 35, 49, 51, 84, 100,
    103–104, 172, 181
Universities. *See specific university*
University of Illinois Committee on
    School Mathematics (UICSM),
    11
unlawful, 95
unpatriotic, 14, 92
unprecedented, 13, 24, 142, 165,
    186, 192, 209, 212
unrealistic, 32, 72, 77, 203
unum v. pluribus, 65, 66
uptight, 34
urbanization, 29, 32, 56
Utah, 168
utopian, 74

validity, 33, 78
values, 30, 54, 55, 78, 118,
    150–151
Values and Teaching, 54
Values Clarification, 55, 150–151
values clarification, 2, 53–58, 78,
    120, 150–151, 186, 210
vandalism, 95
vanguard, 36, 120
vehicle, 41, 54, 103, 116, 125, 157
veil, 205
Vermont, 115–117
veto, 133, 141
Vietnam war, 25, 27, 29, 40, 79, 87,
    96, 144, 204
vigilante, 141
violence, 91–96, 108, 128, 153
Virginia, 91, 93, 144
virtues, 60, 101
visions, 4, 5, 13, 74, 97, 153, 168,
    207
Vonnegut, Kurt, 154
vouchers, 107

walkout, 94
Wall Street Journal, 137
Wallace, George, 118, 125
Ware, Art, 114
wars, 9, 12–13, 17–18, 24, 33, 46,
    48, 51, 64, 87, 91, 109, 115,
    119, 125, 134–136, 208. *See
    also* cold war, Vietnam, World
    War II
Warsaw, Indiana, 149–153
Warsaw Community Education
    Association (WCEA), 151–152
Washington, Booker T., 32
Washington, DC, 120–132, 137,
    151, 156
Washington Elementary School, 149
Washington Post, 137
watchdog, 3, 121, 126
Watergate, 79, 96, 137
Waterman, Alan T., 11
Way It Spozed To Be, The, 37
WCHS television, 93
WCR television, 137
wealth, 69, 80, 97, 126, 180, 182
weapons, 12–13, 17, 109, 123–124,
    132–136, 202, 208
weapons system, 17, 109, 123–124,
    136, 202
Weber, George, 124
Weber, Lillian, 61
Weekly American News, 108, 115
Weingartner, Charles, 38, 41, 42, 53
Welch, Robert, 122
Wesleyan College, 164
West, Cornel, 64
West Virginia Human Rights
    Commission, 93
Weyrich, Paul, 123
What Do Our 17 Year Olds Know?,
    174
Whites, 31, 33, 34, 48, 67
whitewashing, 198
Whitney Estate, 19
"WHO DO WE EAT?," 109

"Widener to Wichita," 134
wife-swapping, 116
Wild Orchids and Trotsky, 68
Will, George F., 159
Williams, Reub, 152
Wilson, James Q., 159
Wingspread Conference, 144–145
Winterhalter, Nadine, 115
Winters, Bonnie A., 64
Wisconsin, 143, 144, 167
Witchcraft, 48
Witchita, Kansas, 134
women, 27–30, 56, 65, 70, 73, 84,
    117, 150–152, 165, 185, 191
Woods Hole, 15–20, 135. *See also*
    Air Research and Development
    Command, Alpert, Blum,
    Bruner, Cronbach, Gagne, NAS,
    NSF, USOE, Rand, systems
    analysis, weapons system,
    Zacharias
Woodward, C. Vann, 175
worksheets, 194, 197
workshops, 22, 128
world government, 88, 120, 122
world history, 19

world studies, 50
World War II, 12–13, 64, 109, 115,
    119, 134–135

Xeroxed articles, 126

Yale University, 49, 51, 168
Yale-New Haven History Education
    Project, 49, 51
Young Women's Christian
    Association (YWCA), 93,
    218
youth, 13, 28–32, 41–42, 48, 52,
    58–59, 108, 117–119, 166, 182,
    188, 204

Zacharias, Jerrold, 11, 12, 14, 15,
    17, 18, 19, 20, 40, 136. *See also*
    Endicott House, motivations
    of reformers, "Observation,"
    physicists, PSAC, PSSC, Woods
    Hole
Zarbin, Earl, 111–112
zenith, 22, 28, 83
Zykan v. Warsaw Community
    School Corporation, 153